Puerto Rico

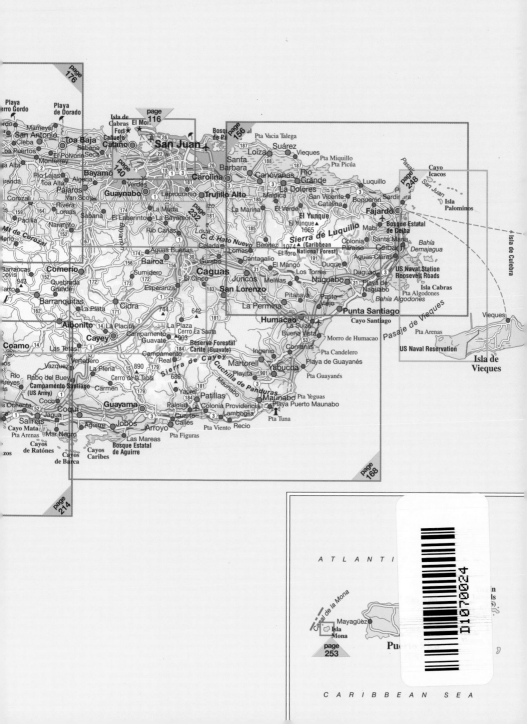

INSIGHT GUIDES

PUERTO RICO

DISCOVERY CHANNEL

APA PUBLICATIONS **L**

Part of the Langenscheidt Publishing Group

INSIGHT GUIDE
PUERTO RICO

ABOUT THIS BOOK

Editorial

Project Editor
Barbara Balletto
Managing Editor
Lesley Gordon
Editorial Director
Brian Bell

Distribution

United States
Langenscheidt Publishers, Inc.
36–36 33rd Street 4th Floor
Long Island City, NY 11106
Fax: 1 (718) 784 0640

UK & Ireland
GeoCenter International Ltd
Meridian House, Churchill Way West
Basingstoke, Hampshire RG21 6YR
Fax: (44) 1256 817988

Australia
Universal Publishers
1 Waterloo Road
Macquarie Park, NSW 2113
Fax: (61) 2 9888 9074

New Zealand
Hema Maps New Zealand Ltd (HNZ)
Unit D, 24 Ra ORA Drive
East Tamaki, Auckland
Fax: (64) 9 273 6479

Worldwide
Apa Publications GmbH & Co.
Verlag KG (Singapore branch)
38 Joo Koon Road, Singapore 628990
Tel: (65) 6865 1600. Fax: (65) 6861 6438

Printing

Insight Print Services (Pte) Ltd
38 Joo Koon Road, Singapore 628990
Tel: (65) 6865 1600. Fax: (65) 6861 6438

©2007 Apa Publications GmbH & Co.
Verlag KG (Singapore branch)
All Rights Reserved
First Edition 1987
Third Edition (updated) 2004
Updated 2007

CONTACTING THE EDITORS
We would appreciate it if readers
would alert us to errors or out-
dated information by writing to:
**Insight Guides, P.O. Box 7910,
London SE1 1WE, England.
Fax: (44) 20 7403 0290.**
insight@apaguide.co.uk

NO part of this book may be reproduced,
stored in a retrieval system or transmitted
in any form or means electronic, mech-
anical, photocopying, recording or otherwise, without prior written permission of
Apa Publications. Brief text quotations
with use of photographs are exempted
for book review purposes only. Information has been obtained from sources
believed to be reliable, but its accuracy
and completeness, and the opinions
based thereon, are not guaranteed.

www.insightguides.com
In North America:
www.insighttravelguides.com

The first Insight Guide pio-
neered the use of creative
full-color photography in travel
guides in 1970. Since then, we
have expanded our range to
cater for our readers' need, not
only for reliable information
about their chosen destination
but also a real under-
standing of the culture,
history and workings of
that destination. Now,
when the internet can
supply inexhaustible
facts, our books marry
text and pictures to
provide those much
more elusive qualities:
knowledge and discernment. To
achieve this, they rely heavily on
the authority of locally based writers and photographers.

In this, the third edition of the
guide, we take you all around
this island-nation and look at the
elements that have given the
country its interesting mix
of "cultural confusion": stylish Spanish architecture,
African-influenced music
and dance, Caribbean cui-
sine with a distinctively
Puerto Rican flair. Discover
the island's equally diverse
landscape – dense moun-
tainous tropical forests,

azure oceans, arid flatlands and the rugged *Cordillera*.

How to use this book

The book is carefully structured to convey an understanding of Puerto Rico and its culture and to guide readers through its sights and attractions:
◆ The Features section, with a yellow color bar, covers the country's history and culture in lively authoritative essays written by specialists.
◆ The Places section, with a blue bar, provides full details of all the sights and areas worth seeing. The chief places of interest are coordinated by number with specially drawn maps.
◆ The Travel Tips listings section at the back of the book offers a convenient point of reference for information on travel, accommodation, restaurants and other practical aspects of the country. Information may be located quickly using the index printed on the back cover flap, which also serves as a handy bookmark.

The contributors

This latest edition was edited by **Barbara Balletto** (who was happy to see her many years of "schoolgirl Spanish" put to practical use), it builds on the earlier editions produced by **Christopher Caldwell**, **Tad Ames** and **Larry Luxner**. Balletto worked with **Gerry Tobin**, a Puerto Rican journalist, who refined the original text written by a team including Luxner, Caldwell, **Sarah Ellison Caldwell**, **Webster** and **Robert Stone**, **Angelo Lopez**, **Adam Cherson**, **Kathleen O'Connell**, **Hanne-Maria Maijala**, **Eleanora Abreau Jimenez** and **Susan Hambleton**.

The principal updater was **Natalia de Cuba Romero**, an island-based writer when commissioned. **Gabrielle Paese**, Sports Editor for the *San Juan Star*, a national newspaper in Puerto Rico, keeps this edition fresh. **Susan Charneco** thoroughly updated the Travel Tips. **Caroline Radula-Scott** edited the original update and **Emma Sangster** proofread the text.

The principal photographers were **Bill Wassman**, **Tony Arruza**, **Robert Fried** and **Bob Krist**.

Map Legend

– – ▪ –	International Boundary
– ▪ –	National Park/Reserve
– – – –	Ferry Route
✈ ✈	Airport: International/Regional
🚌	Bus Station
🅿	Parking
❶	Tourist Information
✉	Post Office
🕆 † ⳨	Church/Ruins
†	Monastery
☾	Mosque
✡	Synagogue
◧ ◨	Castle/Ruins
∴	Archeological Site
∩	Cave
𝚰	Statue/Monument
★	Place of Interest

The main places of interest in the Places section are coordinated by number with a full-color map (e.g. ❶), and a symbol at the top of every right-hand page tells you where to find the map.

CONTENTS

Plaza Colón in
the heart of
Old San Juan.

THE BEST OF PUERTO RICO

Dazzling white-sand beaches fringed by coral reef, steamy rainforests harboring unique flora and fauna, elegant architecture, and thriving markets and malls...

Here, at a glance, are our top recommendations for a visit

BEST BEACHES

- **Luquillo Beach**, east of San Juan, is popular with families and a safe place for children to swim. The kiosks sell afternoon snacks *(see page 160)*.
- **Playa Boquerón** is one of the finest beaches on the island. The fine sands of the wide, curving bay back onto a palm grove, and coral lies beneath its calm waters *(see page 203)*.
- **Playa de Vega Baja** is surrounded by lush countryside and sheltered by a series of weird rock formations running parallel to the sea *(see page 176)*.
- **Crashboat Beach**, named after a shipwreck, is best in the northern section, where the fishermen land their catch and the brightly colored fishing boats rest *(see page 196)*.
- **Isla Verde** is just a minute from all the main resort hotels in San Juan. This white-sand beach is one of the most popular on the island. Rincón is a surfer's paradise, best visited from October through April *(see page 144)*.

FOREST AND NATURE RESERVES

- **Las Cabezas de San Juan Nature Preserve** is an environmental paradise where you can observe most of Puerto Rico's natural habitats *(see page 162)*.
- **El Yunque** receives more than 100 billion gallons of rain per year, making it the perfect habitat for 26 unique animal species *(see page 157)*.
- **Guánica's Forest Reserve** is known for its birdlife as well as its endangered plant species. Some 750 plant and tree species grow here – 16 of them indigenous *(see page 226)*.
- **Boquerón Nature Reserve** is a mangrove forest and noted birdlife habitat *(see page 203)*.
- **Toro Negro Forest Reserve**, up in the mountains, provides great views of both coasts *(see page 240)*.

ABOVE: idyllic Soni Beach, Culebra Island.
RIGHT: Puerto Rico has acres of pristine rainforest.

SNORKELING AND SCUBA DIVING

● **Mona Island**, often called the Galapagos of the Caribbean, has marine life you won't see close to the big island's shores *(see page 254)*.

● **Rincón, Aguadilla and Jobos** on the island's west coast, have unparalleled beauty. Beginners and experienced divers will like **Desecheo Island**, off Rincón and surrounded by a rocky bottom some 120 ft (36 meters) down. Aguadilla's **Crashboat Beach** offers great snorkeling near the old dock and in the caves and reef nearby. **Bahuras Beach**, just west of Jobos, has underwater caverns teeming with tropical fish of all stripes and colors. The coral reef is close to shore and flush with marine life *(see pages 196–7)*.

● **Fajardo** is known for its calm, clear waters and cays and reefs. Icacos offers a narrow stretch of bone-white beach and a coral underworld 20 ft (6 meters) below the sea. Here you can see elkhorn, staghorn, brain, star and other corals *(see page 161)*.

● **Caja de Muertos**, an island off the coast of Ponce, has beautiful coral in calm blue Caribbean waters with a fairly slow current *(see page 223)*.

● **Vieques** is unique for its contrast: rich in marine life in some parts, and completely void in others due to US naval activities. Follow the fish for the best diving spots, but even snorkelers can glimpse sea turtles, rays and the brightest blue coral near Vieques' Sun Bay *(see page 247)*.

ABOVE: scuba divers in Puerto Rico can explore coral reefs and caves in clear blue waters.
BELOW: Clara Cave in Río Camuy Cave Park.

AROUND THE ISLAND

● **Río Camuy Cave Park** has one of the most dramatic subterranean cave systems yet discovered. Trains take passengers between caves and sinkholes that have taken the Camuy River millions of years to erode *(see page 187)*.

● **Phosphorescent Bay** is known for its glowing waters. It has a high concentration of bioluminescence, generated by microscopic organisms in the water. Take a boat trip out into the bay to agitate the trillions of dinoflagellates, and watch them light up *(see page 250)*.

● **Cordillera Central** is an extensive mountainous range that divides the island from east to west *(see page 231)*.

● **Arecibo Observatory** sits in the heart of the karst country, a region of archetypal limestone erosion, and has the largest single-dish radio telescope in the world. It has been silently scanning the universe, making maps of distant solar systems, and listening for messages from other planets since 1960 *(see page 182)*.

● **Tibes Indian Ceremonial Park** is one of the Caribbean's most important Amerindian archeological sites. Visit the museum to find out more about the Amerindian peoples *(see page 223)*.

HIGHLIGHTS OF SAN JUAN

- **El Morro** was one of a ring of forts that held the key to Spanish power in the Caribbean. The watchtowers of the fortress look out to sea and inland across San Juan bay to the coastal plains beyond *(see page 132)*.
- **La Fortaleza** is one of the jewels of San Juan. Now the home of the Governor of Puerto Rico, this fort has undergone numerous changes over the centuries and you will find renovations in the baroque, Gothic and neoclassical styles *(see page 123)*.
- **Iglesia San José** is a true rarity of Spanish Gothic architecture, built in the 1530s. The body of Ponce de León was interred here for over 300 years, before being moved to the San Juan Cathedral in 1908 *(see page 130)*.

- **Casa Blanca** is the oldest house in Puerto Rico and for 250 years was the home of the descendants of Ponce de León. The interior is a museum to life in 16th- and 17th-century San Juan, with rooms full of period furniture *(see page 134)*.
- **San Juan Cathedral** was built of wood and straw in 1521, but was destroyed by a tropical storm only five years later. It was rebuilt with Gothic vaulted ceilings and a circular staircase. Three tiers of white pilasters and arches mount to a simple cross at the cathedral's pinnacle *(see page 126)*.
- **Tapia Theater** was named after the Puerto Rican playwright, Alejandro Tapio y Rivera. and opened in 1832. Today, it stages modern and classical ballet, dance and drama, often by local writers and choreographers *(see page 119)*.
- **La Rogativa** is a bronze statue commemorating the torchlight procession that saved the city in 1797 *(see page 129)*.

BEST MUSEUMS

- The **Pablo Casals Museum** in Old San Juan lets visitors peek at the legacy of the legendary cellist, who was originally from Spain but made Puerto Rico his home *(see page 130)*.
- **Ponce Art Museum**, Ponce. This is Puerto Rico's best place to see the classics, representing schools from around the world *(see page 219)*.
- **Museo de las Américas**, San Juan. The emphasis here is on Puerto Rican life, and you can also get an overview of cultural development in the New World *(see page 131)*.
- **Museo de Arte de Puerto Rico**, San Juan. This converted hospital in Santurce houses works by well known Puerto Rican artists dating back to the 17th century, as well as regional and international works. The museum is also home to Pikayo, one of the city's best

restaurants for gourmet criollo cuisine *(see page 143)*.
- At **Ponce's Museo de la Musica Puertorriqueña** (Musical Instruments Museum), you can see the musical instruments and learn about the history of the island's music, which is rooted in African, European and native sounds *(see page 219)*.

LEFT: El Morro fort in Old San Juan.
ABOVE: Museo de Arte de Puerto Rico in San Juan.
BELOW: sculpture at Ponce Art Museum.

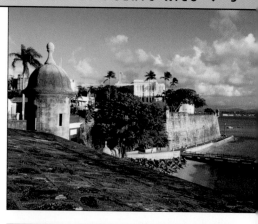

FUN FOR CHILDREN

- The **Parque de las Palomas** in Old San Juan is the perfect place for parents of small children who need to rest their tired feet after a long day of sightseeing in the hilly Old City *(see page 124)*.
- **The Museo del Niño** (Children's Museum) in Old San Juan is a hands-on, educational activity center for kids of all ages. Children can create crafts, play dress-up in a model town and learn the basics of Puerto Rican culture *(see page 127)*.
- **Parque de Bombas**, Ponce. Kids will marvel at the old-fashioned red- and black-striped firehouse that is in the center of the town square. *(see page 219)*.
- **Arecibo Lighthouse and Historical Park** is a fun and educational excursion, with an observation bridge over a small tank containing sharks and rays, replicas of a Taíno indian village, a pirate's ship and a mini-zoo *(see page 178)*.
- **The Mayagüez Zoo** is Puerto Rico's only place to see lions, tigers and bears, as well as explore a forest-style cave that is part of the zoo's new conservation center for reptiles and amphibians *(see page 201)*.
- **Parque de las Ciencias** in Bayamón has displays on archeology, transportation, health and marine eco-systems. A plaza houses models of rockets from NASA *(see page 149)*.

OUTDOOR LIFE

- **Plaza de la Dársena** and **Paseo de la Princesa** are relaxing places to gather and take evening walks. On weekends, artisans set up shop and visitors can buy crafts and listen to live music *(see page 128)*.
- **Paseo de Diego** in Río Piedras is an open-air mall popular with bargain-hunters as well as students from the nearby University of Puerto Rico *(see page 148)*.
- **The Plaza del Mercado** in Mayagüez is a shopping paradise where you can find everything from live chickens to *brazo gitano*, a cake filled with guava paste *(see page 199)*.
- **The Plaza del Mercado** in Ponce spreads across several blocks north of Plaza las Delicias. Here, merchants and customers haggle in an ambiance charged with excitement *(see page 220)*.

ABOVE: sunset at Paseo de la Princesa.
LEFT: kids can play with the birds in the Parque de las Palomas. **BELOW:** an old-style golden bank repository.

MONEY-SAVING TIPS

The Puerto Rico National Parks Service operates small economy cabins in Humacao, Arroyo, Anasco, Boquerón and Marico (Monte del Estado). These no-frills cabins have kitchens and bathrooms, but you supply sheets and towels. They are popular with Puerto Rican families in the summer but are easier to reserve during the high tourist season from November through May. Check availability at www.parquesnacionalespr.com. For those looking for economy without sacrificing comfort, the 17 *paradores*, or small inns, of Puerto Rico are ideal; visit www.gotoparadores.com.

The best transportation bargain in Puerto Rico is the ferry system. For just 50 cents you can cross from Old San Juan to Cataño to tour the Bacardí Rum Factory. The ride is short, pleasant and you get a lovely view both ways. Likewise, the ferry from Fajardo to either Vieques or Culebra is under $5 for a round-trip.

Puerto Ricans are experts at having a good time without spending a lot of cash. There is no charge to use any of Puerto Rico's beaches, save small parking fees. On the weekends, Old San Juan abounds with free activities, from kite flying near El Morro to live music at Paseo de la Princesa. Visit www.gotopuertorico.com for details of special attractions.

A HEADY MIX

Multi-faceted history, colorful culture, breathtaking scenery and distinctive rhythms make Puerto Rico truly a "rich port"

Although the island was originally called *San Juan Bautista* – St John the Baptist – by Christopher Columbus when he discovered it in 1493, it was Juan Ponce de León, the island's first governor, who enthusiastically gave the entire country the name of what was then just the capital: Puerto Rico, meaning "rich port." And it's no wonder, for Puerto Rico is indeed "rich" in many ways. What was once Spain's most important military outpost in the Caribbean has blossomed into not only a marvelous place to live and work for some 3.9 million people with an unparalleled passion for life, but also an "out-of-this-world" vacation destination – an exotic land spiced with beauty, romance and adventure.

The island of Puerto Rico is 100 miles (160 km) long and just 32 miles (51 km) from north to south; if it were to be flattened, however, it would be three times that size thanks to large areas of densely forested mountains. This topography concentrates the population in a few very crowded urban centers, where car ownership is the sixth highest in the world. Meanwhile, up in the mountains, rural life prevails; time ticks by virtually unnoticed, and some farming is carried out using the same methods as five centuries ago.

As a result of its varied landscape, the island has three different kinds of weather: a tropical climate on the beaches of the north coast; endless rains in the lush forests of the mountainous center; and a dry, arid heat along the southern coast. In fact, some people say that weather is born in Puerto Rico.

Puerto Rico overflows with traces of its past: in primitive carvings, in architecture, in cuisine and even in farming techniques. Yet, at the same time, the island has kept up with progress – as its designer stores, art galleries, symphony concerts, communications technology and championship golf courses all attest.

Cultural cocktail

In Puerto Rico, everyone comes from somewhere else. Although the Taíno population had all but vanished within a few years of Spanish colonization, a few poor Spanish farmers intermarried with some remaining Amerindians. Few of these, known as *jíbaros*, remain today, but their cultural imprint survives. Later, African slaves arrived to work on the sugar plantations, as well as other Caribbean islanders seeking jobs. Spanish loyalists sought refuge here, fleeing Simón Bolívar's independence movement in South America.

The French also flocked to Puerto Rico, leaving behind various upheavals in Louisiana and Haiti. Even farmers from Scotland and Ireland in search of a better life ended up on the island,

PRECEDING PAGES: El Castillo San Cristóbal, San Juan; San Cristóbal Canyon.
LEFT: colorful character taking a stroll in Old San Juan.

hoping to benefit from its rich sugar-cane economy. Chinese workers came to build roads in the 1800s; they were followed by Italians, Germans and Lebanese. In 1898, US expatriates sought the island as a home and more recently Cubans, Dominicans and Argentinians have settled here. If ever there was a cultural cocktail, Puerto Rico is it.

Although English is spoken well, Spanish is predominant – but it, too, is a mix, with many words borrowed from both the pre-Columbian Amerindian tongue and modern-day English.

After the struggles of independence, and power tussles with the Dutch and the English, Puerto Rico eventually arrived at a strange but fruitful relationship with the United States. Puerto Ricans enjoy citizen status and can travel freely to and from the mainland; there's no such thing as a Puerto Rican passport. Oddly, they can't vote in US presidential elections, but they *can* vote in the Democratic and Republican primaries – hence presidential candidates sometimes campaign here. A resident commissioner is elected to the US House of Representatives by Puerto Ricans, but although he has a voice he has no vote on legislative matters.

Without question, the relationship with the United States is vital for Puerto Rico's economy: many US corporations have bases on the island, and 2½ million Puerto Ricans spend their working lives on the mainland. Nevertheless, the island likes to keep its distance: in repeated referendums (plebiscites) Puerto Ricans have voted against becoming America's 51st state.

Island spirits

Although Puerto Rico is predominantly Roman Catholic, its Christianity is blended with some Taíno and African traditions, and some say it is spiritism – once banned by Spanish colonial rulers – that is the country's true religion, for it flourishes in many pockets of the island. Spiritists believe that *jípia*, or spirits of the dead, sleep by day and roam the island at night, searching for wild fruit to eat. Even today, modern homes will have a bowl of bright plastic fruit in the kitchen to appease the spirits.

You may spot children wearing bead charm bracelets to guard against the "evil eye"; to look on another person or their possessions covetously may lead to sickness or even death, according to believers. Indeed, spiritism figures in the daily activities of many islanders – through healing, folk medicine and even food. Spiritist literature can be found throughout the island at *botánicas*.

Saints are relied upon to keep the hurricanes away – not always successfully: witness the devastation caused in 1998 by Hurricane Georges, just one of many such storms to plow across Puerto Rico over the centuries. Every town has a patron saint, and *santos*, carved religious figures, are in every home to protect the family. The family unit is still key to local life, with Sunday picnics on the beaches a traditional pastime.

Puerto Rico is an enigmatic, spiritual, magical destination, where the familiar mixes naturally with the exotic. This distinctive, heady mix is examined, explored, and celebrated in the following pages. ❏

RIGHT: *vejigante* fiesta mask dancer.

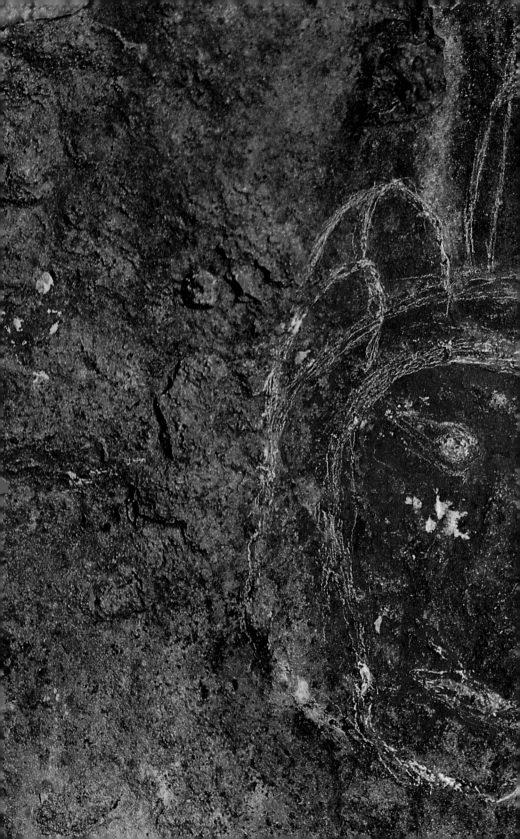

Decisive Dates

ANCIENT TIMES

4500 BC Archaic tribes arrive in Puerto Rico, probably from Venezuela's Rio Orinoco delta.
AD 200–700 Igneri people inhabit the island.
800–1500 Taíno Indian civilization flourishes.

AGE OF EXPLORERS

1493 Columbus lands near Aguadilla, claiming the island for Spain.
1508 Juan Ponce de León establishes first settlement at Caparra.

1510 King of Spain appoints Ponce de León governor of San Juan Bautista, as Puerto Rico is then known.
1516 Entrepreneurs construct the island's first *ingenio* – a factory in which raw cane is ground, boiled and reduced to sugar crystals.
1520s Island officially called Puerto Rico.
1521 Ponce de León dies in Florida: Caparra settlement moved to present-day Old San Juan.
1530 Casa Blanca, Puerto Rico's first real defensive edifice, is completed.
1531 Puerto Rico sends its first sugar exports to Spain.
1532 Army begins building La Fortaleza.
1539 Spaniards begin construction of El Morro fortress.

1580s Governor Diego Menéndez de Valdes improves the island's military preparedness by constructing new fortresses and refurbishing others.
1598 Ginger replaces sugar as Puerto Rico's main cash crop; influenza epidemic wipes out most of the able-bodied population of San Juan.
1625 Dutch captain Boudewijn Hendrikszoon lays siege to San Juan; he retreats after only a month.
1630s–40s King Philip IV of Spain realizes his plan to fortify the entire city of San Juan: seven fortresses linked by stone walls.
1765 Spain sends Alejandro O'Reilly to probe illicit island trade; population estimated at 45,000.
1797 British forces under General Abercromby try to take San Juan; they retreat only a few weeks later.
1812 Spain grants conditional citizenship to island residents.
1813–18 Trade grows to eight times its previous level.
1823 Miguel de la Torres appointed governor.
1824 King of Spain concedes the right of Puerto Rican ports to harbor non-Spanish merchant ships.
1856 Ramón Emeterio Betances is exiled for his criticism of the colonial authorities.
1868 *Grito de Lares* revolt marks beginning of the *independentista* movement.
1887 Luis Muñoz Rivera becomes one of the founders of the Autonomist Party.
1897 Spain declares Puerto Rico an autonomous territory; Muñoz Rivera is appointed Secretary of State and Chief of the Cabinet.

ENTER THE US

1898 Spanish-American War; US troops land at Guánica, bringing the island under American jurisdiction.
1899 Hurricane devastates sugar and coffee industry.
1900 Foraker Act formalizes Puerto Rico's colonial status.
1904 Luis Muñoz Rivera becomes a founder of the Unionist Party.
1910 Muñoz Rivera elected Resident Commissioner to the US House of Representatives.
1917 Jones Act extends US citizenship to Puerto Ricans; labor leader Pablo Iglesias is elected to the new Senate.
1922 Nationalist Party is founded.
1936 Two Nationalist gunmen shoot and kill San Juan's police chief.
1937 Twenty Nationalist protesters are killed by police in the "Ponce Massacre."

PRECEDING PAGES: Taíno petroglyph.
LEFT: Juan Ponce de León.
RIGHT: Luis Muñoz Marín.

1938 Luis Muñoz Marín, only son of Luis Muñoz Rivera, forms the Popular Democratic Party.

1942 Puerto Rico Industrial Development Company established.

POST-WORLD WAR II

1946 Jesús Piñero, appointed by President Truman, becomes the first native governor in the island's history.

1948 Muñoz Marín takes office as the first freely elected governor of Puerto Rico.

1950 Nationalists try to kill President Truman in Washington, and stir up revolt at home.

1952 Puerto Rico made a US commonwealth (July 25).

1954 Nationalists open fire in the US House of Representatives, wounding five Congressmen.

MODERN TIMES

1960s Operation Bootstrap in full swing.

1964 Muñoz Marín resigns from political office.

1967 More than 60 percent of voters choose to retain commonwealth status in islandwide plebiscite.

1968 Luis A. Ferré elected governor.

1976 Carlos Romero-Barceló elected governor.

1978 Police kill two young *independentistas*, sparking the Cerro Maravilla scandal.

1985 Governor Rafael Hernández Colón links Section 936 benefits to President Reagan's Caribbean Basin Initiative (CBI) program, preserving the benefits, provided that Puerto Rico funds development projects of $100 million a year in various Caribbean islands.

1986 A New Year's Eve fire at the Dupont Plaza Hotel kills 97; arsonists are blamed.

1991 Hernández Colón abolishes English as one of Puerto Rico's two official languages.

1992 Pedro Rosselló, after his election as governor, restores English as an official language.

1993 Voters elect to retain commonwealth status; five

days later, Puerto Rico celebrates 500th anniversary of the island's discovery by Columbus.

1996 Rosselló re-elected. Carlos Romero-Barceló re-elected as the Commissioner in Washington, DC.

1998 Hurricane Georges wreaks havoc on the island. Voters reject statehood following a third plebiscite.

2000 Sila María Calderón elected governor.

2003 The US Navy pulls out of Vieques after more than six decades of military exercises. The Roosevelt Roads Naval Station in Ceiba closes the following year.

2006 A budget crisis and subsequent fiscal reform prompts Governor Aníbal Acevedo Vilá to institute the island's first sales tax on consumer goods and services.   ❑

A BEGINNER'S GUIDE TO PUERTO RICAN POLITICS

Contrary to popular belief, Puerto Rico's No. 1 sport isn't baseball – it's politics. No matter where you go in the country, you'll find any number of people enthusiastically discussing and arguing about the political situation. The pros and cons of statehood, commonwealth and independence – as well as the activities of politicians – dominate most conversations.

Puerto Rican voters exceed 80 percent participation at virtually every election, a figure so high it is not found anywhere else in the world where voting is not obligatory.

There are three main "players" on the political stage: the Popular Democratic Party, the New Progressive Party

and the Independence Party, which has a much smaller following than the other two.

The Independence Party, obviously, is pushing for complete independence. It is vocal and highly visible and receives a lot of press coverage and attention – but not a lot of actual votes. A closer battle is fought between those groups who want statehood (mainly the New Progressive Party) and the proponents of commonwealth (the Popular Democratic Party).

So now sit back, sip your cold *cerveza* (beer) and enjoy the lively banter in this politically dynamic country. You may even be invited to join in.

BEGINNINGS

By the time the Spanish came, the native peoples had created a sophisticated culture with ingenious farming techniques and fine handicrafts

Within a year of his triumphant return to Spain with news of his discoveries, Columbus set sail across the Atlantic on a second voyage to the New World. When he discovered Puerto Rico on this 1493 trip, he found plenty of Taíno (and Arawak) Indians already occupying the island.

It has not yet been conclusively determined how or when the Taínos arrived, but much has been learned by the discovery at Loíza of a limestone cave containing artifacts of the early people. Carbon-dating reveals that the island has been occupied since the 1st century AD, and shells fashioned into gouging tools for use in the manufacture of dug-out canoes suggest that the first Indians rowed over from Venezuela, where similar relics have been recovered. There was unquestionably steady communication and trade between the Caribbean islands. In his journal Columbus describes a Taíno canoe which seated three men abreast and 70 to 80 in all. "A barge could not keep up with them in rowing," he wrote, "because they go with incredible speed, and with these canoes they navigate among these islands."

A stratified society

Part of a well-defined Indian culture that extended throughout the Antilles, the Taínos in Puerto Rico lived in a rigidly stratified society. A great king lived on the island of Hispaniola, and district *caciques* – chiefs – governed the districts of Puerto Rico, which the natives called *Borinquen* – "Island of the Brave Lord." Each district had a centrally located capital village where the *cacique* resided. As in medieval Europe, heredity determined status within society, which comprised *nitaínos*, or nobles who advised the *caciques* and enjoyed certain privileges; commoners; and *naborías*, or slaves.

Taíno villages ranged in size from around a hundred people to thousands. The Indians spent most of their time out-of-doors, yet they did

build large bell-shaped thatched houses in which as many as 40 family members slept. These were built around a large open space reserved for public ceremonies and for *batey,* which the Spanish referred to as *pelota* – a ball game. The house of the *cacique* was the largest in town and always fronted on this public

square. At Tibes, in Ponce, an Indian village has been reconstructed from ancient ruins.

The Taínos believed in a polytheistic order of creation. Yocahú, the Supreme Creator, commanded all the gods, the earth and its creatures. The angry god of the winds, Juracán, invoked the eponymous hurricanes. In the central square, the Indians observed religious worship and participated in ceremonial dances. Ceramic icons and clay idols displayed in anthropological museums are evidence of the religious past. South of Arecibo, at the 13-acre (5-hectare) Caguana Indian Ceremonial Park, used for religious purposes eight centuries ago, there are stone monoliths, 10 *batey* balls and other artifacts.

LEFT: ancient Taíno stones at Caguana.
RIGHT: mask at Tibes Ceremonial Park.

Traces of Taíno agriculture remain in Puerto Rico. Their ingenious method of sowing a variety of plants in earthen mounds called *conducos* is still employed by some farmers. The *conduco* system mitigated the problems of water distribution: water-intensive crops were placed at the bottom and those requiring good drainage at the top. Cassava bread, the staple of the Taíno diet, was made by grating and draining the root, which the Indians formed into loaves and baked. They also relied heavily upon yams –sweet *batates* and unsweet *ages* – and among the plants the early settlers sent back to Spain were maize, beans, squash and peanuts. Using *macanas* – stout double broad-swords still used by Puerto Rican farmers – and pointed sticks, the Taínos cleared the thick woods and sowed their fields. Various sources of animal protein supplemented the starchy diet: fish and sometimes pigeon or parrot.

A golden age

In the time left over from farming, fishing and bagging small game, the Taínos developed various handicrafts. Early Spanish settlers in the region greatly admired the Indian woodwork: dishes, basins, bowls and boxes. Most prized of all were the ornate *duhos,* carved wooden thrones used by the *caciques.* The Great Taíno Cacique made a gift of a dozen of these to the Spanish Crown in the 1490s. Indian weavers used cotton and other fibrous plants to make colorfully dyed clothing, belts and hammocks. But the handicraft that aroused greatest excitement among the Spanish was the gold jewelry that the Indians wore as rings in their ears and noses. They neither mined nor panned for gold. When the Spaniards, smitten with desire for the precious metal, coaxed the natives into leading them to their sources, they were taken to beaches where gold nuggets from the ocean floor occasionally washed ashore.

Recent findings have shed more light on these indigenous peoples. The Institute of Puerto Rican Culture has amassed large collections of stones, pottery, tools and skeletal remains. Archeologists are deciphering information from ongoing digs. In Old San Juan, at the Institute of Culture, artifacts and indigenous exhibits, together with a miniature model of a Taíno village on display at Casa Blanca, give some insight into the way of life of the early people in the Old City. ❑

RIGHT: Taíno rock carvings near Cayey.

THE SPANISH SETTLERS

At first the Spanish treated the Taíno population well, but soon the natives were enslaved as their invaders lusted for gold. Then came the trade wars

Fifteen years passed between Columbus's discovery of the island of Boriquen on November 19, 1493, and serious attempts to settle it. The adventurer to the New World came across the island by chance during his second voyage while he was trying to reach Hispaniola. Naming it San Juan Bautista, Columbus claimed it for the Spanish crown and promptly departed. From 1493 until 1508, the approximately 30,000 Taínos living on the island enjoyed a period of benevolent neglect: from time to time, Spaniards sailed to San Juan from Hispaniola seeking to barter with local people for food. These encounters were always very friendly.

Enticing gold

One of the Spaniards who visited the island was Juan Ponce de León. The natives' ornaments and trinkets of gold caught Ponce de León's eye. He felt sure that the area was rich in gold, and he secretly scouted the southern coast for mining sites. In the early summer of 1508 Ponce de León and the Spanish governor of the Caribbean, Nicolas de Ovando, signed a clandestine agreement which granted Ponce de León rights to mine the island on condition that he would yield two-thirds to the king. Secrecy was of utmost importance: Christopher Columbus's son, Diego Colón, had inherited the rights to exploit the island, but his family's megalomaniacal desire for wealth had proved dangerous in the past. Physical abuse, dissolution of tribes and families, and starvation of the inhabitants of Hispaniola had been followed by rebellion and bloodshed.

In July 1508, Ponce de León and a band of 50 men – among them Luis de Añasco, the namesake of the river and village – set off for the island of San Juan Bautista. As they sailed eastward along the northern coast, they made friendly contact with the natives, and Agueybaná, the head *cacique* of the island, provided

Ponce de León with an entry which ensured safe passage for him and his crew. Finally, after six long weeks of searching, the intrepid explorers sighted a suitable site for settlement. In a valley several miles inland on an arm of the Bayamón River, Ponce de León founded the island's first European town, *Caparra* (a

word that might be translated as "blossoming"). In official documents, it was referred to as *Ciudad de Puerto Rico*.

Relations between the Indians and the Europeans proceeded swimmingly. Panning the river beds produced enough gold to persuade Ponce de León that the island merited permanent settlement. He had hoped for a small, strictly controlled group of Spaniards to live and work among the Indians without committing abuses or arousing hostility. However, as soon as King Ferdinand caught wind of Puerto Rico's excellent prospects he directed a number of family friends there. Meanwhile, Diego Colón also entered the scene. Incensed that Ponce de León

LEFT: Ponce de León, Puerto Rico's first governor.
RIGHT: Diego Colón and a bust of his famous father.

had grabbed the island for himself, he granted titles to two of his father's supporters – Cristóbal Sotomayor and Miguel Díaz – and subsidized their establishment on the island. San Juan Bautista was now destined to suffer what Ponce de León had tried to avoid. By a colonial ordinance called a *repartimiento* one of Colón's men enslaved 5,500 Indians, ostensibly in order to convert them to Christianity but in reality to press them into labor.

The enslaved natives were divided and placed "under the protection" of 48 *hidalgos* (minor aristocracy, from *hijo de algo*, meaning "son of a somebody"). A combination of feudalism and

Indigenous resistance

During the winter of 1511, violence erupted, and guerrilla warfare soon spread through the island. Ponce de León responded immediately. Within a few days of the initial outburst he and his captains had captured nearly 200 Indians, whom they subsequently sold into slavery, branding them on the face with the king's first initial. By June, peace once again reigned.

For a few years, the search for Puerto Rican gold continued at the expense of the Indians' freedom and until 1540, when the sources dried up, San Juan Bautista remained one of the New World's foremost suppliers of gold to Spain. To

capitalism, this was the *encomienda* system, and it was employed throughout Spain's 16th-century New World empire. Across the northern coast the Spanish opened mines and panning operations, all supported by the free labor of the natives. The king appointed Ponce de León governor in 1510 but did not empower him to relinquish the *repartimiento*. The mining business proliferated, though there was so much competition for gold that the few who profited were men like Ponce de León, who made their fortunes selling food and supplies to the miners. Moreover, not even Ponce de León could check the Spanish settlers' abuse of the Indians, especially in the remote western end of the island.

assuage the wounded sensibilities of Juan Ponce de León for stripping his office down to little more than a title, King Ferdinand gave him permission to explore the virgin peninsula northwest of the Antilles which the Spanish called *La Florida*.

As people continued to immigrate to the island of San Juan Bautista they brought new commercial enterprises. The days when *hidalgos* left their homeland to strike it rich in New World gold mines were gone. Gradually, the settlers turned to agriculture. Land was plentiful and easy to come by, water was abundant and the climate mild. Labor posed a problem at first, for the Indians had disappeared quickly after the institution of the *repartimiento*. Epidemics of European diseases had swept through the communities of enslaved Indians, devastating the population. Those Indians who escaped fled into the mountainous interior or across the sea to join the tribes of coastal South America. However, West Africans, imported by Portuguese slavers and supplied by the Spanish crown, provided an affordable replacement.

Peasant roots

Two sorts of farm developed. Some islanders, denied political and social status because they were *mestizos* (the progeny of a white and an

on the island) were chiefly interested in profit. After experimenting with a variety of crops, including ginger and tobacco, they finally settled on sugar as the most dependable and profitable cash crop. It was relatively new to Europeans, but their sweet tooth appeared to be insatiable.

In 1516, entrepreneurs constructed the island's first *ingenio* – a factory in which raw cane is ground, boiled and reduced to sugar crystals. A decade and a half later, Puerto Rico sent its first sugar exports to Spain. Ferdinand's successor, Holy Roman Emperor Charles V, was so encouraged by it that he provided a

Indian or black), were unable to obtain large land grants and credit. They resorted to subsistence farming and on their tiny plots raised cassava, corn, vegetables, fruit, rice and a few cattle. Generally, *mestizos* cleared fields in inland regions that would not compete with the large coastal plantations. Puerto Rico's sizeable peasant class blossomed from the seeds of these 16th-century subsistence farmers.

In addition there were, of course, owners of large plantations. Usually of purely European ancestry, these immigrants and Creoles (born

number of technicians and loans for the industry's growth. Peripheral industries burgeoned as well: demand for timber to fuel the *ingenios* and food to fuel the laborers soared, and where sugar is processed, so inevitably is rum produced. Determined to squeeze all the profit possible out of their sugar cane, the Spanish settlers built distilleries soon after harvesting the first sugar crop.

By 1550, there were 10 active *ingenios* on the island, but the restrictive policies of the mercantilist King Philip II led to a major crash in the industry during the 1580s. Eventually it recovered, but throughout Puerto Rico's history sugar would be not only one of the

LEFT: the arrival of Christopher Columbus.
ABOVE: slave labor created the plantations.

island's pre-eminent products but also one of its most troubled industries.

Horses and husbandry

After the collapse of the sugar trade, ginger emerged as the most successful product, and despite edicts from the monarch – who preferred the cultivation of sugar – it flourished until the market bottomed out through a surplus. Animal husbandry was another lucrative industry. The armies that conquered Peru, Central America and Florida rode Puerto Rican horses, and island *hatos* (cattle ranches) supplied the local garrisons with meat.

THE MIGHTY LION

Born around 1460 in San Servos, Spain, Don Juan Ponce de León is known essentially for three things: the discovery of what is now Florida, the conquering and governing of Puerto Rico, and his never-ending search for the mythical Fountain of Youth. Historians believe he sought not only the age-restorative waters but also gold and silver thought to be at the site of the fountain. He explored many regions including the Bahamas and Bimini in his quest, but a poisoned arrow shot into his stomach brought his explorations to an abrupt halt. His epitaph, by poet and historian Juan de Castellanos, reads "Here lie the bones of a Lion/mightier in deeds than in name."

The possibility of foreign aggression remained a constant threat. By the 1520s, the economic and strategic promise of the island – now officially called Puerto Rico – had become apparent. Moreover, the individual with the clearest sense of Puerto Rico's potential and importance was gone. Juan Ponce de León had been fatally wounded in an encounter with Florida Indians in 1521; his remains are interred in the Cathedral of San Juan. Without a leader close to the Spanish king, defensive measures were hard to obtain.

In the year of Ponce de León's burial, the colonialists transferred the capital city from the site chosen by him to a large natural bay to the north, renaming it San Juan. Mosquitoes had plagued settlers incessantly in the old river bank town, and the site proved too small to support increased river traffic as agriculture and industry developed.

Advantageous as the new location was for shipping, it left the people vulnerable to foreign invaders. In the 16th and 17th centuries the French, English and Dutch dedicated themselves to unseating the powerful Habsburg monarchs both at home and abroad. As part of this campaign, they launched attack after attack on Spanish salients in the New World. Many of these attacks were carried out by privateers.

Fortifications

Encouraged by rumors of impending assault by French war vessels, San Juan officials in 1522 initiated the construction of the port's first garrison. The wooden structure had not been completed before they realized it would be insufficient in the face of an attack. The island's first real defensive edifice was not completed until 1530, when descendants of Ponce de León built a house of stone, Casa Blanca, designed to provide a refuge for colonialists in the face of foreign aggression. The house still stands in Old San Juan. But not even Casa Blanca fulfilled the defensive needs of the settlement, particularly given the expected large-scale population growth. Two years later, the army began building La Fortaleza, sometimes known as Santa Catalina. Today it houses the offices of the governor of Puerto Rico, and it holds the distinction of being the oldest executive mansion in the Western hemisphere.

La Fortaleza did little to supplement the defenses already provided by Casa Blanca.

Before it had been completed, army officers informed the crown that it had been built in "a poor place" and begged the appropriation of funds for another fortress. El Castillo de San Felipe del Morro (or, simply, El Morro) was the product of their entreaties. Placed on the rocky tip of the San Juan Peninsula, the fortification, which was finished in the 1540s, did much to assuage the fears of the northern capital's residents.

But Puerto Ricans had more to be concerned with than the French alone. The celebrated "sea dogs" of Queen Elizabeth, Francis Drake and Captain John Hawkins, forcibly seized dozens

colonial policy in the western hemisphere, conferred upon the governor the title of Captain-General and directed him to improve the island's military preparedness. Governor Diego Menéndez de Valdes exercised tremendous initiative during the 1580s. A number of fortresses were constructed during his tenure, including El Boquerón and Santa Elena in San Juan. Menéndez ordered the refurbishing of the land bridge La Puente de San Antonio – now La Puente de San Geronimo – and the strengthening of La Fortaleza. He also requisitioned artillery and ammunition, expanding the troop count from 50 to 209 men.

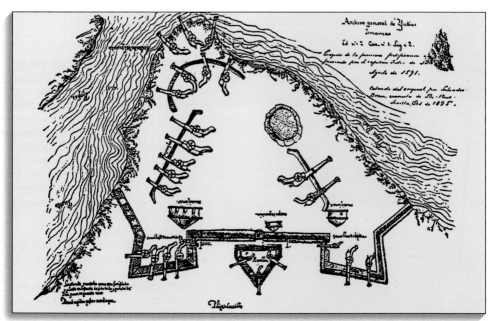

of Spanish cargo ships traveling between the Antilles and Spain. In 1585, open war broke out between the two nations. England's well-known defeat of the Spanish Invincible Armada in 1588 left Spain permanently disabled as a naval power.

More defenses

Towards the end of the 16th century, Puerto Rico received cursory attention. The Council of the Indies, the bureaucracy that oversaw the enforcement and administration of Spanish

Menéndez stepped in just in the nick of time. A string of English assaults launched with the intention of capturing Puerto Rico was thwarted, thanks to sturdy defenses. A historic confrontation in the autumn of 1594 resulted in an English defeat. During one of these battles a cannonball shot through the side of Francis Drake's ship and mortally wounded John Hawkins, who was with Drake in his cabin. Drake was forced to retreat.

Yet the English would not give up. While the Spanish king nearly doubled – to 409 – the number of troops at the San Juan garrison of El Morro, the veteran sea warrior George Clifford, third Earl of Cumberland, secretly

LEFT: foreign navies were a constant threat, hence the heavy fortifications at El Morro (**ABOVE**).

planned an assault. He was aided by an influenza epidemic in 1598, which wiped out most of the able-bodied population of San Juan. As a result, the city was seriously unprepared for the imminent attack.

Influenza's revenge

From a point 80 miles (129 km) east of the capital, Cumberland's troops marched toward San Juan in June, easily taking fortifications as they proceeded. On July 1, the defenders who had been forced to hole up in El Morro surrendered the town. But the same scourge which had weakened the Puerto Ricans now struck the

English conquerors. More than 400 English soldiers died of influenza within six weeks. The Puerto Ricans promptly availed themselves of the British state of weakness. Refusing to acknowledge Cumberland's authority, they engaged relentlessly in skirmishes on the outskirts of the town. On August 27, Cumberland withdrew from the island, destroying two plantations in his wake.

Next the Dutch entered the picture. Determined to bring Spanish dominance of the Caribbean to an end, they commissioned Boudewijn Hendrikszoon to take over the island. Hendrikszoon's fleet of eight vessels arrived in San Juan harbor on September 24,

1625. In the course of the next three days the Dutch slowly advanced, forcing a Spanish retreat into El Morro.

The siege of San Juan lasted a month. Finally, the courageous captains Juan de Amezquita and Andres Botello led surprise attacks on the Dutch trenches on October 22. The next 10 days of battle left the Dutch fleet severely damaged – one ship destroyed and the troops depleted. The island was confirmed as a Spanish domain.

In the 1630s and 1640s, King Philip IV of Spain realized his plan to fortify the entire city of San Juan: seven fortresses were linked by a line of stone walls. The natives were inducted into the provincial district militia.

In control

Having seen off the English and the Dutch, the island was now relatively safe from invaders, and attention was turned to the problem of establishing a strong economic base. But, as a Spanish colony, Puerto Rico was allowed to keep open only one port – San Juan – and was barred from trading with non-Spanish powers. These strictures seriously limited the chances for economic growth.

In the mid-16th century, when the influx of African slaves diminished, Britain threatened Spain on the high seas, and when non-Spanish producers in the West Indies developed more efficient sugar production, the sugar industry collapsed. Virtually nothing was exported in the 1560s and 1570s. In 1572, there was not a single ship in the harbor, and there was a seven-year span in which no European vessels docked at San Juan at all.

The Spanish crown, wishing to convert Puerto Rico into a defensive salient, instituted an assistance program called the *situado*. According to this plan, Puerto Rico was to receive from Mexico 2½ million *maravedies* annually – a substantial sum. Although the *situado* was fraught with problems – such as privateers repeatedly intercepting the money in transit – the erratic delivery of bullion from Mexico kept the island afloat until independent economic development began.

Smugglers all

Ironically, what turned the flagging island economy around was the circumvention of the Spanish mercantilist policies that had been the cause of Puerto Rico's problems to begin with. Refused permanent concessions by the crown, the planters and merchants on Puerto Rico engaged increasingly in illicit foreign trade. Local produce – sugar, livestock, tobacco – was exchanged for slaves, staples, tools and other manufactured goods. By the mid-17th century almost everyone, from clerical authorities to soldiers, from friars to peasants, was involved in smuggling. The coastal towns of Aguada, Arecibo, Cabo Rojo and Fajardo grew into busy centers of illicit international trade.

Word of the proliferation of contraband activity and privateering in Puerto Rico eventually got back to Spain. Recognizing that the island's problems were critical, the king sent a commissioner, Alejandro O'Reilly, to evaluate the state of Puerto Rico. O'Reilly's report of 1765 was remarkably comprehensive and perspicacious. He reckoned the island's population had reached about 45,000: 40,000 free men and 5,000 slaves. Most of the urban inhabitants lived in northeastern coastal towns and earned their livelihood through smuggling and black-market trade. Smuggling was so prevalent that O'Reilly could report extensively on prices, supply, demand and distribution.

In 1765, a Spanish council met to review O'Reilly's report and to formulate a solution to the Puerto Rican problem. Recognizing the need for a stronger enforcement agent to curb contraband trade, Spain more than doubled the *situado* and installed Don Miguel de Muesas as governor. He was instructed to create a sturdy domestic economy. By building bridges and roads, by strengthening defenses, and by improving public education he hoped to promote agricultural prosperity and domestic self-sufficiency.

Despite the ability with which O'Reilly pleaded Puerto Rico's case, Spain continued to see the development of the island's economy as secondary to its importance as the first naval fortification in the New World empire. Further, a population boom – largely attributable to immigration – had more than tripled the number of residents on the island by the turn of the century.

Meanwhile, Great Britain had its eye on Puerto Rico and was showing a readiness to acquire it. In 1797, after Napoleonic France and Spain had declared war on Britain, a British fleet of 60 vessels manned by 9,000 troops under the command of General Abercromby landed at Boca de Cangrejos. On April 17, they took Santurce and quickly laid siege to the walled capital. Militia detachments from around the island arrived and launched a counterattack. Abercromby ordered a retreat on May 1.

Shifting control

Napoleon's invasion of Spain in 1808 sent shock waves through the empire and led to a complete reorganization of colonial rule. As control over the transatlantic territories became

weakened, several countries in the Americas won independence from Spain. A provisional assembly called the *Cortes* was convened in Spain to rule in the name of the deposed King Ferdinand VII. Fearing that Puerto Rican separatists who sympathized with the rebellious colonialists in South and Central America – Mexico and Venezuela particularly – would instigate revolutions at home, the *Cortes* invited Puerto Rico to send a delegation to Cádiz in 1809.

An island Creole by the name of Ramón Power Giralt went as the colony's emissary and was elected vice president of the assembly. He pushed for reforms designed to ameliorate the

---

LEFT: relics at Casa Blanca, Puerto Rico's first fort.
RIGHT: the patron saint of sailors.

social and economic ills of the island. Puerto Ricans gained status as Spanish citizens; tariffs on machinery and tools were dropped; a university was founded; and measures were taken to improve island industry. The *Cortes* disbanded in 1814 when Napoleon retreated and King Ferdinand VII returned to the throne. But the king, wary of the independence fever pervading the colonies, left in place a fair number of Power Giralt's reforms in a *cédula de gracias* (royal decree) granted in 1815.

During the 10 years from 1795, trade between the United States and the Spanish West Indies grew by a factor of six. Household goods, food and, to a minor extent, slaves were

supplied by the United States in exchange for West Indian staples such as sugar, coffee, rum and spices. In 1803, Puerto Rico sent 263,000 pounds of sugar to the United States, and the amount exported grew yearly. In 1807, the US president, Thomas Jefferson, placed an embargo on all trade with the Spanish West Indies, which cut exports by more than half, but after Napoleon Bonaparte's invasion of the Iberian Peninsula Jefferson lifted the embargo.

Not long after it was lifted, new difficulties floated into Puerto Rican harbors. Trying to respond to the threat Napoleon's armies posed on Spain's borders, the Spanish governor

called upon its colonies to ship an extraordinary supply of resources which could be used to outfit and maintain its own troops. With most profitable products going to Spain, Puerto Rico's economy suffered. And added to all these woes was the War of 1812 between Great Britain and the United States. The British blockade of the North American coast severely hampered American trade. Puerto Rico, by then one of the major suppliers of sugar to America, had nowhere to turn.

Increasing independence

The recovery following this tumultuous period included tremendous growth in the island economy. Power Giralt's economic reforms remained in place and, for the first time since their institution, began to have a real effect. Not only was trade with the wealthy United States permitted, but the tariffs were also decreased significantly. The *cédula de gracias* declared by Ferdinand VII in 1815 ended the Spanish trade monopoly in Puerto Rico by permitting trade with other countries. However, according to the dictates of the king, only Spanish vessels were allowed to carry on the exports.

Once again, the colonial governors took exception to Spanish policy. Disobeying the king's orders, they gave right of entry to ships regardless of their origins. Also, under a civil intendancy plan instituted by Power Giralt, an independent official was appointed to oversee financial affairs, rather than their being left in the hands of the governor. Alejandro Ramírez Blanco filled the post first. During his tenure he opened several ports, abolished superfluous taxes, and increased the export of cattle.

Between 1813 and 1818 Puerto Rican trade expanded to eight times its previous level, and in 1824 the king finally relinquished the last vestiges of mercantilism, conceding the right of Puerto Rican ports to harbor non-Spanish merchant ships. The future of the Puerto Rican economy became clear to many. Spain was neither a reliable nor a tremendously profitable trading partner, and the more Puerto Rico moved away from its dependence on the mother country, the faster its economy would develop. ❏

Left: the US flag flies prominently outside the University of Puerto Rico.
Right: slave market in Puerto Rico.

SELF RULE AND THE UNITED STATES

"It wasn't much of a war, but it was all the war there was," said Teddy Roosevelt.

Even so, the Spanish-American War marked a turning point for Puerto Rico

In 1820 the population of Puerto Rico was estimated at 150,000. By 1900 it had mushroomed to about a million. The character of society had changed drastically; for the first time, agitators for Puerto Rican autonomy were vocal and posed a serious threat to the Spanish government. Increasingly, the royally appointed governor and the army would be identified as impediments to the achievement of Puerto Rican independence. In 1820 Pedro Dubois had scarcely initiated a recruitment program when he was discovered by the government. The governor incarcerated Dubois at El Morro and had him executed before a firing squad.

Three years after the Dubois incident, another event in the struggle for autonomy took place. After the restoration of Ferdinand to the throne in 1814, a series of governors with absolute power ruled Puerto Rico. On the first day of 1820, an army commander declared the liberal reformist constitution of 1812 to be still in effect. One by one officials of various districts joined him. The already weak king, hoping to avoid an all-out revolution, had to concede, and decided to resurrect the *Cortes,* disbanded in 1814. José María Quiñones went to Spain as the representative from Puerto Rico in 1823. He submitted a plan to introduce more autonomy to the island colonies, particularly in the administration of domestic affairs.

The *Cortes* approved the Quiñones proposal, but its intentions fell to pieces before it could see them through. In 1823 the constitutional government of Spain collapsed. The king returned to absolute power and appointed the first of 14 governors of Puerto Rico who exercised unlimited authority over the colony, collectively staging a 42-year reign of oppression and virtual martial law.

The first of these dictators was Miguel de la Torre. Hanging on to the governorship for 15 years, Torre imposed a 10pm curfew and

established the *visita* – an island-wide inspection network that allowed him to keep abreast of activity in the colony and maintain tight security. Although Torre's reign was oppressive, it had some benefits. He took control of the country's development, built roads and bridges and brought in huge numbers of black

BETANCES.

slaves to foster sugar production, contributing significantly to the lasting development of the local economy.

Subversive beards

In 1838 a group of separatists led by Buenaventura Quiñones plotted a putsch. Word of the conspiracy leaked out and several of the participants were executed; the others were exiled. Declaring beards subversive, the new governor banned the wearing of facial hair. Subsequent governors passed laws aimed at the suppression of blacks (following the historic slave rebellion on Martinique) and instituted the *libreta* laws which required all inhabitants of

---

LEFT: battling in the Spanish-American War.
RIGHT: a "subversive beard", Dr Ramón Emeterio Betances spoke out against the authorities.

Puerto Rico to carry passbooks and restricted unauthorized movement. It was a troubled time for the beautiful island; between 1848 and 1867, seven consecutive military dictators governed the island, taking advantage of the institutions put into place by the Torres administration. To add to the colony's misery, in the 1850s a cholera epidemic swept across the island, claiming the lives of 30,000. Ramón Emeterío Betances, a doctor renowned for his efforts against the epidemic, was exiled in 1856 for his criticism of the colonial authorities.

Intimidated by the growing separatist fervor in Puerto Rico and Cuba, and by the Dominican

1870s under the aegis of the Puerto Rican Revolutionary Committee. Covert satellite organizations formed in villages and towns across Puerto Rico, centering around Mayagüez. On September 23, 1868, several hundred men congregated at a farm outside the northwestern mountain town of Lares. Marching under a banner that read *Libertad o Muerte. Viva Puerto Rico Libre. Año 1868* ("Liberty or Death. Long Live Free Puerto Rico. Year 1868") they took the town and arrested its officials. They elected a provisional president and proclaimed the Republic of Puerto Rico. The Republic would be short-lived. Troops sent by the governor met

Revolution in 1862, the crown of Spain invited Puerto Rico and Cuba in 1865 to draft a colonial constitution in the form of a "Special Law of the Indies." The documents which emerged called for the abolition of slavery, freedom of the press and speech, and independence on a - commonwealth basis. While the crown dragged its feet in granting these concessions, in Puerto Rico the angry governor, José María Marchessi, exiled several leading reformists, including the recently returned Betances. Fleeing to New York, they joined with other separatist Puerto Ricans and Cubans.

From New York the autonomists directed the independence movement during the 1860s and

the rebel front at San Sebastián and won an easy victory. Within six weeks the echoes of the "Grito de Lares" – "the Shout of Lares" – had died completely, although it has retained lasting symbolic importance in the Puerto Rican independence movement.

Brief independence

Puerto Rico did enjoy a brief flash of autonomy in 1897. The Autonomist Party voted to fuse with the monarchist Liberal Party of Spain after forming a pact with its leader, Mateo Sagasta, which guaranteed Puerto Rican autonomy if the Liberals came to power. On the assassination of the Spanish prime minister

Sagasta became Spain's leader; he immediately declared Puerto Rico an autonomous state.

Adopting a two-chamber constitutional republican form of government, as agreed with Sagasta, the Puerto Ricans elected a lower house of assembly and half of the delegates to the upper house. The governor was still appointed by Spain, but his power was carefully restricted. The new government assumed power in July 1898. Later that month General Nelson A. Miles of the United States landed on the

> ## LAST PRIZE?
>
> When the US "won" Puerto Rico, only an eighth of the population was literate, and only one out of 14 children attended school.

southern coast with an army of 16,000 men. It was the beginning of the Spanish-American War and the end of short-lived Puerto Rican autonomy.

The US steps in

"It wasn't much of a war, but it was all the war there was," Teddy Roosevelt reflected on the Spanish-American War. On August 31, 1898, Spain surrendered. The Puerto Rico campaign had lasted only two weeks, the whole war less than four months. General Miles tried to assuage the inhabitants' anxiety about annexation

ABOVE: 19th-century Spanish currency.

as a United States protectorate, however, telling them: "We have come … to promote your prosperity and to bestow upon you the immunities and blessing of the liberal institutions of our government." His assurances did not pacify everyone. Emeterío Betances, now aging, issued a warning to his fellow Puerto Ricans: "If Puerto Rico does not act fast, it will be an American colony forever."

On December 10, 1898, the Treaty of Paris, which settled the final terms of Spain's surrender, was signed. In addition to a large reparations payment, the United States won Puerto Rico and the Philippines from Spain, but Puerto Rico wasn't exactly a grand prize at the time. Its population had reached about a million. A third were blacks and mulattoes who generally had little capital or land. Two percent of the population owned more than two-thirds of the agricultural land, yet 60 percent of the land owned was mortgaged at high interest rates.

It ain't over till it's over

The United States set up a military government, and Puerto Rico was placed under the charge of the War Department. Assuming a hard-headed approach to underdevelopment and a lagging economy, the first three governors-general enjoyed almost dictatorial power. They introduced American currency, suspended defaulted mortgages and promoted trade with the United States. They improved public health, reformed tax laws and overhauled local government.

But to many Puerto Ricans, autonomy was still vital. A leading autonomist leader, Luis Muñoz Rivera, organized a new party in an attempt to reach a compromise between the separatists and the US government. The Federal Party and its ally, the new Republican Party, advocated cooperation with the United States, especially in commercial matters, full civil rights and an autonomous civilian government. But not even the conciliatory approach Muñoz Rivera endorsed satisfied the McKinley administration. The colonial governor-general, George W. Davis, reported to the president that "the people generally have no conception of political rights combined with political responsibilities."

As if political turmoil were not enough, Mother Nature interfered in the form of Hurricane San

Ciriaco in 1899. Three thousand people lost their lives, and the damage to property was immense. The hurricane devastated the vital sugar and coffee crops and left a fourth of the island's inhabitants without homes. The US Congress awarded only $200,000 to the island in relief payments.

Puerto Rico faced an unhappy future. The economy was on the brink of collapse, the hostilities with inept American administrators continued, and there were the apparently insurmountable difficulties of illiteracy and poverty. Things began to look up in 1900, when the Secretary of War, Elihu Root, proposed a program

culturally and economically if its bonds with the US were to strengthen.

Puerto Rico looms large in recent American history. It was the first non-continental US territory and served as the test case for the formation and implementation of colonial policy.

Special interest groups in the United States polarized into two lobbies. The agricultural contingent, fearing competition from Puerto Rican producers whose labor costs were lower, allied with racists who dreaded the influx of the "Latin race" which would result from granting American citizenship to Puerto Ricans. And as proof of Benjamin Franklin's observation

for the gradual introduction of autonomy for Puerto Ricans which President McKinley endorsed. However, though Puerto Rico was suddenly closer to autonomy than it had been since before the Spanish-American War, the path to home rule was not yet clear.

The big debate

For the next 48 years, Puerto Rico and the US had a strange colonial-protectorate relationship. While it was widely acknowledged that the latter possessed enormous wealth from which the former stood to benefit, Puerto Ricans also feared that Betances' prediction would come true – that Puerto Rico would be swallowed up

that politics makes strange bedfellows, these opponents of the administration's Puerto Rican colonial plan found themselves under the blankets with liberal Democrats who opposed imperialism of any sort.

The burgeoning of a colony

With the passing in 1900 of the Foraker Act *(see box on facing page)*, Puerto Rico took on a new colonial status, but reception of the Act could have been better. An immediate challenge

---

ABOVE: US and Puerto Rican flags fly harmoniously over El Castillo San Cristóbal.
RIGHT: American medical officers at Coamo Springs.

to its constitutional legality brought it before the Supreme Court of the United States where the majority declared that constitutionality was not applicable in an "unincorporated entity" like Puerto Rico. Dissenting Chief Justice Fuller wrote that it left Puerto Rico "a disembodied shade in an intermediate state of ambiguous existence."

Reluctant US citizens

On the eve of the United States entry into World War I in 1917, President Wilson approved the Jones-Shafroth Act granting US citizenship to all Puerto Ricans. This Act affronted many Puerto Rican statesmen. For years they had pressed for a break from the US and now, in blatant contradiction of their demands, Congress was drawing them in even more. Muñoz Rivera, the Resident Commissioner, had beseeched Congress to hold a plebiscite – but to no avail. The "Catch-22" of Puerto Rico's relationship with the US had emerged full-blown. The more political maturity the colony showed, the more fervently nationalists agitated for independence. The more hostile to the US the colony seemed to American lawmakers, the more reluctant they were to give any ground.

THE FORAKER ACT

On April 2, 1900, US President McKinley signed a civil law that established a civilian government in Puerto Rico. Although officially known as the Organic Act of 1900, it was more commonly referred to as the Foraker Act for its sponsor, Charles Benson Foraker.

The new government had a presidentially appointed governor, an Executive Council comprising both Americans and Puerto Ricans, and a House of Delegates with 35 elected members. There was also a judicial system with a Supreme Court. All federal laws of the United States were to be in effect on the island. In addition, a Resident Commissioner chosen by the Puerto Rican people would speak for the colony in the House of Representatives, but have no vote. The first civil governor of the island under the Act was Charles H. Allen, inaugurated on May 1, 1900, in San Juan.

An initial 15-percent tariff was imposed on all imports to and exports from the United States, and the revenues would be used to benefit Puerto Rico. Free trade was promised after two years. The colonial government would determine its own taxation programs and oversee the insular treasury. Ownership of large estates by American corporations was discouraged by prohibiting businesses to carry on agriculture on more than 500 acres. However, this clause was rarely enforced and capital-rich firms from the US moved in.

During this period of strong antagonism between Puerto Rico and the US, the island's economy and population grew rapidly. Better health care resulted in a drop in the death rate.

Meanwhile, employment and production increased, and government revenues rose. Big US corporations pocketed most of the profits from this growth, and Congress assured them of continued wealth. In contrast, the average Puerto Rican family earned between $150 and $200 a year; many *jíbaros* had sold their own little farms to work for farm estates and factories.

Pablo Iglesias, a disciple of Samuel Gompers, one of the great fathers of American trade

unions, led the move to organize Puerto Rican laborers. By 1909 the labor movement, organized under Iglesias' leadership as the Free Federation, identified itself with the labor union movement in the US. It even assumed the task of Americanizing Puerto Rico. "The labor movement in Porto [sic] Rico," Iglesias wrote, "has no doubt been, and is, the most efficient and safest way of conveying the sentiments and feelings of the American people to the hearts of the people of Porto Rico."

A 1914 cigar strike and then a 1915 sugar cane strike brought useful publicity. Iglesias was subsequently elected to the new Senate of Puerto Rico in 1917.

Trouble-shooting

The Great Depression of the 1930s nearly undid Puerto Rico. Two hurricanes accompanied the collapse of the economy – San Felipe in 1928 and San Cipriano in 1932 – destroying millions of dollars' worth of property and crops. Starvation and disease took a heavy toll on the population during the Depression. Across the island, haggard, demoralized people waited in long queues for inadequate government food handouts. But out of the poverty and deprivation, a new voice emerged.

It belonged to Pedro Albizu Campos, a former US Army officer and a graduate of Harvard Law School. He was of a generation of Puerto Ricans who were children at the time of the United States' takeover. Equipped with a great understanding of the American system, he used it to become a leader of militant revolutionaries. Albizu Campos's accusation was that (according to both American foreign policy and international law) the United States' claims on Puerto Rico were in fact illegal, since Puerto Rico was already autonomous at the time of occupation.

The strength and seriousness of Albizu Campos's Nationalist organization were made abundantly clear on February 23, 1936. Two of his followers, Hiram Rosado and Elías Beauchamp, shot and killed the chief of police of San Juan. The assassins were arrested and summarily beaten to death, and Albizu Campos and seven key party members were imprisoned in the Federal Prison in Georgia.

A year later, however, the party was still strong. Denied a permit to hold a demonstration in the town of Ponce, a group of Albizu Campos's followers dressed in black shirts assembled to march on March 21, 1937. As the procession moved forward to the tune of *La Borinqueña* – the Puerto Rican anthem – a shot rang out. The origin of the gunfire has never been determined, but within moments police and marchers were exchanging bullets. Twenty people were killed and another hundred wounded in the panic-stricken crossfire that subsequently ensued. The governor called the affair "a riot"; the American Civil Liberties Union labeled it "a massacre." The event is still remembered today as *La Massacre de Ponce*. ❏

LEFT: the Puerto Rican national crest.
RIGHT: sugar-cane harvest near Guayama.

MODERN TIMES

Colony or commonwealth? Or independent state? Luis Muñoz Marín helped decide the issue with the innovative "Operation Bootstrap"

The United States began to export Puerto Rico's share of the New Deal in 1933, but it was not a winning hand. President Franklin Roosevelt sent a string of appointees to the Governor's Mansion in San Juan, but their efforts proved inadequate and aggravating to many Puerto Ricans. Then, from amidst the crumbling political parties, a brilliant star in Puerto Rico's history appeared.

Luis Muñoz Marín, son of the celebrated statesman Luis Muñoz Rivera, had served in government since 1932 and had used his charm and connections with the American political élite to bring attention to the plight of the colony. In 1938, young Muñoz Marín founded the Partido Democratico Popular (PDP), running on the slogan "Bread, Land and Liberty," and adopting the *pava* – the broad-brimmed straw hat worn by *jíbaros* – as the party symbol. In 1940, the *populares* took over half the total seats in the upper and lower Houses.

A people's governor

Muñoz Marín, elected leader of the Senate, decided to try to work with the new governor to achieve recovery. The appointee, Rexford Guy Tugwell, was refreshingly different from his predecessors. Able to speak Spanish and evincing a genuine compassion for the Puerto Ricans, he seemed promising. Muñoz Marín's good faith paid off. By improving the distribution of relief resources and by proposing a plan for long-term economic development, contingent upon continued union with the United States, Muñoz Marín convinced Tugwell that Puerto Rico was finally ready to assume the responsibility of electing its own governor.

As a first step, the United States appointed Puerto Rico's resident commissioner, Jesús Piñero, to the post. In 1946, Piñero became the first native governor in the island's history. Simultaneously, the US unveiled plans for the

LEFT: tuna plant, Mayagüez. Industries such as this boomed under Operation Bootstrap.
RIGHT: Uncle Sam's daughter.

popular election of Puerto Rico's governor, demonstrating new confidence in the colony.

The people elected Muñoz Marín, of course. In 1948 he took office as the first popularly elected governor and put forward his proposal for turning Puerto Rico into an associated free state. Learning from the newly independent

Philippines, where instant autonomy had crippled economic and social progress, the US delayed endorsing Muñoz Marín's plan.

However, in 1950, President Truman approved Public Law 600, the Puerto Rican Commonwealth Bill. It provided for a plebiscite in which voters would decide whether to remain a colony or assume status as a commonwealth. As the latter, Puerto Rico would draft its own constitution, though the US Congress would retain "paramount power." In June 1951, Puerto Ricans voted three to one in favor of the commonwealth.

Two disturbing events punctuated the otherwise smooth transition to commonwealth status. On the very day that President Truman signed Public Law 600, a group of armed Nationalists marched on the Governor's Mansion, La Fortaleza. In a brief skirmish a policeman and four Nationalists were gunned down. Simultaneously, outbursts in five other towns left over a hundred casualties, including 27 dead. The violence extended beyond Puerto Rican shores. Two Puerto Ricans from New York traveled to Washington and made an attempt on the president's life a month later. In March 1954, four Puerto Rican Nationalists fired into the House of Representatives from the visitors' gallery, wounding five Congressmen.

Muñoz Marín resigned from political office in 1964 but his party remained in power. In 1966, a commission determined that commonwealth, statehood and independence all deserved consideration. Seven months later the PDP, pushing for a decision, passed a bill mandating a plebiscite. Muñoz Marín re-entered the fray in support of continuing as a commonwealth. He argued that Puerto Rico had been placed fourth in the worldwide rate of economic progress only due to its relationship with the US. Further, he claimed, statehood could easily bring an end to the independent culture of Puerto Rico. His arguments held sway; two-thirds of the ballots in 1967 were cast for commonwealth status.

Muñoz Marín had long ago recognized that the key to averting future economic catastrophe lay in avoiding a dependence on agriculture. Relying heavily on one or two crops left Puerto Rico subject to too many risks: weather, foreign production and interest rates. The government established the Puerto Rican Industrial Development Corporation in 1942 to oversee the development of government-sponsored manufacturing. When the state plans floundered, the administration canceled the program and initiated a new plan, known as Operation Bootstrap. Aimed at developing an economy based on rum, tourism and industry, the program sent dozens of public-relations agents to the mainland on promotional tours extolling the Puerto Rican climate, geography, economy and people.

During the early years of Operation Bootstrap, manufacturing jobs quadrupled to over 20,000, but between 1950 and 1954 over 100,000 Puerto Ricans moved to the mainland in order to take advantage of the postwar labor market. In New York, Puerto Ricans became the archetypal Latinos, later celebrated in *West Side Story*. A slowdown followed the resumption of peace, but in 1955 manufacturing contributed more to the economy than agriculture for the first time ever.

Operation Serenity

As a complement to Operation Bootstrap, the government instituted a program entitled "Operation Serenity," which had the uplifting of the arts as its objective. Programs to promote music and art were administered by the Institute of Puerto Rican Culture. The thinking at the time was that "man cannot live by bread alone." Poster-making got its start at the Department of Community Education, where serigraph and lithograph techniques were developed. Puerto Rico's new-found skill of poster-making promoted government instructional films and art exhibits, and portrayed local history. A large group of artists and filmmakers were able to develop their skills through the Community Education programs.

Today, the production of Puerto Rico's imaginative posters goes back to those days in the 1950s when the islanders began to pick themselves up from their meager conditions.

LEFT: Luis Muñoz Marín, Puerto Rico's brilliant political star and the first popularly elected governor.
RIGHT: Rita Moreno in *West Side Story*.

Tax holiday

Operation Bootstrap later evolved into Section 936, a clause in the US Internal Revenue Code that partially exempted manufacturers from having to pay federal income tax on profits earned by their subsidiaries located in Puerto Rico. Although 936 was phased out in 2005, some 2,000 factories still operate throughout the island, churning out everything from Microsoft software to Bumble Bee tuna, all for the huge American market.

In 1985, when Section 936 was first threatened by congressional budget-cutters, former governor Rafael Hernández Colón came up with a novel approach to save it: he offered to link 936 to President Reagan's Caribbean Basin Initiative (CBI), a trade program designed to help the struggling economies of Central America and the Caribbean. As a result of the deal, Section 936 was extended for 20 more years, and Puerto Rico ended up funding at least $100 million worth of development projects per year in selected CBI beneficiary nations.

The island's heavy dependence on US federal aid programs and local government jobs have led some to call Puerto Rico a "welfare state". Critics of the island's political system say the same Operation Bootstrap that created jobs for

POPULAR CULTURE: A PUERTO RICAN HALL OF FAME

Rita Moreno's fiery performance in the 1961 film of *West Side Story* not only made her a household name around the globe, it also set the stage for a string of Puerto Ricans to make their mark on popular culture. José Ferrer and Raul Juliá also enjoyed much success in the world of film. Benicio Del Toro has followed in their footsteps, winning a prestigious Academy Award in 2000 for his role in the movie *Traffic*. Jennifer López and Roselyn Sánchez have also made their mark in Hollywood, while Ricky Martin is known for both his success as a singer and as a TV star.

Celebrities on the music scene have included José Feliciano and salsa singer Marc Anthony, while Tito Puente took his distinctive form of Latin jazz to international audiences. He died in 2000.

Puerto Rico has also had its share of household names in sport. Topping this list is baseball Hall-of-Famer Roberto Clemente, with other baseball greats including Hiram Bithorn (the first Puerto Rican to play in the major leagues), Orlando Cepeda, Ivan Rodriguez and Roberto Alomar.

Achieving fame in the ring were boxers Félix "Tito" Trinidad and Héctor "Macho" Camacho, while jockey John Velázquez is well known in horse-racing circles. The world of golf, too, has its famous Puerto Rican: Juan "Chichi" Rodríguez, now retired from the Seniors Tour in the US.

Drug Country

Mention Caribbean drug exports and people are likely to think of cigarette boats streaking across the water in the dead of night transporting bales of marijuana. But in the case of Puerto Rico, manufacturing drugs means making perfectly legal pharmaceutical products for export around the world.

Around $33.3 billion worth of chemical products, including $31.1 billion in medications, were produced and exported in 2002, making pharmaceuticals Puerto Rico's most important industry and

accounting for more than a quarter of its gross domestic product.

In the same year there were 171 chemical companies with established plants on the island, including 77 pharmaceuticals. They churn out products from Anacin (for headache relief) to Zantac (an over-the-counter ulcer medicine). Around 25 percent of pharmaceuticals manufactured in the US are shipped from Puerto Rico including 16 of the world's top-20 selling prescription drugs such as Viagra, Lipitor and Xanax. But don't look for "Made in Puerto Rico" on the label; as part of the United States, there is no separate identification. And don't look for lower prices on prescription drugs on the island; most are shipped out and back in. Pharma-

ceuticals came to the island as a result of the now-defunct Section 936, a job-creating clause of the United States Internal Revenue Code. For years this tax exempted companies from paying federal income tax on profits generated by Puerto Rican operations. The law is no more, but its benefits for companies already on the island extend until 2005.

In 2003 the governor, Sila Maria Calderón, worked on proposals in the US Congress to establish new federal tax incentives in order to retain these drugmaking giants beyond 2005. They may stay. Abbott Laboratories has spent $350 million on a factory specializing in manufacturing biotechnical products in Barceloneta – the largest single expansion in Puerto Rican history. The project will create 200 permanent and more than 800 temporary jobs. Currently, Abbott employs more than 2,300 people and manufactures nutritional, pharmaceutical, diagnostic, chemical and agricultural products on the island. Other companies include ICN/Roche Pharmaceuticals, American Home Products Corp., Bristol-Myers Squibb Co., Eli Lilly Industries and Johnson & Johnson.

Healthcare products, such as intravenous solutions, blood-pressure kits and thermometers, are also manufactured here. Puerto Rico's largest private employer is Baxter Healthcare Corp., with 6,000 workers in nine factories and three service centers. Among its products are pathogens that will make donated blood more secure.

One of the first drugmakers to set up shop here was Searle & Co. (now Pharmacia), which in 1969 established a huge factory in Caguas. In the mid-1980s, the island surpassed New Jersey in US drug production and eventually became the world's pharmaceutical capital.

Today, state-of-the-art drug factories are found even in remote mountain towns. The industry is most prevalent, however, in Carolina (in Metropolitan San Juan) and along the northern coast. Hidden behind high fences, drug factories generally have the greenest lawns anywhere, thanks to the rich chemical effluents in the waste water. Their workers are well paid: in 2001 they received around $14 an hour compared to the federal minimum wage of $5.15. Some towns are almost entirely dependent on drug companies. In Humacao, for example – in addition to the Roche/ICN manufacturing plant – Medtronic assembles pacemakers, Sandoz makes Ex-Lax and Syntec produces birth-control pills, all within 10 minutes of each other. ❏

LEFT: pharmaceutical production in Caguas.

island residents also contributed to the system's current bloated payroll and Puerto Ricans' belief that the government must provide for them. The central government employs one-fourth of the 1.2 million people working on the island.

In 2006, Governor Aníbal Acevedo Vilá, faced with a $738 million fiscal year-end shortfall, ordered a two-week, partial government shutdown that put 100,000 people out of work.

While it is hoped that the budgetary woes will eventually be resolved by the implementa-

GREAT STRIDES

Today, Puerto Rico has an 89 percent literacy rate – a big improvement over 1898, when only an eighth of the population could read.

star resorts and vacation homes in areas such as Río Grande and Piñones. Tourism currently accounts for just 7 percent of the island's GNP.

Despite economic troubles, residents, even the poorest, enjoy a relatively high standard of living; Puerto Rico has a per-capita income of around $14,000. Though far less than the poorest US state, Mississippi, it tops most Caribbean islands and outranks any in Latin American nation. In fact, the island's per-capita income is said to be grossly underestimated, owing to the

tion of the island's first ever sales tax on consumer goods and services – initially set at 7 percent – the work stoppage actually sparked an economic recession.

Although manufacturing still accounts for 42 percent of economic output, the island's Section 936 low-cost lure has disappeared. Now Puerto Rico may be forced to reduce the government payroll and compete in the global economy. Indeed, one option being explored by the governor is to place greater emphasis on luxury tourism, with the planned construction of five-

ABOVE: a well thought out political statement on a hidden wall.

Treasury department's inability to capture, via income tax, a thriving underground economy of cash and bartering.

The belief in an underground economy is fueled by visible prosperity, such as all houses built of concrete, unlike most other Caribbean islands. Virtually every Puerto Rican owns a TV and telephone; there are 1.5 million cars on the island, almost one for every two inhabitants; and fuel consumption is half of the Caribbean total.

On the other hand, Puerto Rico is plagued with overpopulation, high unemployment, water contamination, deforestation, a high incidence of HIV/Aids and a frightening number of serious crimes. Around 800 murders are committed every year on the island, making it one of the most violent places in the Caribbean outside Haiti. Sociologists blame many of the problems on the identity crisis caused by Puerto Rico's unusual political status.

Under commonwealth status, Puerto Ricans are exempt from US federal income tax, though they do pay personal income taxes to their own government, and are subject to the US Army draft. Proportionately more Puerto Ricans died in Vietnam – all having been sent there by a president for whom they could not vote. To date more than a quarter of a million Puerto Ricans have served in the US Armed Forces.

Because Puerto Rico is not an independent nation, there is no Puerto Rican passport; travel to the US mainland is unrestricted. Some 2½ million now live in the US, about half of them in New York City. These *Nuyoricans*, however, still maintain close links with their homeland.

Although island residents cannot vote in US presidential elections, they *can* vote in the Democratic and Republican primaries. Puerto Ricans also elect a resident commissioner to the US House of Representatives who has a voice – but no vote – on legislative matters.

Two parties are fighting to change that. The Partido Nuevo Progresista (PNP), founded in 1968, wants to make Puerto Rico the 51st state.

This, the party claims, would rapidly give the island economic parity with the rest of the US, though it wants to keep sufficient sovereignty to participate separately in the Olympics and the Miss Universe contest.

At the other end of the spectrum is the Partido Independentista Puertorriqueño (PIP). The PIP dreams of a republic free of US influence. These *independentistas* make lots of headlines, but they rarely win more than 5 percent of the island votes.

A third party, the Partido Democratico Popular (PDP), favors continued commonwealth status and sees both statehood and independence as potential economic and social disasters. Continued plebiscites show a narrow majority opposed to statehood, with the majority preferring the status quo.

The controversy continued in 1998, which marked the 100th anniversary of the US presence in Puerto Rico. In December, another plebiscite saw about 51 percent voting for the fifth alternative on the ballot – "None of the Above" – narrowly defeating the 46 percent who opted for statehood. Less than 3 percent actually favored independence.

Weather woes

In 1998, Puerto Rico sustained huge losses as Hurricane Georges wreaked its havoc. The death toll was 12, with widespread loss of both the natural environment and man-made structures. It was estimated that about 80,000 homes were destroyed. When Georges struck, the island had just recovered from four other hurricanes that caused great devastation. Immediately after Georges' swath of destruction, Puerto Rico was declared a disaster area by former US President Bill Clinton. The estimated loss in property was $2 billion. The US Congress allocated $74 million in emergency funds to help with the recovery, while a group of Federal Emergency Management Agency officials was on hand within days to help residents. The sting of severe weather conditions lingers into the 21st century. In 2004 parts of Puerto Rico suffered from flooding when the island was hit by tropical storm Jeanne. ❏

ABOVE: prelude to disaster: waves crash on the rocks near San Juan as Hurricane Georges draws near.
RIGHT: one of Puerto Rico's major attractions is its golf courses, like Las Palmas near Humacao.

PEOPLE AND SOCIETY

*Nearly everyone comes from somewhere else. But the wide range of ethnic types
has forged a proud and dynamic Hispanic culture*

There is a song, one among many, which stands as the most evocative of what it means to live in the paradise which is Puerto Rico. If it does not exist in fact – there is squalor amid the great natural beauty, a certain sadness amid the promise – this paradise exists in the heart.

Written by José Manuel Rivera, *Mi Tierra Borincana* extols with deceptive simplicity the reasons to endure the *tapones* (traffic jams) in San Juan, the ineptitude of certain bureaucracies, and even the preciousness of certain resources – water in particular – that Continentals (non-Puerto Ricans from the mainland who come to live here) all too frequently take for granted.

"*How beautiful it is, to live in this dreamland! And how beautiful it is to be the master of the coquí's song!*" as the song says. "*What an advantage it is to reap the coffee of this great gift!*"

In a certain sense the lyrics are themselves an illusion, yet in another they're very real. For while life on the island for natives and immigrants alike is not what it was 20 or even 10 years ago – there is more crime and unemployment in the bigger cities; its working class works harder for what seems to be less and less – its lure, for those who truly love Puerto Rico, is not diminished.

Living anywhere within the commonwealth requires a balance of cleverness, common sense, and hard realism for Puerto Ricans and Continentals alike. Opulence is hardly uncommon among those who can afford it – in the wealthier suburbs of San Juan, for example, a modest-looking three-bedroom house with a small yard can cost upward of $200,000 – but even so the display of wealth isn't encouraged.

Look beyond the suntanned tourists enjoying the sunshine on the beaches, the glass-fronted modern buildings of metropolitan San Juan and the coastal factories, and you'll see the attraction of what remains: a Caribbean countryside of small, colorful towns filled with local people, always ready with a smile and a greeting, chatting peacefully in the plaza,

selling their produce at roadside stands or taking a stroll in the night air.

The Puerto Rican people are a friendly and passionate lot, vivacious and expressive in their conversations – and their dancing. Music and food are two essential elements which the people – young and old – use to help them celebrate life to the fullest.

Sense of pleasure

What's important here is a sense of belonging, acquired largely through willing readjustment to Puerto Rico's pace. And the attitude behind it is certainly quite a healthy one. It's an attitude which sees work not as an end in itself, but

---

PRECEDING PAGES: Spanish colonial house, Guayama; loading plantains.
LEFT: a typical smiling Puerto Rican welcome.
RIGHT: costumed children on parade in Old San Juan during the Carnival.

merely as a means to fund subsequent enjoyment. Weekends are taken very seriously, and major holidays, especially Christmas, even more so. In the United States, Christmas lasts perhaps a week; on the island the celebrations begin in late November and don't completely stop until the middle of January.

In addition to Christmas Day, Puerto Ricans celebrate Three Kings Day, or Epiphany, on January 6. Following tradition, local children cut grass (to feed the Wise Men's camels), put it in boxes and place these under their beds on

> ### RELIGIOUS TIES
>
> Some 85 percent of Puerto Ricans are members of the Roman Catholic Church.

Local produce

Although the University of Puerto Rico's ambitious School of Agriculture continues to experiment with ways of growing the kinds of produce that now have to be imported, fruits and vegetables that are easily found throughout the United States are widely available in supermarkets. Yet, there are still trucks along almost every major road selling homegrown oranges – *chinas* – at about $8 for a large bag. Despite the incursion of a horde of mainland products of dubious nutritional repute, *comida*

January 5, just before they go to sleep. The next morning, the grass is gone and gifts have been left mysteriously in its place – much to the innocent delight of the youngsters throughout the island.

During this extended holiday period, it's presumed by residents that there will be company, people coming from far away to visit or just neighbors stopping by from roughly December 15 (also the official start of the tourist season, which ends on April 15 of the following year) until the last *pasteles* (tamales) are eaten and the last glasses of *coquíto* (a delicious mixture of milk, rum, vanilla, cream of coconut and cinnamon) consumed.

criolla is still the food of the day in most households.

The traditional cuisine is heavy food, rich with an invigorating assortment of beans, from *arroz con habichuelas* (rice with either small pink beans or kidney beans) and *arroz con gandules* (pigeon peas) to *lechón asado* (whole roast suckling pig) prepared almost exclusively for holidays and large family gatherings, and its counterpart, *pernil* (fresh picnic ham in most Stateside butcher shops and supermarkets). Both the suckling pig and ham are seasoned with *adobo*, a thick, fragrant paste of garlic, vinegar, peppercorns, and herbs such as cilantro, culantro and oregano.

Strangely, for a place with so much marine life – grouper, yellowtail, spiny lobster, squid, sea snail, conch and shark – Puerto Ricans prefer chicken and pork. However, red snapper (*chillo*), shrimp (*camarones*) and lobster (*langosta*) are enjoyed by the locals, as is salt cod – known as *bacalao* – which is a staple. Seafood lovers will find plenty of good restaurants to choose from, as well as local *fondas*, where specialties such as *mofongo relleno* (fried mashed plantain) with *mariscos* (seafood) are firm favorites. The most popular local snacks include *alcapurrias*, meat or crab fritters *(see also "Puerto Rican Cuisine," page 75)*.

Automobiles are bought for either practicality or show, and those who buy for show know they're taking risks. Amazingly – or possibly not, given the great influence of US culture – Puerto Rico consumes half the gasoline in the Caribbean. The Urban Train, a light railroad system, was completed in 2004, with further sections due to be completed by 2020.

Other developments include the use of the internet, which has become just as popular in Puerto Rico as anywhere else in the world. Many internet-access companies have cropped up in recent times, as well as establishments for the sale and servicing of computers.

Cars, computers and crime

With or without the benefits of a *siesta*, quality eating, still done mostly during the lunch hour, tends to make the pace of transacting business a little slower: even, perhaps, more sensible. Only behind the wheels of the island's 1.5 million cars – Puerto Rico ranks sixth in the world for the ratio of motor vehicles to people; nearly 2.5 autos per household – is there any indication that anyone is in a hurry. Here, assertive driving is considered an asset.

Schools teach computer science, and wireless internet access is widespread in tourist areas and in most urban centers.

Despite the progress, the island's poverty is still a sad and consistent fact of life. It explains in part the decorative but restrictive iron grillwork known as *rejas*, found on almost every home. As in most modern countries, it's wise to be cautious with belongings. Petty crime is a reality; however, violent crime is generally restricted to poorer areas and it is almost unheard of in areas frequented by tourists.

Tragically, violent crime, everything from carjacking to murder, plagues Puerto Rico like never before. On December 31 each year, local

LEFT: goat salesmen at a local flea market take shelter from the rain.
ABOVE: two wheels are as good as four in San Juan.

newspapers announce a new high in the annual homicide tally. Surveys consistently show that voters are far more concerned about increasing crime than anything else. The violence is blamed largely on drugs – as is the island's severe HIV/Aids problem. Politicians haven't found solutions to any of these problems, but on the enforcement side the government has taken measures to increase the number of police officers and to put harsher prison sentences into force for drug dealers; it has also carried out an increasing number of drugs and arms raids. Criminals are punished with the full weight of the US federal law.

Barrios and barriers

In the meantime, Puerto Ricans have responded to crime and gaps in police protection by closing neighborhoods to outsiders. Today, all new residential development is gated. Older neighborhoods, such as Parkville, Caparra Heights and Torrimar, long ago barricaded their streets with electronic gates. The closed neighborhoods, unheard of 20 years ago, are considered essential to protect property and fight crime. And until the crime rate comes down, the trend is sure to continue.

Puerto Rico's ills may also be attributed to sheer overpopulation. Because of traditionally high birth rates and medical advances that caused the death rate to plummet shortly after the Spanish-American War, Puerto Rico's population jumped to about a million by 1900, and now stands at around 3.9 million. This gives the island a population density of nearly 1,100 per sq. mile (425 per sq. km), among the world's highest. Only Bangladesh, the Maldives, Barbados, Taiwan, South Korea and the city-states of Hong Kong and Singapore are more crowded. Indeed, if it weren't for the safety valve that allows Puerto Ricans unrestricted travel to the American mainland, the island might have 5 million people today.

For administrative purposes, Puerto Rico is divided into 78 municipalities. They range in size from Arecibo and Ponce, with more than 100 square miles (260 sq km), to 6 square-mile (15 sq-km) Cataño. In terms of population, the largest *municipio* is San Juan, with more than 430,000 people; the smallest is offshore Culebra, with only 2,000.

Driving in Puerto Rico is on the right-hand side, unlike in the nearby Virgin Islands, where motorists drive on the left. Adding to the confusion is the fact that the island adheres half-heartedly to the metric system, which means that all distances are posted in kilometers, and gasoline is sold by the liter. Nevertheless, temperatures are still given in Fahrenheit rather than Celsius, and speed-limit signs are still in miles per hour (in order to accommodate the speedometers of American-made cars). This is unlikely to change as long as Puerto Rico remains under the US flag.

Español sí, inglés no!

A far more contentious issue is the language debate. For 90 years the island had two official languages, Spanish and English. Then, in 1991, former Governor Rafael Hernández Colón – citing Puerto Rico's "cultural heritage" – abolished English as an official language. This won him Spain's Prince of Asturias Award and praise from the *independentistas*, but sparked an outcry from many local educators and business people.

The controversy heated up further when Hernández Colón's pro-statehood successor, Pedro Rosselló, took office in January 1993. One of the first things he did was restore English's official status, making Puerto Rico once again bilingual.

However, regardless of the law, fewer than a

fourth of Puerto Ricans are completely bilingual; outside the big cities you will find it useful to know at least a few basic Spanish words and phrases to help you when you are traveling around.

Puerto Rico is a place of which it can truly be said everyone comes from somewhere else. There are the traces of Taíno and Carib blood left in the fine, high cheekbones and caught in the depths of the beautiful eyes of many of those whose families have lived on the island for

> ### THE LONE STAR
> Although officially adopted in 1952, Puerto Rico's flag was first used in 1895; its "lone star" was the "guide of the patriots."

Patriotism

Despite all varieties of political difference, pride is universal and strong. Though US flags fly alongside all Puerto Rican flags in public places (by law), and schoolchildren sing *The Star Spangled Banner* before *La Borinqueña*, the island's own beautiful anthem, being Puerto Rican always comes first. This isn't without its paradoxical side. The people who've chosen to live here, Puerto Ricans and Continentals alike, love the island intensely yet know that things are far

generations. In fact, in the town of Loíza, east of San Juan, the evidence of the island's slave-trading days is impossible to ignore. There are women with skin the color of *café con leche* – the strong coffee with hot milk which is a staple on every Puerto Rican breakfast table – who have tightly curled hair that is naturally auburn, and children with liquid blue eyes and blond hair whose faces are exotically beautiful, thanks to any number of forebears – including traders, pirates, artisans, slaves and colonists.

LEFT: selling oysters.
ABOVE: family party on Flamenco Beach, Culebra.

from perfect – which is where patience, cleverness and common sense come into play. The Ports Authority (Autoridad de Puertos), for example, is the only municipal agency that consistently makes a profit. Yet those who rely on the ferries it operates between Fajardo, Vieques and Culebra have a well-honed sense of humor toward its less-than-pristine equipment. It might take two hours. It might take six. *Así es la vida.* That's life.

Along with the islanders' resilient humor, there is also an ongoing sense of rebellious resentment in the face of authority, especially towards the US Navy. This became acute in 1970, when Culebrans were kept off Flamenco

Beach – as they had been for decades – during practice bombing runs. "Enough," said 2,000 people all at once. The red flag went up to keep people off the beach; the majority of the population headed straight for it, loaded with picnic coolers. They were going to picnic until the US Navy stopped its target runs so close to their beach. Three years later, the Navy finally listened to them and agreed to leave Flamenco Beach alone.

In 1999, the controversy of the naval presence in Vieques blew up as David Sanes, a civilian worker for the Navy, was accidentally killed by naval ordnance. Protesters stormed the island, including independence advocate Rubén Berríos, along with a group of his cohorts, who camped out on the island for almost a year until the authorities arrested them. It seems that the protests have succeeded. The Navy finally left the island in May 2003. The land has been turned over to the US Department of the Interior.

Poetry, poverty and politics

In conclusion, Puerto Rico is a place where beauty coexists on occasions with squalor; a place where politics and poetry very often merge; a place where its most celebrated leaders, among them Luis Llorens Torres and Luis Muñoz Marín, were also poets.

The island's poorer residents cherish the things that have no price tags: family, friends and the pleasure, challenging as it can be, of living here. Even the tradition of family, however, has changed, moving from the old extended collection of various uncles, aunts and grandparents to a more nuclear one.

There is poverty, certainly, a chronic ache to those who love their island. But art flourishes here too, with the craftworkers, the musicians, the composers, the playwrights and the painters and sculptors and actors. It gives Puerto Rico's beauty a face which is proud yet edged in sadness, exotic yet utterly recognizable.

The country's aforementioned national anthem, *La Borinqueña,* which, unlike other nations' songs that speak glowingly of military might and triumph over adversaries, sums up the flavor. It celebrates a reality which is at the same time an ideal, *"a flowering garden of exquisite magic. A sky, always clear..."* ❑

LEFT: street party during the San Sebastián festival.

A LAND OF FANTASTIC FESTIVALS

Puerto Ricans express their zest for life through a succession of exuberant celebrations. Many have their origins in the island's strong Catholicism

No matter where or when you go, Puerto Ricans always seem to be celebrating something – be it a saint's feast day or a cultural tradition. First and foremost are the *fiestas patronales*, or patron saint festivals, during which each town honors the area's patron saint. Incredibly, there are 78 of these, beginning on January 6 and continuing straight through December 12, and the festivities at each last 10 days. So, in theory, you can party your way around the island nonstop.

And this isn't even taking into consideration the *other* festivals, which all celebrate something, no matter how insignificant it may seem.

In April, for instance, Juana Díaz hosts the Maví Festival, which honors *maví*, a fermented drink made from the bark of the ironwood tree.

With farming being a dominant occupation, harvest festivals abound. Yauco and Maricao both have Coffee Harvest Festivals in February, while the picturesque western town of San Germán marks the end of the island's sugar harvest in April with an appropriate celebration.

If you have to choose, three of the best festivals are the Carnival in Ponce (February), where the *vejigante* masks were first created; Loíza's *fiesta* of Santiago Apóstol (July) and the Hatillo Masks Festival (December).

All feature music, dancing, ornate masks and costumes, games, religious processions, shows, parades, drink and food, food, food. It's hard not to join in the dancing, and easy to forget about the diet.

◁ **ROYALTY FOR A DAY**
San Juan's Children's Parade at Carnival time is a kid's dream come true.

△ **ANYTHING GOES**
Parades feature costumed marchers, bands, floats – and generally anyone who wants to tag along.

◁ **SPIRIT CHASERS**
Garishly dressed masked *vejigantes* roam the streets during the island's *fiestas patronales* to chase away evil spirits.

△ **GLITTERING COSTUMES**
Festival time brings out revelers in the most fantastic and glamorous outfits.

◁ **TIME TO DANCE**
An essential element of *any* festival is music and dance. Folk dances include the *bomba*, of pure African origin, and the *plena*, which blends elements from the island's many cultures.

THE CATHOLIC CONNECTION

With all the colorful costumes and riotous behavior, it is easy to forget that many of Puerto Rico's festivals – particularly the *fiestas patronales* – have religious roots. Religious candle processions (such as the one above, during the capital's San Juan Bautista festival) with statues, or *santos*, often kick things off, and many Masses are held throughout each festival.

Puerto Rico is strongly Catholic, with many convents, monasteries and even one or two shrines where the Virgin Mary has appeared to the faithful. But this Catholicism has, over the years, been blended – like everything else in Puerto Rico – with animist elements of African and Taíno origin. Some of the elements are simple superstition: at midnight during the San Juan Bautista festival on June 24, thousands fill the beaches and walk backward into the sea (or nearest body of water – even a pool will do!) three times to renew good luck for the coming year. Beach parties, together with the usual dancing and music, round off the occasion.

THE LANGUAGE OF PUERTO RICO

Although English and Spanish are both designated "official" languages,
it's Español that rules the heart – and tongue – of most Puerto Ricans

Even before Columbus's fleet "discovered" the island in 1493, Puerto Rico was in a state of cultural unrest. Invading Carib tribes from South America were threatening the native Arawaks, as they had many other cultures throughout the Caribbean. When the local Arawaks met the invading Caribs, what language was created? The Arawak name for the island, Borikén, is still used (*La Borinqueña* is the Puerto Rican national anthem), and the Caribs live on in the word Caribbean. Many Puerto Rican municipalities go by their pre-Columbian names, for example Caguas, Arecibo, Mayagüez, Yauco and Guaynabo. The Arawaks feared the god Juracán, while we fear hurricanes. And the *hamacas* in which the early Indians slept are just as popular today under the name of hammocks.

If the Arawaks welcomed the Spaniards as a strategy to ward off the Caribs, they miscalculated. A wave of Spaniards swept across the island. Eventually there came battle and disease, which obliterated the native Arawak population. Then came sex, producing the first Puerto Ricans and the first people who could claim to speak a truly Puerto Rican Spanish. The Spanish of the earliest Puerto Ricans, like that of their modern descendants, can be said to reflect either a pronunciational sloppiness or an Arawak love of diphthongs. For example, Spanish words which end in *ado* are pronounced as if the *d* were silent. Humacao is an Arawak name, but *pescao* will get you fish anywhere on the island. A good stew is an *asopao*, but if your *fiao* (credit) isn't good enough, you won't be served one in any restaurant.

Puerto Rico's first Africans were brought as slaves, mostly from west-central Africa. They brought with them another language; they also had many musical instruments, including the drums, and countless customs and attitudes which have found their way into the lives of everyone. The *baquine*, a festival of mourning for the death of an infant, is a ritual of African origin, and is usually the scene of a great deal of rum, dancing and *lechón asado* (roast suckling pig). By the mid-19th century, the Africans made up a fifth of the population, and such customs penetrated Puerto Rican society.

Integration of the races has worked smoothly in Puerto Rico, and it is said that *él que no tiene dinga tiene mandinga*, a phrase which attributes some amount of African ancestry to virtually all Puerto Ricans. The Mandinga were one of the more populous of the West African tribes, brought to Puerto Rico to harvest sugar cane, coffee and tobacco.

The farmers of those crops, black, white and *mestizo*, gradually became the Puerto Rican *jíbaros*. The most famous record of the *jíbaro* was written by Manuel A. Alonso, a doctor whose writings fit into the Latin American literary movement known as *costumbrismo*. In 1849, his book *El Gíbaro* was published in

---

PRECEDING PAGES: talking it over at El Combate.
LEFT: hanging out in Arecibo.
RIGHT: street talk in Calle San José.

Barcelona, and in it there are invaluable accounts of a *jíbaro* wedding, dances and cock-fights, Christmas celebrations and the arrival of the magic lantern in the hills. Equally important is the portrait of mid-19th-century *jíbaro* speech patterns. In Alonso's verses we can hear the *jíbaro* dialect in its purest form. He mentions foods such as *lechón asado*, *toytiyas* (tortillas) and *maví* (a drink made from tree bark).

For all the eccentricities of the Puerto Rican tongue, it is important to remember that the language of the island is Spanish, albeit a Spanish heavily influenced by other nationalities, and that Puerto Rican Spanish shares many oddities

with the Spanish of its Caribbean neighbors – such as *seseo*, by which *s* sounds are muted, and sometimes disappear altogether, at the end of syllables. Matches are *loh fohforoh* rather than *los fosforos* and *graciah* means thanks. *Yeismo* is another confusing variation; this involves pronouncing the Spanish *ll* and *y* sounds as English *js*, so as to render a word like *Luquillo*, the island's most popular beach, as "Look here, Joe."

Those who live in Puerto Rico also practice an important non-verbal language in everyday dealings. For example, wrinkling the nose usually means, "What is that?" Both hands raised palms front means "Wait a minute," and when

an individual tweaks his or her cheek it means "I like that." A movement akin to washing of the hands means "It's done."

Spanish spoken here

The granting of United States citizenship to Puerto Ricans in 1917 signaled the advent of English as the first Germanic language to become part of the Puerto Rican dialect. The startling result of this last infusion is Spanglish, a colloquial Spanish which may be as familiar to a North American as it is to a Spaniard. Spanglish consists not only of a shared vocabulary but also of the terse sentence construction characteristic of English. The first penetration of English into Puerto Rican Spanish seems to have come from English labels on consumer products.

Indeed, men still sit at bars nursing *un scotch* while their children look on, chewing *chicles*. The introduction of American commerce was no less confounding in other ways. When the first American cash registers were introduced in San Juan's grocery and department stores, a whole generation stood paralyzed at checkout counters when the "No Sale" tab, marking the end of the transaction, flipped up. *No sale* in Spanish translates as "Do not leave."

Spanglish truly entered its heyday only with the mass migration of Puerto Ricans to the United States in the 1940s. This exodus created a generation of so-called *Nuyoricans*, who returned to their native island with the baffling customs and speech patterns developed on the streets of New York. Or they would send letters home with news, and, if they had no money, they would send the letter *ciodí* (cash on delivery).

Letters to the Cordillera would have to be transported by *un trok*. Perhaps there would be bad news, that a son had been *bosteado* by the *policías* for dealing in *las drogas*. More often the letters would just contain idle chatter, or discussions of the decisions of the world *líderes*, or of how a brother had won a pool game by sinking the important eight ball in the corner *poquete*.

Puerto Ricans love pool, but if Puerto Rico and the Spanglish language have an official sport it has to be *el béisbol*, or baseball. Everyone knows that Roberto Clemente (from Carolina) and Orlando Cepeda (from Santurce) were Puerto Rico's greatest hitters of *jonrones* and *dobles* (home-runs and doubles). Most Puerto Ricans would say their ballplayers were *wilson*, meaning "very good." Some things have remained little changed, though. Dollars are sometimes called *dolares*, but more often *pesos*. Quarters are *pesetas*, nickels *vellones* and pennies *centavos*.

Language means more to the people of Puerto Rico than just about anything else. Most Puerto Ricans fear the loss of their language through the influence of other cultures, especially if the island were to become a state of America. One of the first questions a Puerto Rican will ask a visitor is *"Habla español?"* If

RAYMOND: *Cómo estamos, broder?* (How we doin', brother?)
PAPO: *Na' mas se me estalló la tabla.* (I just cracked my surfboard.)
RAYMOND: *Qué chavienda!* (What a drag!)
PAPO: *Estuve gufeando en un tubo y fua! se me fue la tabla contra esas rocas por ahí.* (I was goofing around in a tube, when, boom! my board flies into those rocks over there.)
RAYMOND: *Ea rayo!* (Gee whiz!)
PAPO: *Ay, pero mira a esa jeba. Vamos a rapiarla.* (Oh, will you look at this babe. Let's rap.)
RAYMOND: *Oye, guapa, ven aca un momento.* (Hey, cutey, come here a minute.)

the visitor responds positively, then he or she will be welcomed into the fold graciously.

Spicy talk

Puerto Rico's beaches have been the stage for dialogs in many languages, but none are as spicy as those you'll hear on the beach at Piñones between two *playeros* when the midwinter swells are up:
PAPO: *Oye, 'mano, que pasa?* (Hey brother, what's happening?)

LEFT: Añasco men exchange the day's news.
RIGHT: the Friday flea market in San Sebastián is the scene of many a lively conversation.

MARTA: *No seas cafre o te parto el coco.* (Don't be rude or I'll break your head).
PAPO: *De dónde tú eres?* (Where you from?)
MARTA: *De Guaynabo y a ti que te importa?* (Guaynabo, and what do you care?)
PAPO: *A ver si quieres pon pa' San Juan.* (To see if you'd like a lift to San Juan.)
MARTA: *Bueno, sí.* (Well, okay.)
PAPO: *Cógelo suave, Raymond.* (Take it easy, Raymond.)

Having such a rich and vibrant oral tradition, Puerto Ricans love good conversation, and, with at least four linguistic families from which to draw, enjoy a speech that is all at once cryptic and colorful. ❑

PUERTO RICAN CUISINE

Junk food is threatening to squeeze out local dishes. But you can still find tasty concoctions from Taíno roots, African flavors and Spanish traditions

Carib and Spanish destruction of Puerto Rico's native Taíno tribes, for all its ruthlessness, was far from complete. It has been said that Puerto Rican society today reflects its African and Indian origins more than its Spanish ones, and there is much truth in that. Non-Spanish ways live on in customs, rituals, language and all aspects of life, and one can see in many facial features the unfamiliar expression of the Taínos, a race otherwise lost to us forever. But nowhere is the Taíno influence more visible, or more welcome, than in Puerto Rican cuisine, one of the great culinary amalgams of our hemisphere.

Imagine a Taíno man – call him Otoao and set his caste at *naboría,* one of the higher agricultural castes in the Taíno hierarchy – rising one sunny morning after having won a glorious victory the previous day over the invading Caribs. This victory was cause for an *areyto,* the Taíno ritual that either preceded or followed any happening of even the remotest importance. Births, deaths, victories, defeats... it's *areyto* time. *Areytos,* like other socio-religious Taíno festivals, required intricate preparations for whatever food and drink was to be served, and, as a *naboría,* Otoao was in charge of hunting and fishing for the tribe.

Not that Otoao's wife Tai had it terribly easy. As a *naboría* woman (a woman's caste was determined by that of her husband), Tai was responsible for the cultivation and harvesting of the fields *(conucos)* as well as the preparation of the meals. These were elaborate, and the Taínos managed to get an astounding range of food on the banquet table.

The menu that evening included roast *jutías* (young guinea pigs) seasoned with sweet red chili peppers, fried fish in corn oil, fresh shellfish and a variety of freshly harvested vegetables. Among the vegetables were *yautías* (starchy tubers similar to potatoes and yams),

corn, yams, cassava and the same small red chili peppers used to season the *jutías.* Bread was *casabe,* a mixture of puréed cassava and water cooked between two hot rocks. For dessert, the Taínos had fresh fruit picked from the extensive variety available throughout the island. The culmination of the celebration was

the drinking of an alcoholic beverage made from fermented corn juice.

This activity was accompanied by the ceremonial inhalation of hallucinogenic fumes thought to make the warriors fitter for battle. The Taínos made hallucinogens of many sorts, the most common of which used the hanging, bell-shaped flowers of the *campana* tree to make a potent and mind-bending tea.

Most of the dietary staples of the Taínos survive in the Puerto Rican cuisine of today, albeit some in altered form. Puerto Rican cooking is now an amalgam of Taíno, Spanish and African traditions. Much of this intermingling took place early in the island's history, with

PRECEDING PAGES: an island favorite, roast suckling pig *(lechón asado).* **LEFT:** picking green peppers. **RIGHT:** a display of Puerto Rican cuisine.

Spanish colonists incorporating a variety of their own ingredients and techniques into the native cuisine, most of which were found to blend surprisingly well. A tremendous addition to this culinary mélange was made by the Africans brought as slaves shortly thereafter.

African tradition is responsible for what is perhaps the greatest achievement in Caribbean cooking – the combination of strikingly contrasting flavors which in other culinary traditions would be considered unblendable. One of these savory concoctions is *pastelón*: ripe plantains layered between well-seasoned ground beef and usually served with rice.

Surprisingly, many of the agricultural staples that look indigenous to the island were in fact brought to Puerto Rico from other parts of the world. Among the great variety of crops imported were coffee, sugar cane, coconuts, bananas, plantains, oranges and other citrus fruits, ginger and other spices, onions, potatoes, tomatoes, garlic and much more. These products, in combination with those already present, were to mold what was to become the Puerto Rican culinary tradition.

It is ironic that among these imports are several for which Puerto Rico was to become renowned. Puerto Rican coffee, for example,

Food from around the world

As different ingredients and cooking techniques were introduced to the island by its early settlers, a local culinary tradition began to take shape. Most important of the early imports were the Spanish cattle, sheep, pigs, goats and other grillable creatures, which the islanders had never tasted but took to with zeal. Along with the animals came an almost infinite number of vegetables, fruits and spices from the farthest reaches of Spain's vast colonial empire. A subtler, but no less important, influence on the Puerto Rican food supply was the introduction of European farming methods and agricultural equipment.

especially that from the region around Yauco, was long considered by Europeans the best coffee in the world. And the plantain, arguably the most popular staple in Puerto Rican cuisine, is something of a national symbol – almost as the leek is to the Welsh. A man who is admired for his honesty and lack of pretension is said to have on him the *mancha del plátano*, or "stain of the plantain."

Myths and misconceptions

Puerto Rican cuisine is as eclectic as it is varied. Local food has earned a reputation it most decidedly does not deserve for being hot, fiery and spicy. In fact, although it is prepared with a multiplicity of richly varied spices and condiments, Puerto Ricans tend to season their food more subtly than one might imagine. The base of a majority of native dishes is the *sofrito*, an aromatic and well-seasoned sauce made from puréed tomatoes, onions, garlic, green peppers, sweet red chili peppers, coriander, anatto seeds and a fairly arbitrary handful of other spices. This *sofrito* adds a zesty taste to stews, rices, stewed beans and a variety of other dishes, but only the blandest of palates would consider it to be piquant.

Native Caribbean flavors are evident in the majority of Puerto Rican recipes. The most

Social traditions of old

Puerto Ricans have very successfully kept alive not only the culinary but also many of the social traditions of their Taíno forebears. Christmas time on the island is not complete without rice, *gandules* (pigeon peas), *lechón asado* (roast suckling pig), *pasteles* (tamales made from plantains and *yucas* filled with a flavorful meat stuffing) and, as dessert, a *majarete* made with rice flour, coconut milk, grated coconut pulp, sugar and spices. During Lent, seafood dishes include the traditional *serenata*: codfish in a vinaigrette sauce served with tomatoes, onions, avocados and boiled tubers.

popular dinner dishes are stewed meats, rice and beans, and an enormous selection of fritters. Rice dominates many local main courses; expect a big heap with *arroz con pollo* (chicken – or another meat – served with rice sometimes cooked in coconut milk). Popular desserts include *flan* (custard), made of cheese, coconut or vanilla; and *guayaba con queso* (candied fruit slices with cheese). Fruit is popular and plentiful, and includes mango, papaya, passion fruit, banana, pineapple and grapefruit.

LEFT: street-corner temptations.
ABOVE: Puerto Rico has many fine restaurants, such as La Mallorquina in Old San Juan.

Though Puerto Rico is far too small to have many truly regional cuisines, a number of dishes are limited to particular areas of the island. For example, seafood dishes tend to be accompanied by *sorrullos* (corn fritters) in most of the restaurants on the south coast, from Salinas to Cabo Rojo. The same is true of the great variety of fritters available in the food shacks of Luquillo, a most rewarding 30-minute trip from San Juan for anyone interested in local cuisine. Bayamón and its environs offers a truly unusual snack in *chicharrón*, a sort of massive pork crackling sold on the highways in and out of the city. It's definitely an acquired taste, but once you've acquired it, you'll understand why there are so many hefty individuals wandering the streets.

The island offers a great variety of restaurants for tourists and local consumers. Typical restaurants serving local food are only rarely luxurious or expensive. In fact, among Puerto Ricans, a rule of thumb applies that the shabbier the establishment, the better the food. The best native creations are found at modest little local *fondas*, where the prices are as reasonable as the food is distinguished. In a *fonda*, you can pick up a generous plate of rice and beans, *biftec criollo* (steak), *tostones* (fried plantains), salad, a can of beer and dessert for about $8. If

you can afford to splurge the extra 80¢, you can pick up one of the better cups of coffee you will have in your life. At the low end of the economic scale are delicious sandwiches made with a mixture of red meats, cheeses, tomatoes and other ingredients. Among the most popular are *cubanos* and *media noches*. The *cubano* consists of pork loin, ham and Swiss cheese on *pan de agua* (similar to French bread), while the *media noche* is smaller and uses egg bread. At the pricey end of the scale is *asopao*, probably Puerto Rico's most widely loved native dish. This thick stew can be made with chicken, pork or seafood, and is invariably worth every penny paid for it.

International cuisine

In addition to restaurants serving up traditional fare, you'll find a large assortment of places in which to savor food from different countries. Puerto Rico has become a proving ground for all sorts of global cuisine. Chinese food has practically become a staple, with fast-order restaurants found everywhere. Spanish restaurants, too, abound. The Puerto Rican *panadería* (bakery) is usually Spanish in style and includes a wide assortment of local and Spanish delicacies. The famous Cuban sandwich is very popular, as are Spanish *tortillas* – a thick pie-like dish of eggs, potatoes and onions.

Italian food, however, is probably consumed more than any other type. Pizza parlors can be seen everywhere, and home delivery is very common. German specialties are limited to a few choice restaurants, but Mexican eateries run hot and heavy in the San Juan metropolitan area. (Traditional Puerto Rican food lacks the hot spices of Mexico, but islanders still tend to indulge in the torrid fare at times.)

Even Thai and Japanese restaurants can be found, and *sushi* is gaining in popularity with supermarkets preparing it to go.

While Puerto Ricans love to eat in *fondas*, it does not mean their palates are unsophisticated. The US obsession with food has sparked a Puerto Rican culinary revolution. Restaurants in the tourist areas of Old San Juan, Isla Verde and the Condado attract thousands of food lovers annually with their fusion of traditional island ingredients, international flavors and gourmet presentation. Chefs such as Pikayo's Wilo Benet and Robert Trevino, co-owner of the Parrot Club, Aguaviva and Dragonfly restaurants, are internationally renowned for their innovative cooking. The culinary trends have even inspired food festivals in Old San Juan, the largest of which is the biannual SOFO (South of Fortaleza Street) Culinary Fest (call 787-723 7080).

If "gourmet" international food is not your style, rest assured that eateries serving hamburgers and fries, hot dogs, crispy fried chicken and other exceptional "junk food" are ubiquitous throughout the island. Fast-food restaurants have become a way of life in the large population centers, including Burger King, McDonald's, KFC, Wendy's and Pizza Hut.

LEFT: San Juan is a hub of culinary delights.
RIGHT: plain, simple and filling.

The franchise fast-food boom has played another significant role in motivating local eateries to dispense wide varieties of food such as plantain fritters, stuffed potatoes and seafood salad, while employing novel merchandising techniques to promote them. Advertising for these establishments has become a billion-dollar industry in itself.

Making it on your own

Armchair connoisseurs who have no plans to visit Puerto Rico in the near future and who live far enough from New York City to be unable to procure a pre-cooked Puerto Rican

each). Fry in vegetable oil until slightly browned. Drain off oil. Mash with other ingredients. Shape into balls and serve in chicken stock. Otherwise, shape into hamburger-shaped patties and serve with *carnecita* (see the following recipe) – both dishes will provide a rewarding change of pace.

Carnecita
Ingredients:
2 lbs pork (the leaner the better)
adobo (see below)
Cut pork into one-inch cubes. Marinate in *adobo* for 24 hours. Fry in olive oil. Serve with *mofongo*.

delicacy will be happy to find that the dishes are fairly easy to cook – once you've got the correct ingredients.

Here's a recipe for *mofongo abreu*, a hearty, typically Puerto Rican plantain dish that makes a first-rate lunch or dinner.

Mofongo abreu
Ingredients:
3 green plantains (plus vegetable oil for frying)
¼ cup olive oil
1½ tsp. salt
½ cup grated pork rind
2–3 garlic cloves
Cut plantains into sections (about six pieces

Adobo
Ingredients (enough for 2 lbs of meat):
¾ tsp. salt
⅛ tsp. ground pepper
¼ tsp. ground oregano
1 pressed medium garlic clove
1 tbsp. olive oil (optional)
1 tsp. vinegar (optional)
Stir all this up well. Slather it on the *carnecita* and refrigerate it for a day or so. Fry it all up, eat it with *mofongo*, and you'll realize it is a tasty concoction indeed. It just might make you want to head down to this Spanish-speaking, Caribbean island and sample the full range of a truly unusual cuisine. ❑

ISLAND ART

It's the range that surprises. Flamboyant modern painting sits alongside remarkable folk art and a vast Taíno legacy of ancient art

Be warned that Puerto Rico's art scene offers delights to the mind and senses as meaningful and alluring as those of its landscape. This may mean entering a room of carved religious figures *(santos)* in the middle of a bustling city and finding yourself enveloped in their holy silence; or wandering into a museum or gallery in Old San Juan, only to find yourself as taken by a beautifully land-scaped 17th-century courtyard as by what you see on the walls; or talking to a local artist or scholar and finding that his passion for the island and its craftsmen is yours.

To be sure, there are frustrations. In San Juan the problem centers around a glut of a good thing; finding the best is often a confusing task, with charlatans working next to some of the great artists of the day. Difficulties out on the island are more logistical, with many of Puerto Rico's fascinating local museums hiding in out-buildings on the edges of towns. But even the most cursory foray into the island's artistic past and present will be rewarding.

Museum isle

The Institute of Puerto Rican Culture in Old San Juan owns a vast amount of the island's cultural inheritance, and can guide you to almost anything you fancy. Old San Juan itself is particularly fortunate as an artistic center; besides its 12 museums, it has a dozen con-temporary art galleries, a few co-operatives and craft shops of all descriptions.

If buying art interests you as much as just looking at it, Old San Juan is certainly the spot to begin your shopping spree. You'll find fine *santos* and other crafts at Puerto Rican Art & Craft, and prints as well as paintings at Sin Título, Coabey, Atlas Art and Botello. You can also see the work of future arts luminaries at

the exhibition hall of the School of Visual Arts (Escuela de Artes Plásticas) in front of El Morro fort.

New Museum of Art

The Museo de Arte de Puerto Rico in Santurce, which opened in 2000, has given the island

great prominence as the cultural leader in the region. This converted hospital, designed in the 1920s' neoclassical style, is a masterpiece in itself. The building houses a 400-seat theater, upscale restaurant, meeting rooms and a lavish garden. Works by well-known Puerto Rican artists date back to 1600, and the collection also includes regional and international works.

The museum of the University of Puerto Rico in Río Piedras, San Juan, exhibits only a fifth of its collection, but that small proportion is of top quality, from pre-Columbian art to the strongest and most respected painters of the present day.

But the last word on international art must go to the Museo de Arte de Ponce, envisioned

---

PRECEDING PAGES: sculptor Jan D'Esopo relaxes amid her creations.
LEFT: street artist in Old San Juan.
RIGHT: carved religious figures *(santos)* were an early art form.

by the late Governor Luis A. Ferré and executed by architect Edward Durrell Stone. Here, in a series of dramatically sunlit hexagonal rooms, art reflects the full range of the drama of human life. From the simplest of faces in Jan van Eyck's *Salvator Mundi* to an overpopulated *Fall of the Rebel Angels* to Rossetti's wonderfully confrontational *Daughters of King Lear*, you'll find it impossible not to be moved. *(See also page 222.)*

Art for heart's sake

Many of Puerto Rico's greatest achievements have been in the folk arts, and these retain a

by people who had prayed to particular saints for intercession in healing parts of the body. You can find such *santos* in the Cristo Chapel in Old San Juan. Though *santos* by the great masters are difficult to come by, there's hardly a home on the island where you won't find at least one *santo* of some sort, greatly revered and passed on from generation to generation.

Ancient heritage

The Caguana Indian Ceremonial Ballpark near Utuado gives haunting echoes of pre-Columbian life and culture. Here, early Taíno Indians played *batú*, a more civilized version

broad appeal. *(See pages 88–9.)* Most notable are the Puerto Rican *santos*, arguably the island's greatest contribution to the plastic arts. These wooden religious idols, evoking an uncanny spiritual quiet, vary greatly in size and shape. The baroque detail of the earliest pieces reflects both their period origins and the tastes of a Spanish clientele. But as Puerto Rico began to develop a stronger sense of colonial identity, as well as an artisan tradition, *santeros* began to carve figures of a striking simplicity.

The proof of the healing powers of *santos* is said to be attested to by the presence of *milagros* ("miracles"), small silver appendages in shapes of parts of the body. These were donated

of the balancing game favored by Mexico's Mayans, in which one had to keep a small ball suspended in the air for long periods of time, hitting it only with shoulders, head and ankles. This version is only "more civilized" on the strength of the fact that the early Taínos were not sacrificed to the gods if they dropped the ball, as their Mexican counterparts were. The dolmen-like stones surrounding the *bateyes*, or playing spaces, show great feeling for the ideal spatial relationship between art and nature.

Similar evidence of the vast Taíno legacy is found at the university museum in Río Piedras, which holds the cultural heritage of the island. Recent digs have been especially abundant in discoveries, some of them dazzling in quality. Amid the expected – amulets, potsherds, tools – are some baffling curiosities, like stone collars: great solid yokes at once regal and unwearable. In one intriguing case concerning Puerto Rico's early Taínos, men bend and sway together in entranced harmony. In another are two partially exposed skeletons, a few broken possessions at their sides.

For all the diversity of Puerto Rico's many cultural traditions, it was not until the 18th century that the island produced its first major artist in the Western tradition: José Campeche (1752–1809). In spite of never having left the

which hangs in the Institute of Puerto Rican Culture that one sees Campeche at the height of his powers. The eponymous *Governor Ustariz* stands in a magnificent room, with sunlight entering from behind. In his left hand are the first plans to pave the streets of San Juan; outside in the distance are men laboring busily to make his dream into a reality. It is truly a triumphant picture.

A more accessible painter, and something of a local hero in Puerto Rico, is Francisco Oller (1833–1917). His work is housed in all three main sources: the Institute and the museums at Ponce and Río Piedras. To this

island and having been exposed to European painting only through prints, Campeche still managed to create paintings of mastery. His religious works show a weakness for sentimentality, with their glut of *putti* and pastel clouds, but the inner peace which Campeche succeeds in displaying in his main holy figures dispels all doubt as to his stature as a truly inspired and talented artist.

There are two such masterpieces in the Ponce museum, but it is in a formal portrait

day, the extent of his influence on Puerto Rican painting is immeasurable.

Unlike Campeche, Oller lived and traveled abroad throughout his life. He studied under Courbet, was an intimate of both Pissarro and Cézanne, painted European royalty, and yet remained loyal to – and fiercely proud of – his island homeland. He was a Realist with Impressionist ideas, able to paint gorgeously everything he saw. He was adept at all genres: portraits, still lifes and landscapes – such as *Hacienda Aurora*, resonating with the vibrant colors of Puerto Rico which are just as much in evidence today.

A piece of work which defies reproduction is Oller's *El Velorio* (The Wake). An

LEFT: the Centro de Bellas Artes in Santurce.
ABOVE: artwork on display in a gallery at the Tibes Indian Ceremonial Park near Ponce.

enormous painting, it covers an entire wall in the university museum and illuminates the common man's universe in a fashion that recalls the work of Breughel. Here people laugh, cry, drink, sing and dance, while on a lace-covered table an almost forgotten, stone-white dead child lies strewn with flowers.

Oller's legacy to Puerto Rican painters has been one not only of technique but also of theme. Since his time, island painters have taken an overwhelming pride in Puerto Rico's diverse populace and landscape. Miguel Pou and Ramon Frade were among the earliest to follow Oller's lead, doing some spectacular

genre work in the early part of the 20th century.

At the Institute, Frade's painting *The Jíbaro* is a splendid homage to Puerto Rico's country farmers. Shyly surveying us with a bunch of plantains in his arms, this tiny old fellow appears to be a giant, with the land miniatured at his feet and his head haloed by a cloud.

The 1940s saw a rise in printmaking, which has left that medium one of the most vibrant in Puerto Rico to this day. Funded by the government, printmaking projects lured a slew of fine artists, many of whom are still active. Of particular note are Rafael Tufiño, Antonio Martorell, José Rosa and Lorenzo Homar. Posters by Ramón Power illustrate some of the clarity

and strength from which the best of Puerto Rican artists continue to draw.

Over the past 30 years, almost all Puerto Rican artists have studied abroad, and the consequence has been a broadening and an increasingly avant-garde range of artistic attitudes. Some artists have remained abroad, like Rafael Ferrer, whose work is as popular in New York as it is in San Juan, and Paris resident Ricardo Ramírez.

Others have returned to work and teach, producing an art with a distinctively Puerto Rican flavor. Myrna Báez falls into this category, her canvases interweaving past and present, inner and outer space. Her *Homage to Vermeer* shows a lone figure in an interior surrealistically touched by landscape. Reflectively, she seems to have loosed a phantom of tropical hubris as she opens the drawer of a nearby table.

The large fraternity of Puerto Rico's artists shows reverence and sensibility for the island and its people. Color plays an integral part in style and technique. The art of Augusto Marín, Angel Botello, Francisco Rodón and Mari Mater O'Neill can be obtained in Puerto Rico and in New York auction houses for hefty prices.

Rafael Tufiño's woodcut ink prints tell the story of Puerto Rican life at mid-century. A group of Tufiño's pictures are often on display at the Tourism Company's headquarters in Old San Juan. Luis Cajiga paints dazzling flamboyant trees and humble *piragua* vendors. Jorge Zeno's and Sylvia Blanco's imaginative techniques are good examples of surrealistic art, while John Balosi's sculptures and paintings of horses are treasured for their originality.

Viewing opportunities

Gallery nights, when many of Puerto Rico's talented young artists are discovered, are held in Old San Juan on the first Tuesday of each month from 6–9pm. Two of the country's leading art galleries can be found on Calle del Cristo in Old San Juan: Atlas Art and Galería Fósil Arte.

Another excellent occasion to get more than a taste of local talent is at the San Juan Biennial Graphic Art Exhibition, which covers the spectrum of imaginative techniques and styles of Caribbean artists. ❑

LEFT: grand stairway at the Museo de Arte de Ponce.
RIGHT: detail of Myrna Báez's *Homage to Vermeer*.

FOLK ART WITH A FLAVOR ALL ITS OWN

Many of Puerto Rico's handicrafts have evolved out of necessity, and focus on function as well as form, but some of it is just plain fun...

Puerto Rico's most exquisite form of "folk art" actually borders on "fine art": *santos*, the carved religious figures that have been produced here since the 1500s. (*See page 84.*) But over the centuries, the country's folk art has expanded into many other areas, with today's artisans producing a great variety of paintings, non-religious sculpture, jewelry and many other more quirky – and collectible – artifacts.

Usually bursting with bright colors, Puerto Rican folk art has an almost childlike quality. Many times folk artists base their themes on the nature around them: roosters, iguanas, and the tiny *coquís* (tree frogs) are frequently depicted.

Old San Juan is the best place to see – and purchase – local folk art. The Institute of Puerto Rican Culture is a great source of information about the country's arts and crafts, but buyers should head for the two weekend craft markets – one on Plaza de la Dársena in front of Pier 1 (11am–10pm) and the other in Paseo de la Princesa (noon–8pm). Just before Christmas each year, the Bacardi Artisans Fair, held in the distillery grounds, features more than 100 booths displaying everything from stone necklaces to musical flutes.

◁ **EXPERT HANDS**
Bobbins flying, a lady from Moca keeps alive the 500-year-old craft of making *mundillo*, or tatted fabric.

◁ **HOME FOR SALE**
A craftsman proudly displays his intricate model of an island home at the San Sebastián Hammock Festival.

△ **ESSENTIAL ART**
Music is an integral part of life to a Puerto Rican, and the *cuatro* guitar – skillfully crafted by local artisans – plays an important role.

SCARY ART: *VEJIGANTE* MASKS

An unusual – and popular – form of folk art in Puerto Rico is the grotesque, colorfully painted masks that are one of the highlights of the island's many festivals. Artisans (such as the *ponceño* above) have been producing the horned, spike-toothed, speckled *papier mâché* creations for centuries – some historians believe the practice dates back to ancient Taínos; others link it to medieval Spain or tribal Africa. Traditionally the masks were black, red and yellow – symbolic of hellfire and damnation. Brightly costumed *vejigantes* don the masks and roam the streets at carnival time, in an attempt to scare sinners back into the church. Ponce and Loíza are the island's mask-making centers; their carnivals provide a chance to see masks in action.

◁ **THE ART OF RELAXING**
Dating back to Taíno times, hammock-making remains a favorite pastime of the islanders – perhaps second only to actually lying in them!

△ **FOLK FRESCOS**
When it comes to artistic expression, any wall will do. Puerto Rico is full of small buildings adorned with colorful scenes of local life.

RHYTHM OF THE TROPICS

Salsa is king, but the sounds range from the percussion of traditional instruments
to the classical music encouraged by Pablo Casals, who made his home here

Just before he died, the world-renowned Argentinian composer Alberto Ginastera visited Puerto Rico in order to attend the world première of one of his works commissioned by the Pablo Casals Festival. During an interview at the Caribe Hilton, Mr Ginastera's thoughts turned to the song of the *coquí*, the tiny frog that is found only in Puerto Rico and is famous for its persistent and ubiquitous nocturnal calls. "It is the only natural song that I know of," said Mr Ginastera, "which is formed of a perfect seventh." The *coquí* sings a two-note song – "co … kee!" – and these two notes are a perfect seventh apart. It should come, therefore, as no surprise that the island's natural sounds have their unique man-made counterpart. The music of Puerto Rico is salsa.

From settlement to salsa

Puerto Ricans have always excelled in music, and the somewhat haphazard course of the island's history has given it a multitude of traditions from which to build a distinctively Puerto Rican sound. The earliest settlers were as enthusiastic about their music as any Spaniards; but, deprived of their native string instruments, found themselves in the position of having to create their own. As a result, there are at least half-a-dozen string instruments native to the island.

In the absence of many tonal instruments, the settlers were forced to make do with simple percussive ones, which are ready to hand in the various gourds, woods, shoots and beans native to this land. The arrival of West African slaves, who brought with them a well-developed and long history of percussion-based music, accelerated this trend.

Even now, Puerto Ricans are very adept at making music with whatever happens to be within grabbing distance. No one *owns* a

PRECEDING PAGES: the highly acclaimed Puerto Rico Symphony Orchestra.
LEFT: folk music figures prominently in island life.
RIGHT: drumming out a *bomba* beat.

musical composition in Puerto Rico, as one does in other countries. Play a Puerto Rican a piano tune he likes in a bar room or café, and you won't believe your ears when you hear the rhythmic sounds he gets out of a spoon, a wood block, a bead necklace or even his knuckles on the table.

No lack of formality

To be fair, there is a somewhat formalized genre of this very type of music. It's collectively called *bomba y plena*, but the two are completely different types of music that are coupled with dance. Together, they are the most popular forms of folk music in Puerto Rico.

The *bomba* is purely African in origin and came over with the black slaves who were forced to work on the country's sugar plantations. It's essentially a marriage of drumming and dancing: one egging the other on in a rhythmic competition of sorts. The northeastern town of Loíza is a particularly good place to experience a typical *bomba*.

Plena, on the other hand, is a blend of elements from the island's many cultures – even ancient Taíno – and generally involves a handful of musicians creating different rhythms on an amazing variety of hand-held percussion instruments. Some resemble hand-held tympanis, some Irish *bodhrans*, some tambourines. Many of them are homemade, and have become a type of "folk art" of sorts, as well as functional instruments. The custom of *plena* originated in Ponce, but today you can hear its distinctive sounds at any patron saint's festival and occasionally at Plaza de Armas or Plaza de la Dársena in Old San Juan.

Traditional music is still performed widely, especially during holidays and festivals. At family parties and get-togethers, there are usually guitarists, *güiro* (gourd) players and pianists playing the long-established music of the people – particularly such standards as *Flores Negros* and *Somos Novios*. Television and radio stations showcase popular singers and groups, such as Chucho Avellanet, Danny Rivera, Ednita Nazario, Lucecita and Nydia Caro. The "Tropical Salsa" renditions of balladeers Chayanne, Ricky Martin and Marc Anthony command large audiences at concerts held at the Coliseo de Puerto Rico and Centro de Bellas Artes or at town plazas.

Contemporary music ranges from the traditional-but-modern sounds of *plena libre* to merengue singers like Olga Tañon, Elvis Crespo and Melina León. The 21st century brought a new beat, reggaeton, a uniquely Puerto Rican fusion of hip-hop, with sounds ranging from reggae to rock to salsa, all with an underground beat. Artists such as Tego Calderón, Daddy Yankee, Don Omar and Calle 13 not only hold sway in the island's top radio stations and clubs, but have crossed over into the US market as well.

Classical sounds, too

This is not to neglect the achievements of this small island in the more traditional forms. It is a haven for the opera, and has its own company; Justino Díaz, the island's finest male vocalist, has impressed critics from New York to Milan, and Puerto Rico's "Renaissance Man," composer Jack Delano (who died in 1998), made his mark on the classical scene.

The Puerto Rico Ballet Company stages classics as well as original local productions at the Centro de Bellas Artes (Performing Arts) in Santurce, while the Puerto Rico Symphony Orchestra – despite being relatively young – is probably the best in the Caribbean, and has premièred works by some of Latin America's finest composers, many of them at San Juan's Casals Festival, the Caribbean's most celebrated cultural event, held for two weeks in January each year (exact dates vary). The orchestra and the Children's Chorus have drawn much attention internationally.

It is Pablo Casals who, more than any other Puerto Rican resident, is responsible for the upsurge of interest and proficiency in classical performance in Puerto Rico in recent years. Born in Catalonia in 1876 of a Puerto Rican mother, Casals was recognized almost before World War I as one of the greatest cellists of his era. After leaving Spain in 1936 as a protest against the Spanish Civil War, he settled in the French Pyrenees, where the first Casals Festival was held in 1950. He visited his mother's homeland in 1956, and spent the final years of his life in Puerto Rico.

In 1957, at the invitation of Governor Luís Muñoz Marín, he founded the Puerto Rican Casals Festival, which must rank as the greatest cultural event in the Antilles, and a formidable one even by world standards. In later years, Casals went on to form the Puerto Rico Symphony Orchestra and the Puerto Rico Conservatory of Music. On his death at the age of 97 in 1973, he considered himself a Puerto Rican; his compatriots consider him one of their national heroes.

Rhythm of the tropics

Salsa is what happens when Afro-Caribbean music meets big-band jazz. Its roots may be found in the early explorations of the late Puerto Rican Tito Puente and Cuban musicians in New York City clubs following World War II. After serving three years in the United States Navy, Puente studied percussion at the prestigious Julliard School on New York's West Side. He was soon playing and composing for top bandleaders such as Machito and Pupi Campo, and he quickly proceeded to establish his own orchestra.

In an interview in *Latin US* magazine, before his death in 2000 at age 77, Puente was asked to define salsa. "As you know, salsa in Spanish means 'sauce,' and we use it mostly as a condiment for our foods," he said. "Salsa in general is all our fast Latin music put together: the merengue, the rumba, the mambo, the cha-cha, the guaguanco, boogaloo, all of it is salsa… in Latin music, we have many different types of rhythms, such as ballads (boleros), rancheros, tangos, and, of course, salsa."

The salsa band is usually composed of a lead vocalist and chorus, a piano, a bass, a horn section and a heavy assortment of percussion instruments (bongos, conga, maracas, *güiros*, timbales, claves, and the ever-present cowbell – a *jíbaro* touch). The overall effect is mesmerizing; the rhythm contagious. It is unquestionably highly danceable music and you will hear it everywhere.

Salsa (the center of which is now thought to have shifted *back* to Puerto Rico from New York) has firmly placed the island on the map of popular music, with more and more young *salseros* getting in on the act every day – and not just in Puerto Rico.

"It's totally unexpected to see Belgians, Swedes, Finns and Danes swing to the Latin

SPICY SAUCE

Salsa literally translates as "sauce": in a musical sense, the "sauce" that makes parties happen.

Beat… the bands there are playing more salsa than we are," said Puente.

A musical evolution

Puerto Rican music has evolved into the salsa beat; music has played a crucial role in Puerto Rican society and culture for as long as there have been Puerto Ricans. During Spanish rule, the *danza* was the chief form of entertainment for the *criollo* aristocracy; it reached its high point in the late 19th century when Juan Morel Campos and other masters gave it a popularity

that resounded back to Spain. This highly stylized tradition of music and its accompanying dance movements are preserved by several local ensembles in Puerto Rico. The *danza* is characterized by a string orchestra, woodwind, and a formal ambience. *La Borinqueña*, the Puerto Rican national anthem, is a *danza*.

A more popular and widely practiced Puerto Rican musical tradition is the *aguinaldo*, a song performed around the Christmas and Three Kings holiday, usually in the form of an *asalto*. The *asalto* is a charming tradition which dates back to the 19th century, and perhaps earlier. It goes along with the unrestrained partying of the holiday season. It is

LEFT: Puerto Rican folk music is almost inevitably accompanied by lively dance.
RIGHT: Tito Puente, often referred to as the "king" of Puerto Rican salsa.

customary at an *asalto* to feast on *lechón asado* (roast suckling pig), *yuca* (a local potato-like root), *arroz con pollo* (chicken with rice), *gandules* (pigeon peas) and *palos de ron* (well, okay, so they have some rum). Following the feast, a group of noisy celebrants stumbles from house to house, waking the residents and singing *aguinaldos*. The members of each household are expected to join the *asalto* as it moves throughout the surrounding neighborhood. Recordings of these genial songs are available as performed by a *parranda* or *trulla*, which is any professional group of *aguinaldo* singers.

fueled by the audience. The similarity between the traditional *décima* and the more modern verbal duelling of today's rap DJs is striking.

Star performers

In Puerto Rico, salsa is king, but who is the King of Salsa? No one really agrees, but lists generally include Willie Colón, Panamanian singer-turned-politician Rubén Blades, the late Hector Lavoe, El Gran Combo de Puerto Rico, and the Fania All-Stars. Puerto Rico's biggest salsa star is Gilberto Santa Rosa (a protégé of Willie Rosario), affectionately known as "Gilbertito." In addition to salsa, merengue groups from the

The *décima*

The *décima* is arguably the most appealing form of traditional Puerto Rican music. It is the vehicle through which the *jíbaro* expresses his joys and frustrations; it is the poetry of the Puerto Rican soul. Instrumentation for the *décima* consists of a number of three-, four- and six-stringed instruments (called appropriately the *tres, cuatro* and *seis*); a minimal rhythm is kept up by claves or the *güiro*.

The trademark of the *décima* is verbal improvisation. Often, two singers will alternate stanzas, trying to outboast each other with rhyming tales of luscious fruit, pretty women or physical prowess. The verbal jousting is significantly

nearby Dominican Republic have become very popular. In fact, it is the preferred dance music at many Puerto Rican parties.

Some locals, led by Olga Tañon, Elvis Crespo and Melina León, have been able to cash in on the fast-paced merengue sound. Local salsa musicians in Cuba and Puerto Rico compete in playing the most infectious melodies, but it is said the latter are more avant-garde in their approach.

Willie Colón and his band have produced some of the most inspired salsa music to date. The album *Siembra*, a collaboration with Rubén Blades in 1978, is easily one of the hottest classics. The songs on *Siembra* show the rhythmic complexity which lies at the core of salsa, as well as the thematic motifs which tie all of salsa together. Like the *plena* singers of old, today's salsa vocalists often tell a story filled with satire or a social commentary. *Pedro Navaja*, for example, tells the story of a street tough and his inevitable demise. Blades croons the final verse, describing the scene after a gunfight:

"And believe me people, although there was noise, nobody came out. There were no busy-bodies, no questions asked, and nobody cried. Only a drunk bumped into the two bodies, and picked up the revolver, the knife and the dollars

Colón's talent sparkles in other collaborative efforts. His 1977 recording with Celia Cruz, entitled *Only They Could Have Made This Album*, is a superb example of salsa's African roots. The songs from *Pun Pun Catalu*, *Rinkinkalla*, and *Burundanga* make use of African linguistic and musical references. *Burundanga* is an outgrowth of the music of *santería*, the Afro-Caribbean religious cult.

Of the bands, El Gran Combo (de Puerto Rico) has had great success since the early 1960s, probably owing to its songs' optimism and enthusiasm. It has great talent, a good sense of humor, and a massive popular following.

and marched off; and stumbling, he went on his way singing off-tune the chorus that I bring you that gives the message of my song. Life gives you surprises, surprises will give you life, Oh, God!"

He who lives by violence dies by violence; Colón and Blades are not the first salsa singers to choose this emotive theme for a musical starting point.

The road to a better future is not always easy to follow, and the song *Resignación* suggests an amusing relief for the "estress" of making a fulfilling life for one's self:

"Tell me Mr Psychiatrist, what should I do?/I've lost my friends and my woman, too./I'm going to prescribe 'bothers me not' potion/Along with an ointment and salve of 'and so what'/And if you know English and things continue ugly/Take five pills of 'I don't care'."

Whatever the individual's taste, salsa continues to be one of the hottest forms of popular music in the world today. ❏

LEFT: a couple dancing to the music of a local band in Vieques.
ABOVE: the "town character" struts his stuff at the San Sebastián Hammock Festival.

A SPORTING LIFE

Baseball, basketball and volleyball fire the Puerto Ricans' competitive spirit but there is plenty for the visitor to do on and off the island's tropical waters

When the first ball was thrown in the Taíno *batú*, sport was born in Puerto Rico. All that remains of this early interest in sport are the ruins of the Taíno game courts south of Arecibo at the Caguana Ceremonial Ballpark and the Tibes Indian Ceremonial Park near Ponce, where early people played a game much like soccer.

Today, baseball games have replaced the Taíno diversion. The 20th century brought a wealth of action to Puerto Rico, but it all started with the US's national pastime, which became the island's most popular sport. This is not surprising, since the climate enables baseball to be played virtually every day of the year.

The amateur leagues set up their schedules so that there are games on most days. The Winter League, which includes many professional players from the minor and major leagues, slates its games from October to January. Teams represent Manatí, Bayamón, Caguas, Carolina, Ponce and Mayagüez. In February, the Caribbean Series is held, with teams representing Puerto Rico, the Dominican Republic, Venezuela and Mexico. The game has produced such luminaries as Roberto Clemente, Orlando Cepeda and Rubén Gomez, with current stars including Ivan "Pudge" Rodriguez, Carlos Delgado, Carlos Beltrán, Bernie Williams and Jorge Posada.

Hoop dreams

Although baseball has been the sport most identified with Puerto Rico, since the 1990s basketball has ranked a close second. This sport draws much interest because of the island team's success in international competitions such as the Olympics and the Pan-American Games. Puerto Rican teams have even given the powerful US entries a run for their money. The Superior Basketball League fields 12 teams in Santurce, Arecibo, Bayamon, Carolina, Caguas, Coamo, Morovis, Ponce, Guayama, Guaynabo, Humacao

and San Germán. The season runs through spring and summer, adjusted annually to accommodate the island basketball team's international participation in the Olympics, Pan Am Games and other events. Most basketball games in Puerto Rico are played in indoor coliseums. In the Central American-Caribbean Games, held

every four years, island basketball teams have dominated such countries as the Dominican Republic, Colombia and Mexico.

International competition has become so important that the majority of Puerto Ricans prefer to have their own representation rather than to be part of the US teams. This option of Puerto Rican representation in the Games, as well as participation in world beauty contests, is considered to be one of the arguments against statehood status.

Puerto Rico has produced a large group of champion boxers, tennis players, golfers – and even a horse that won the Kentucky Derby, Bold Forbes. Horse-racing draws great interest around

---

PRECEDING PAGES: underwater treasures.
LEFT: windsurfer sets sail.
RIGHT: aspiring Roberto Clementes.

the island, even though there is only one race track – El Comandante in Canóvanas. Offtrack betting agencies in every town are usually full on racing days, which are every day except Tuesday and Saturday.

Puerto Rico's boxers have won gold medals in international competition. More than 50 professional pugilists have held champion status in every weight category except heavyweight. Boxing enthusiasts acknowledge and revere the accomplishments of José "Chegui" Torres, who held the light heavyweight title back in the 1960s. Three-

DUFFER'S DELIGHT

Puerto Rico's 17 golfing facilities include a total of 22 courses. The island's Golf Association honors local legends in their Hall of Fame.

Punta Borinquen and Aguirre, with a public driving range in Bayamón. All hotel courses are available at higher rates. Puerto Rico's most famous golfer, Juan "Chichi" Rodríguez, has retired from the Seniors Tour in the United States. He devotes much of his time to his own golf resort, El Legado, in Guayama.

Watersports of all types feature, naturally, and boating marinas are at Isla Grande, Boca de Cangrejos, Fajardo, Ponce and Mayagüez. Surfing has become a way of life in areas like Rincón, where international events

time world champions include Wilfredo Gómez, Wilfredo Benítez and Felix "Tito" Trinidad, all of whom are still considered among the best pound-for-pound fighters in the world.

For the net set, tennis courts abound around the island, especially at the hotels and resorts. The public may use the facilities for a fee. A few internationally known tennis players have emerged from the local courts, such as Charlie Pasarell and Gigi Fernández. The Baldrich Tennis Club in Hato Rey provides 10 regulation courts for use at a nominal cost.

Golf is a natural for the island, with championship courses mainly found at the resorts. Public courses are available at reasonable rates in

have been held. Windsurfing is a natural choice for the waters of the Atlantic and the Caribbean. On any given day, the colorful sails flash by. Ocean kayaking has gained popularity in recent times, with kayaks for rent on the placid Condado Lagoon. On the beaches and in the parks, racquetball, volleyball, soccer and even touch football attract large crowds.

Anglers can indulge in all types of fishing, although deep-sea fishing is particularly good, with billfish plentiful. Marlin as heavy as 500 lbs (227 kg) have been reeled in. The record marlin catch of 604 lbs (274 kg) is held by Carmina Méndez Miller, a retired broadcaster, who stands less than 5 ft (1.5 meters) tall.

Something different

For a country that is considered *machista*, Puerto Rico's fascination with women's volleyball is notable. Some sports writers suggest it may be the short shorts the players wear, but whatever the cause, the semi-pro leagues fill arenas all over the island. Even the high-school levels get a great deal of media attention, sometimes nudging the baseball and basketball news to less prominent sports pages.

The college players, who studied on the US mainland, were getting important experience by playing for free in the summer Puerto Rico pro leagues when school got out. The result has

catering vans for picnics along the way, right through to raucous four-legged pub crawls that include anyone who's managed to raise a horse in his backyard.

The Puerto Rican *pasofino* horse, descended from the first Andalusian horses to be brought to the island by the Spaniards, is said to be the only breed actually born with a Lippizaner-style gait. Small-boned and gentle, even a complete beginner will generally feel comfortable astride one of these horses.

Sports bars provide a full complement of National Football League games on TV during the season. Shannan's Pub in Guaynabo shows

been that Puerto Rico is breaking into the ranks of the world's top-10 national selections. But the attention has caused US college sports ruling body, the NCAA, to deny amateur status to college players who play with any pro leagues, even if they aren't paid.

In four-legged sports, a favorite weekend activity is *cabalgatas*. Derived from the Spanish word for horse – *caballo* – these are trail rides that can range from elegant *paseos* on fine US$50,000 *pasofino* horses accompanied by

all of Sunday's games. And cable TV brings college and pro games into homes weekly during the season.

The grand San Blas Half-Marathon, held in the southern Coamo area every year, draws hundreds of contestants from around the world and attracts thousands of spectators. Often the event is won by runners from Kenya.

Unquestionably, the islanders' interest in a wide variety of sports is growing at an accelerating pace. And it's a far cry from the Taíno games of ancient times: modern technology, such as computerization and electronic communication, promises new dimensions to the already booming field. ❑

LEFT: taking to the fairways on one of the island's lush golf courses.
ABOVE: surfer "soul arches" at "Wilderness," Ramey.

PLACES

*A detailed guide to the entire island, with principal sites
clearly cross-referenced by number to the maps*

P uerto Rico? That's beaches, right, and *paradores,* and old
Spanish forts tossed in with a few frosty rum drinks? Well,
yes and no. You won't want to miss Old San Juan's colorful
streets, or the chance to stand on El Morro's walls, looking out into
the Atlantic at the ghosts of 16th-century British invaders, and you
certainly shouldn't leave the island without tasting a *piña colada* –
but there are far more places to see and understand than those
fringed with surf and sand.

We've started this section of the book in Puerto Rico's most populous area, San Juan. Old San Juan, an eight-block area on a small
peninsula, harks back to the 1500s, while only a few miles away, in
Hato Rey and Río Piedras, modern commerce is being conducted in
sleek steel-and-glass corporate offices.

If metropolitan San Juan is the most humanly populated area of the
island, then the northeast is the most geographically diverse. The
range of terrain in the region, from beaches to dense rainforest to
secluded islands, is staggering. Here, too, you'll find the island's
best beach and some of the finest yachting.

As you head west from San Juan, exploration of the northern part
of the island reveals one of the largest cave networks in the Western
hemisphere, as well as the oddly scaled karst mountain region. Limestone formations rise above the island's most historic cities – Arecibo,
Lares, San Sebastián.

The western reaches of Puerto Rico feature beautiful beaches,
surfers' paradises and towns worth discovering, such as metropolitan Mayagüez and architecturally rich San Germán.

In the south of the island, you'll realize fully the relaxed pace of
life in Puerto Rico. There's Ponce, a pearl of a city on the coast, but
if you're tired of the urban hustle you'll never be at a loss to find a
quiet place to sit in the sun.

The heart of the island is the Cordillera Central. Here, the Ruta
Panoramica will take the adventurous driver from one end of the
range to the other, affording spectacular views all the while.

But don't let the island's boundaries stop your explorations: off its
shores lie three other islands with charms all of their own: Vieques,
Culebra and Mona. ❑

PRECEDING PAGES: San Juan skyline at dusk; ancient and modern at the
Old Casino in San Juan; boats on the quay, San Juan Yacht Club.
LEFT: Playa las Palmas, Punta la Galiena.

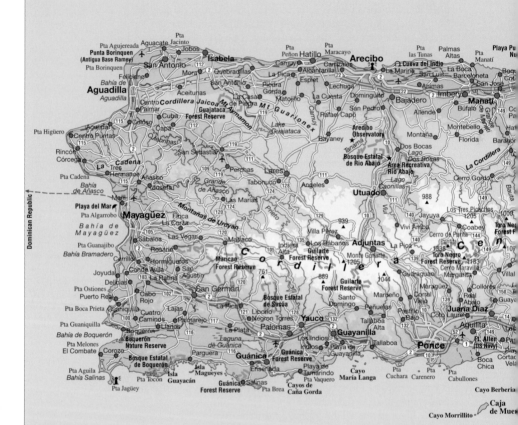

N

0   10 miles
0   10 km

O C E A N

Playa
Cerro Gordo
Playa
de Dorado
Isla de
Cabras
Fort
El Morro
San Juan
Bosque Estatal
de Piñones
Pta Vacia Talega
Mameyito
San Antonio
Toa Baja
Sabana
Cañuelo
Santa
Barbara
Loíza
Suárez
Vieques
Pta Miquillo
Pta Picúa
Los Puertos
Polvorin
Seca
167
26
187
188
187
Vega Alta
Monterrey
22
Cataño
18
26
Rio Lajas
Toa Alta
2
Bayamón
2
Lomas
Verdes
1
Carolina
Cañovanas
Río
Grande
Luquillo
La Cordillera
Cayo
Icacos
Cayo
Lobos
Isla de Culebra
Pajaros
Van Scoy
Algeria
Guaynabo
Laprocomio
181
3
La Dolores
Playa
Sardiñera
Pasaje de San Juan
Corozal
164
Rivera
Lomas
174
52
Carrizo
Alto
Trujillo Alto
La Marina
El Verde
185
El Yunque
Boquerón
Fajardo
Isla
Palominos
Naranjito
152
Sabana
El Laberinto
La Bayamorisa
181
La Mina
181
San Vicente
Catalina
El Yunque
1065
Mabi
Santa
Maria
Bosque Estatal
de Ceiba
Bahía
Demajagua
Sonda de
Vieques
Mil de Corazon
167
Rio Cañas
Loíza
Lake
C. d. Hato Nuevo
Benítez
Celada
Colonia
Paraiso
1074
Sierra de Luquillo
(Caribbean
National Forest)
El Toro
191
Aquas Claras
Ceiba
Isla de Vieques
Berio
Aguas
Buenas
Gurabo
Lomas
El Mango
Duque
Daguao
3
US Naval Station
Roosevelt Roads
Isla Piñeros
Isla Cabras
Pasaje de Vieques
barancas
943
Comerio
152
Sumidero
156
Bairoa
30
Cantagalio
Los Torres
Naguabo
31
Playa de
Naguabo
Pta Algodones
Bahía Algodones
Carro
Quebrada
Grande
172
173
Esperanza
El Cinco
Caguas
183
Juncos
31
Melillas
Pitahaya
Pasto
Viejo
Mosquito
Pier
Barranquitas
162
Cidra
52
San Lorenzo
30
La Permina
Humacao
Punta Santiago
Cayo Santiago
Mosquito
Aibonito
14
La Placita
1
744
La Plata
171
642
181
La Suiza
Buena Vista
Morro de Humacao
Pta Arenas
US Naval
Reservation
Coamo
14
Cayey
Cerro La Santa
903
Reserva Forestal
Carite (Guavate)
Ingenio
Comunas
53
Pta Candelero
Mount Pirata
Cayo
de Afuera
Isla de Vieques
301
Las Tetas
Vazquez
Campamento
Guavate
184
Campamento
Real
Martorell
Yabucoa
Playa de Guayanés
890
15
La Plena
Cerro de la Tabla
686
901
Playita
Pta Guayanés
153
Rabo del Buey
Sierra de Cayey
184
181
Cuchilla de Panduras
Maunabo
Campamento Santiago
(US Army)
Carmen
179
Yaurel
Patillas
Palmas
Colonia Providencia
Playa Puerto Maunabo
Pta Yeguas
Coco
Guayama
3
Cuarto
Lamboglia
Rocio
Pta Tuna
Coqui
Jagua
1
Jobos
Calles
Pta Viento
Salinas
Mar Negro
Arroyo
Las Mareas
Pta Figuras
Cayo Mata
Pta Arenas
Aguirre
Cayos
de Ratónes
Cayos
de Barca
Cayos
Caribes
Bosque Estatal
de Aguirre

S E A

116

Old San Juan

0   200 yds

0   200 m

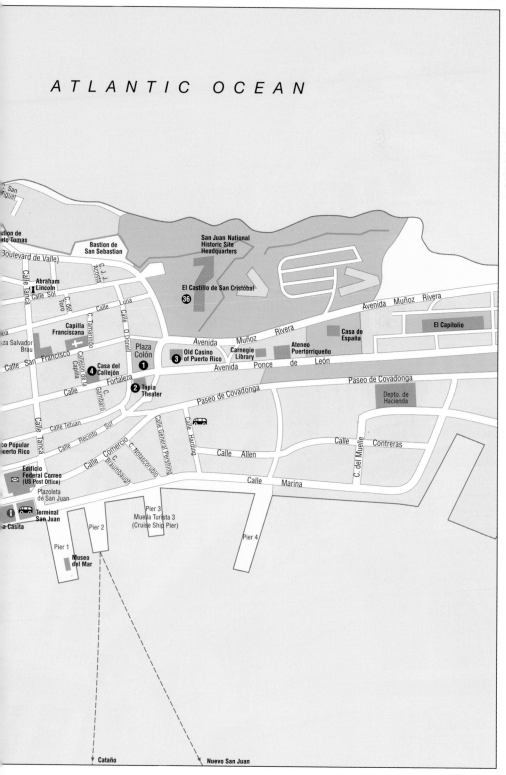

ATLANTIC OCEAN

OLD SAN JUAN

There's a wealth of architectural treasures in this oldest of American cities. Fortunately, many of them aren't swamped by the hordes of cruise-ship tourists

San Juan

No matter how much history is crammed within the cobblestoned streets of Old San Juan, no matter how seductive the pastel and wrought-iron Spanish colonial houses may seem, no matter how chock-to-the-brim with opportunities for socializing and partying this city may be, it is something altogether more spiritual that attracts Puerto Ricans and visitors alike to San Juan.

There is something in the place that traps travelers and forces them to move at the old city's pace. If you've rushed through Old San Juan, you certainly have not been there. Get a good pair of walking shoes and ramble; a car is as much a liability as it is an asset here, anyway.

This oldest of American cities has iron streets, cobbled with *adoquines*, or blocks of slag, from the lowland smelting mills of Spain's 16th-century empire. (The stones were brought over by the Spanish as ballast for their ships.) It has two of the most invulnerable forts ever constructed, which are connected by walls that circle a peninsula, and some of the finest restaurants and bars in the Caribbean. And the city is full of art galleries.

It is also full of some of the narrowest sidewalks you'll find anywhere. So be careful with traffic. It might be mentioned at this point that even within its tiny area, Old San Juan has an endless supply of undiscovered attractions to enjoy. These are what lead second-time visitors to call for a taxi to Old San Juan as soon as they step off the plane at Luis Muñoz Marín International Airport.

Into the city

As Puerto Rico's Spanish history begins with Columbus, an exploration of Old San Juan could naturally begin in the **Plaza Colón ❶**, or Columbus Square, a quadrangle built around a commemorative statue of the explorer. It is here that the high-speed, heavily trafficked *avenidas* Ponce de León and Muñoz Rivera give way to the narrow and scarcely navigable grid that is Old San Juan. If you're without a car this will be your last stop on the municipal bus, or *público*. If you are driving, you should now start looking for a place to park.

Located at the southeastern corner of the Old San Juan quadrant, Plaza Colón is an ideal spot for fanning out on a walking tour of the city. The square itself offers a good introductory stroll. On its south side is the **Tapia Theater ❷**, a tasteful, ochre, hacienda-like structure dating from 1826 and beautifully restored in the mid-1970s (box office open Mon–Fri, 9am–4pm).

For all its other cultural achievements, Puerto Rico has produced very little internationally known theater,

PRECEDING PAGES: strolling along one of Old San Juan's many-hued streets. **LEFT:** colonial style in Old San Juan. **BELOW:** monument to Christopher Columbus in Plaza Colón.

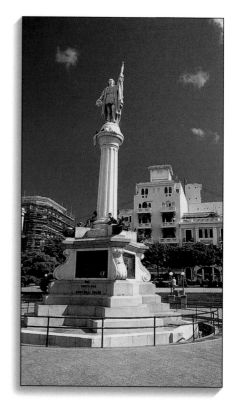

TIP

A good way to get around the old city is by using the free small yellow buses that go to El Morro and El Castillo San Cristóbal (and points between the two), which run every 5–8 minutes from 7.30am to 7.30pm, reducing in frequency later in the evening. Stops (*paradas*) are marked.

BELOW: view of Old San Juan from just offshore.

although playwrights such as Myrna Casas have won prizes in New York; Alejandro Tapia y Rivera (1826–82), after whom the theater is named, is the earliest and perhaps most notable exception. Today the theater premières plays by contemporary international dramatists. Across the street from the theater on the plaza's eastern side is the **Old Casino of Puerto Rico ❸**, built shortly after Puerto Rico became a US colony early in the 20th century but harking back architecturally to the Spanish reign, it is now the Government Reception Center.

Ironically, if somewhat predictably, the path most tourists take into Old San Juan is the least characteristic of the city. **Calle Fortaleza** is, at least for three blocks, as cluttered with souvenir shops, jewelry shops and shoe stores as any place in the city. Fortunately, Calle Fortaleza is just as crowded with architectural wonders. The first right along the street is **Callejón de la Capilla**, a romantic, lantern-lit alleyway that arcs uphill to Calle San Francisco.

At the corner of Fortaleza and Callejón de la Capilla, the **Casa del Callejón ❹**, an 18th-century residence, houses two charming museums – one dedicated to colonial architecture and the other to the Puerto Rican family – but both are closed indefinitely for restoration.

Continuing on Calle Fortaleza, you can turn right on Calle Tanca for a bit of relaxation in the sloping Plaza Salvador Brau, or make a left toward the piers of San Juan Port. Nearby at the waterfront, **Plazoleta de San Juan** teems with eager visitors who purchase souvenirs and folk art from local artisans.

Most ports which serve a large number of cruise ships end up looking rather like jungles of cranes and heavy machinery. San Juan, which takes more cruise traffic than any other port in the Caribbean, is an exception. The port not only benefits from the tastefulness of its more utilitarian maritime buildings (the

pink, mock-colonial **US Customs House** ❺ is a good example of this) but has a beautiful cityscape as well.

The waterfront has become even more attractive now that the ambitious $120-million **Frente Portuario** complex is finished. This Mediterranean-style mega-project offers 200 condominium apartments across three buildings, the 242-room Sheraton Hotel and Casino, two office towers, a 603-space parking garage and 110,000 sq. ft (10,200 sq. meters) of retail space.

Frente Portuario, designed to ensure that it blends in with the rest of Old San Juan, features picturesque cobblestone-like paved boulevards lined with wrought-iron lamps and red-tiled roofs. Visitors can browse through art galleries, eateries and boutiques.

The government has already spent $100 million on renovating half a dozen cruise-ship ports along the waterfront. Some of the world's largest cruise ships, including Royal Caribbean Line's *Monarch of the Seas* and its twin sister, *Sovereign of the Seas*, regularly call here. From Pier 2 you can also take the ferry to Cataño, home of the Bacardi rum distillery. At 50 cents a passenger, this ferry is truly one of Puerto Rico's great bargains.

Plaza de Hostos is an oasis of shade in a square full of *adoquines*. Named for the 19th-century scholar, it provides a haven for sunburnt tourists and locals alike; the square must be the dominoes capital of the Caribbean. Looming over the plaza is the original office of the **Banco Popular de Puerto Rico** ❻, which has to be one of the great modern architectural triumphs of the Caribbean region. This brawny, 10-story edifice, built in the mid-1930s, is a fine example of Art Deco. Heavy cameo eagles brood over the impressive main entrance, which is lettered in sans-serif gilt intaglio. Elongated windows with

Map on pages 116–7

The Spanish flavor of Old San Juan's architecture is evident from any angle.

BELOW: the old city is full of romantic little side streets.

prominent pastel mullions run the full height of a faintly apsidal façade. The bank presents various exhibits of historical interest during the year.

The area is particularly fortunate in its culinary offerings. Calle Fortaleza has a number of first-rate restaurants, ranging from Dragonfly (Asian Latino) to Tantra (Indian).

Whether approaching uphill on Calle Cruz from Plaza de Hostos, or via Calle Fortaleza from Plaza Colón, almost all travelers pass through the workaday heart of Old San Juan, centering around the **City Hall** (Alcaldía) ❼ (open Mon–Fri; closed pub. hols; tel: 724-7171) and the adjacent **Plaza de Armas** ❽. City Hall was designed to be a replica of Madrid's. What works in Europe seems rather somber for the Antilles, but it is an attractive building nonetheless, one whose charms are enhanced by the fact that small businesses operate within the same arch-covered block as the local government.

The plaza, originally known as Plaza Mayor, is no less historic. Built in 1521, it was the first square in the newly established city. It also served, in the days before soldiers were permanently billeted in San Juan, as the training field for Spanish soldiers sent out from Europe in order to defend the island – hence its current name. Stone paving of the plaza began in 1840, but it was completely remodeled in the late 1980s.

Nonetheless, the main streets along the Plaza de Armas have the unpretentious likeability of a business district, rather than the imposing sense of history of much of Old San Juan.

Calle San Francisco is a friendly mix of tourist shops and government buildings, while the part of Calle Fortaleza just south of the plaza is an engaging few blocks of restaurants and department stores.

The City Hall, or Alcaldía, was built in stages from 1604 to 1789 and underwent extensive alterations in 1841. Free English-language Old City tours can be arranged by appointment (tel: 977-4825).

BELOW: the broad, open Plaza de Armas was remodeled in the 20th century.

La Fortaleza

Calle Fortaleza grows more dignified as it approaches **La Fortaleza** ❾ itself (open Mon–Fri; closed pub. hols; tel: 721-7000 ext. 2211). This chalk-white wonder of a fortress is the oldest continuously inhabited executive mansion in the Western hemisphere. Its construction began in 1532 and was completed in 1540, and it serves to this day as the residence of the Governor of Puerto Rico. It is an architectural wonder, but strategically it was always inadequate. This was apparent even to the Spanish architects, who decided that the gnarled peninsula on which La Fortaleza was being built did not command enough of San Juan Bay to protect completely against invasion from the sea. Accordingly, construction of the massive fort at the tip of the San Juan Peninsula – El Morro – began in the 1540s. *(See page 132.)*

The 1588 sinking of the Spanish Armada made the West Indian possessions of the Spanish Crown more vulnerable than ever, with the result that even more Puerto Rican colonists clamored for greater fortification. By 1595, Queen Elizabeth I had dispatched Sir Francis Drake, whose ambitions included not only a great bounty of gold but all the Spanish lands of the New World as well. Drake arrived in San Juan in late November of that year. He stopped across the bay at Isla de Cabras, and launched several dozen ships from there. Ten would never go back to England, and a total of 400 English sailors would rest forever beneath San Juan harbor. Drake's own cabin was torn apart by a mortar shell during the invasion.

Perhaps the Spanish grew complacent after the first thwarted invasion of their colonial capital, for in June 1598 the Duke of Cumberland was able to land a force of about 1,000 men in the area of Puerta de Tierra, and then march

Map on pages 116–7

TIP

Guided tours of the public areas of La Fortaleza (in English every hour; in Spanish every half hour) depart from the main gate on Calle Fortaleza.

BELOW: bright bougainvillea at La Fortaleza border a serene view over the bay.

Campeche paintings and a gold-and-silver altar can be seen through the Cristo Chapel's glass doors.

into San Juan. The 400 Spanish soldiers defending the city were suffering from tropical diseases but put up valiant resistance, enduring a 15-day siege inside El Morro before capitulating. The English flag flew over the walls of La Fortaleza. The British were hounded by Spanish colonists almost immediately, but it was less Spanish resistance than British *lack* of resistance to the same diseases that led them to give in. In a matter of several weeks after the invasion, Cumberland sailed for home, having lost over 400 men, to leave San Juan to recover in peace for another 27 years.

The year 1625 saw the final occupation of La Fortaleza during colonial times. A Dutch fleet under the command of Boudewijn Hendrikszoon swiftly moved into San Juan Bay and set up a beachhead between El Morro and La Fortaleza. The Dutch burnt much of the city to the ground, including a large portion of La Fortaleza. Reconstruction began in 1640; the building was expanded in 1800 and 1846.

Romantic road

Calle del Cristo (Christ's Street) is the most alluring of Old San Juan's thoroughfares, an intoxicating avenue of sights and sounds, of romance and history. Running from a point high above San Juan Bay, Calle del Cristo arches to an even higher perch above San Juan's Atlantic shore, where El Morro looks sternly out to sea. It can claim Old San Juan's most popular park, most underrated museum and most famous chapel.

This adventure in *adoquines* begins at the **Parque de las Palomas** (Pigeon Park) ❿, a part of the city walls which thousands of pigeons have made their home. Fabulous views of San Juan Bay and the distant suburbs of Bayamón

BELOW: children frolic with feathered friends in Parque de las Palomas.

ARCHITECTURE IN THE OLD CITY

From an architectural standpoint, La Fortaleza really captures the essence of all of Old San Juan: it is an amazing blend of building styles through the ages, from its 16th-century core to its 19th-century façade. La Fortaleza and El Morro – both World Heritage Sites – are perhaps the most outstanding, but throughout the streets of the old city are fine examples of medieval, Gothic, baroque, neo-classical and even Arabian architecture. Most buildings are in excellent condition, partly owing to the painstaking efforts of those who restored them (who worked from many original plans and used, whenever possible, original materials, like *ausubo*, or ironwood, beams) and partly because Old San Juan's sandstone walls and fortresses prevented any modern expansion.

There are some 400 historically important structures in this part of the Puerto Rican capital city, some of which are considered to be the finest examples of Spanish colonial architecture in the New World. Those of particular note include San Juan Cathedral, with a baroque façade but medieval core; San José Church, the only truly Gothic structure under the US flag; and the Dominican Convent, a 16th-century white building that now houses the Institute of Puerto Rican Culture.

and Guaynabo make Parque de las Palomas a popular spot for lovers and an even more popular spot for aspiring ones.

Building with love

Love almost certainly played a decisive part in the construction of the quaint **Cristo Chapel** or Capilla del Cristo ⓫ (open Tues 10am–4pm; free). Romantic legend has it that, during an 18th-century horse race, one of two competing riders failed to make a left turn onto Calle Tetuán and plummeted over the cliffs, seemingly to his death. When he survived, astounded locals constructed a chapel to commemorate Christ's intercession.

Others claim that the race was really a duel over a comely young woman between two chivalrous *enamorados*. One fell to his death, and the chapel was built both to commemorate the tragedy and to block off Calle del Cristo to prevent such a mishap from ever occurring again.

The peninsula stretching below the Cristo Chapel is known as **La Puntilla**. Today it accommodates the **Arsenal de la Marina** (opening times vary; tel: 787-722 1709; free), a former Spanish naval base that houses the Fine and Folk Arts Divisions of the Institute of Puerto Rican Culture and three excellent art galleries.

A short walk up Calle del Cristo on the right is one of Puerto Rico's most enchanting and least-known museums. The **Casa del Libro** ⓬ (open Tues–Sat, 11am–4.30pm; closed pub. hols; free) is a breezy, parqueted sanctuary which is dedicated to the history of books and printing. Within its walls are nearly 5,000 rare sketches, illustrations and ancient manuscripts, as well as work by local artists and illustrators. Two of the museum's most prized possessions are royal mandates, signed in 1493 by Ferdinand and Isabella of Spain, concerning the

Map on pages 116–7

TIP

You can get many discounts and special offers on historic site tours, folklore shows, lodgings, meals and more by joining Puerto Rico's LeLoLai VIP program for a small fee. Phone 787-721 2400 ext. 2715 for more information.

BELOW: dusk settles on Calle del Cristo, with the Cristo Chapel providing a romantic backdrop.

provisioning of Columbus's fleet for his second voyage, which resulted in the discovery of Puerto Rico. Another precious work is one of only six known copies of the first printing of the Third Part of the *Summa* of St Thomas Aquinas, dating from 1477.

Next door, the **Centro Nacional de Artes Populares y Artesanías** or Popular Arts and Crafts Center ⓭ (open Mon–Sat 9am–5pm; free), run by the Institute of Puerto Rican Culture, houses a collection of paintings from the 18th century to the present. Island crafts are for sale at the shop inside.

If you build up an appetite exploring this oldest and best-known street of the old city, don't worry: half a dozen eateries crowd this end of Calle del Cristo. In addition, any aesthetic overdose one suffers on the south part of the street can be cured with a bracing *piña colada* in one of the bars on the north side. A plaque around the corner on Calle Fortaleza claims that a bar which once occupied the site of what is now a jewelry store was the birthplace of the *piña colada* in 1963. According to long-time imbibers, however, the coconut, pineapple and rum drink was concocted well before then.

A cathedral and a convent

Ascending Calle del Cristo, even the most skeptical travelers will begin to see what they came to San Juan for. On the right, usually bathed in sunlight in the afternoon, is **San Juan Cathedral** ⓮ (open daily 8.30am–4pm; donation), a fabulous beige-and-white structure that must count among the most important houses of worship in the West. It was built in 1540 and carefully restored in the 19th and 20th centuries, and the beauty of its exterior is immediately perceptible. Three tiers of white pilasters and arches mount to a simple cross at the

In front of San Juan Cathedral stands a gnarled tree – a living gesture of international friendship from dozens of North and South American nations.

BELOW: the much-photographed cupolas of San Juan Cathedral.

Map
on pages
116–7

cathedral's pinnacle. The three brick-red and white cupolas are among San Juan's most photogenic sights.

But the interior of the cathedral is not as easy to appreciate for anyone who thinks of cathedrals primarily in their French, German or British incarnations. For one thing, the floor is of black parquet, which seems to belie the solemnity of the building. The brown and ochre *trompe l'oeil* ceiling is pretty, but it appears too close to the worshipper's eye. The cathedral really needs several visits but will in time reward the most discerning.

Among its highlights are **Ponce de León's marble tomb**, with an understated virgin warrior glancing down at the body and the red script of the epitaph, and the glittering blue statue of **La Virgen de Providencia**, Puerto Rico's patroness, located nearby. A relic of San Pio, a Roman martyr, is in a glass case containing a macabre plaster figure of the saint, behind the altar. There's another such effigy, of a prostrate Jesus, in the **Chapel of Souls in Purgatory**, which is in the cathedral's right nave.

Directly across Calle del Cristo is **Hotel El Convento ⓫**, established in 1651 as a convent for Carmelite nuns, San Juan's first. When the nuns moved to Santurce in the early part of the 20th century, the convent fell into disrepair. It was restored in 1996 and turned into the five-star, 100-room luxury hotel with a casino – much to the anger of the nuns, who argued that slot machines were a sacrilege to the memory of their sisters buried underneath. Though few of the fixtures are originals, the decor fits in harmoniously with the concept of a nunnery-turned-hotel.

Next door is **Museo del Niño** (open Tues–Thurs 9am–3.30pm, Fri 9am–5pm, Sat and Sun 12.30–5pm; entrance fee), which has interactive exhibits and covers topics such as dinosaurs, space, music and the human body.

BELOW: religious crafts for sale in the old city.

History aside, San Juan natives view their city as a place to have fun.

One block away from El Convento, the **Center for Advanced Studies** – originally built in 1842 as a religious school for young men – houses a fine library of the Caribbean and Puerto Rico. Besides its academic value, the center can be a haven for weary tourists and locals.

Steps and statues

Across Cristo from San Juan Cathedral, between the fork of two of San Juan's oldest and most pleasant *adoquine* streets, lies the lush **Plazuela de las Monjas** (Nuns' Square), a perfect spot for an urban picnic. The square looks out not only on the cathedral and El Convento but also on the **Casa Cabildo**, San Juan's original City Hall, which now houses an interior-design company.

A walk down **Caleta de San Juan** will take you to the massive wooden **San Juan Gate ⑯**, built in the 1700s and the only one of three original portals remaining. Sailors weary of their voyages used to moor their ships in San Juan Bay, ferry themselves ashore, enter through the gate, and walk to prayer services via Caleta San Juan, which describes a conveniently straight line between the gates and the main altar of the cathedral.

BELOW: modern sculpture in an ancient city: dramatic lines of La Rogativa.

Through the gate is **Paseo de la Princesa ⑰**, a romantic bayfront promenade that skirts the **Old City Wall ⑱**, or *muralla*. Built of sandstone from 1635 to 1641, it measures up to 20 ft (6 meters) in thickness and at one time completely surrounded the colonial city, guarding it against enemy attacks. Along the *paseo* – an immaculate, landscaped pedestrian boulevard facing the sea – are various statues, a large fountain, and kiosk vendors selling everything from cotton candy to *guarapo de caña* (sugar-cane juice). Various family activities, such as concerts and children's theater, are scheduled here on many weekends. The old

La Princesa ⓲ jail (open Mon–Sat 9am–4pm; free), midway along the promenade, now houses the Tourism Company offices, an art gallery and a museum featuring the actual jail cells used centuries ago.

Continuing up Recinto del Oeste, past more examples of fine colonial architecture, you reach a modern sculpture, **La Rogativa** ⓴, showing the Bishop of San Juan followed by three torch-bearing women, which commemorates the failure of an English siege of the city in 1797. The legend runs that General Sir Ralph Abercromby led a fleet of British ships to take San Juan in a rapid, all-out assault by land and sea. When this plan failed, Abercromby ordered a naval blockade, which lasted two weeks, while the residents of San Juan began to suffer from dysentery, losing hope of the arrival of Spanish reinforcements from the inland settlements. The governor called for a *rogativa*, or divine entreaty, to the saints Ursula and Catherine. All the women of San Juan marched through the town carrying torches, to the accompaniment of loud ringing of tocsins. Abercromby, believing reinforcements had arrived, quit San Juan, never to return.

A short walk back down Recinto del Oeste brings you to **El Museo Felisa Rincón de Gautier** ㉑ (open Mon–Fri 9am–3.45pm; free). This little museum is the former home of Felisa Rincón de Gautier, or "Dona Fela," one of San Juan's most popular mayors, who led the city from 1946 to 1968 and was noted for her flamboyant style. The home-turned-museum contains many items belonging to the late Dona Fela, including her impressive collection of hand fans – as well as a film clip from the 1950s which shows the mayor bringing a plane-load of snow to the island from New York so that the children of San Juan could have a snowball fight.

Map on pages 116–7

From Paseo de la Princesa the waters of San Juan Bay look enticing – but they are considered too polluted here for swimming. The more adventurous locals and visitors, however, do often swim to the right of the big pier outside the San Juan Gate.

BELOW: bustling street market in Plaza San José.

The walk back to the cathedral on **Caleta de las Monjas** is full of surprises, chief among them the "step streets" leading up to the left toward *calles* Sol and San Sebastián. At the top of the first, **Escalinata de las Monjas**, is the old Palace of the Bishop of San Juan. The second, **Calle Hospitál**, is a favorite of artists and photographers.

With all the historical legacy San Juan offers, it's sometimes easy to forget to view the city as its natives view it: a place to have fun. **Calle San Sebastián** is perhaps the pre-eminent place in the old city in which to do just that. Perpendicular to the top of Calle del Cristo, it's a place of museums and old homes whose many bars and spacious plaza make it a mecca for *sanjuanero* youth.

Plaza San José 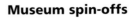 is the focal point of the street, paved with rosy Spanish conglomerate around a statue of Ponce de León made from English cannons melted down after the first invasion. The plaza draws strolling locals on warm weekend evenings, and fun-loving tourists throughout the year. Live concerts of traditional music often take place here.

San Juan's **Dominican Convent** ㉓ (open Mon–Sat 9am–5pm) dominates the plaza. Built in 1523, this mammoth, white, elegantly domed structure has seen as much history as any building on the island, having housed both English and Dutch occupying forces over the centuries.

The convent now houses the craft and book store of the **Institute of Puerto Rican Culture**, the body which more than any other has been responsible for the renaissance in Puerto Rican scholarship and art over the last several years. Under its auspices the parts of the convent not used for office space have been converted to cultural use. A beautiful indoor patio is the scene of many concerts and plays, and it now serves as the focus for the magnificent San Juan Museum of History and Art. The old convent library has been restored to its original 16th-century decor.

Museum spin-offs

A complex of museums has sprung up around the Dominican Convent. The **Museo Pablo Casals** ㉔ (open Tues–Sat 9.30am–4.45pm; entrance fee), which abuts the convent, is a petite, gray, two-story townhouse storing memorabilia of the legendary cellist who moved to Puerto Rico in 1956 and lived here until his death in 1973. It includes manuscripts, instruments, texts of his speeches to the United Nations, and cassettes of his music which can be heard on request. A Casals arts festival takes place every year. *(See page 94.)*

Another interesting visit to consider in the Dominican Convent area is the **Museo del Indio** (open Tues–Sat 9am–4pm; free), which concentrates on the indigenous cultures of Puerto Rico.

Next to the Convent is the stunning and unusual **San José Church** ㉕. Built shortly after the convent in the 1530s, San José is the second-oldest church in the western hemisphere; just San Juan Cathedral, a half-block down the street, is older. The Gothic architecture of the structure is a true rarity; only the Spanish arrived in the New World early enough to build Gothic churches, and just a handful exist today. The interior of San José certainly has far more charm than that of the nearby cathedral.

TIP

If your feet need a break, consider a ride on a *calesa* (horse-drawn carriage) reminiscent of old colonial days. The carriages are based just off Pier 1 at the San Juan Harbor front. Night rides are particularly enchanting.

BELOW: the Puerto Rican flag proudly displayed in a San Juan doorway.

Map
on pages
116–7

A wooden crucifix of the mid-16th century, donated by Ponce de León, is one of the highlights, as is the 15th-century altar brought from Cadíz. In addition, the great Puerto Rican painter José Campeche is buried here.

Across from the Plaza San José is the **Cuartel de Ballajá ㉖**, built as a hospital, and later home to Spanish troops. This structure was the centerpiece of the restoration of Old San Juan in time for the 500th anniversary in 1992 of Columbus's arrival in the New World. A black granite tablet inscribed in Spanish offers maps of the area and tells how the building was restored.

Directly in front is the three-level **Plaza del Quinto Centenario ㉗**, which looks out over the Atlantic. Dominating this plaza, at the center of an eight-pointed pavement design, is the controversial **Totem Telurico**, a terracotta (some say phallic) sculpture by local artist Jaime Suárez that symbolizes the blending of Taíno, African and Spanish cultures. Nearby is a fountain with 100 jets of water; it is supposed to symbolize five centuries of Puerto Rican history.

On Ballajá's second floor is the **Museo de las Américas ㉘** (open Tues–Sun 10am–4pm; free), which provides an overview of cultural development in the New World. Among its colorful exhibit of crafts in the Americas are a replica of a country chapel and examples of Haitian voodoo and *santos*.

Across the plaza from the Cuartel de Ballajá, along unmarked Calle Beneficiencia, is the stately **Antiguo Asilo de Beneficienca** or Old Home for the Poor ㉙ (galleries open Wed–Sun 9am–4.30pm; free). The building, constructed in the 1840s to house the destitute, today serves as headquarters for the Institute of Puerto Rican Culture.

Climb the stairs, go through an ornate foyer and enter the room to your left. Here you'll find an impressive exhibit on the Taíno artifacts. On your right

After Ponce de León's death in Cuba in 1521, his body was brought to Puerto Rico and laid to rest in San José Church, where his descendants worshipped. Later, in 1908, his remains were moved to San Juan Cathedral.

BELOW: ancient and modern come together again: a US Coast Guard helicopter flies over El Morro.

The Port of San Juan Lighthouse sits at the highest point of El Morro and marks the channel entrance to San Juan Harbor.

is a small exhibit of Puerto Rican religious statues. Two huge interior court-yards are used for various cultural activities; surrounding them are the institute's main administration offices.

The Spanish colonists considered San Juan chiefly as a military stronghold, and held military architecture as their first priority. It is not surprising, then, that contemporary *sanjuaneros* are proudest of the breathtaking forts, unique in the Western world, that their antecedents left them.

El Morro

El Castillo San Felipe del Morro, simply known as **El Morro** ③⓪ (open daily 9am–5pm; entrance fee), features a maze of secret access tunnels, dungeons, lookouts, ramps, barracks and vaults. Declared a World Heritage Site by the United Nations, El Morro falls under the auspices of the US National Park Service. Free tours in English and Spanish are given daily.

This, the larger of the city's two forts, commands San Juan Bay with six levels of gun emplacements and walls that tower 140 ft (43 meters) over the Atlantic. Its guns were capable of aiming at any ship within El Morro's field of vision, no matter the distance, and the walls themselves, connected with the system that encircles Old San Juan, are 20 ft (6 meters) thick.

The fort's first battery was completed in the 1540s, but it was not until 1589, when Juan Bautista Antonelli arrived with a team of other Spanish military engineers to begin raising a true bulwark along the edge of the peninsula, that the fort was completed. When Sir Francis Drake attacked in 1595 he was roundly repulsed, but Cumberland's land attack from the Condado succeeded in piercing El Morro's still vulnerable rear approach.

BELOW: entrance to El Morro.

The English held the fort for three months, until dysentery took the lives of nearly half their men. It would be the last time El Morro would fall, even holding out against the Dutch siege of 1625 and the American gunnery fire which rained upon it during the Spanish-American War of 1898.

Today, visitors appreciate El Morro (which means "headland" in Spanish) more for its breathtaking views and architecture than for the protection it gives them. The approach to the fort is over a vast, 27-acre (11-hectare) parkland, once the former drill square for the soldiers and currently a haven for kite-flyers and strolling lovers. A gravel path through the green leads over a moat and into the massive structure, crossing El Morro's main courtyard surrounded by beautiful yellow walls and white archways. Here you will discover a souvenir shop and a museum, both of which are useful in orienting the traveler to the fort's layout and long history.

The massive archway facing over San Juan Bay on the west side of the courtyard is the entrance to what looks like the longest skateboard run in the world: a huge, stone, step-flanked ramp leading to the lower ramparts. This is the most popular of the fort's various sections, affording views of the surf crashing below, and profiling the fort from the ocean side, as its invaders saw it.

Back on the upper level of El Morro, a left turn through the courtyard patio leads to another ramp, this one twisting rightward toward the **Port of San Juan Lighthouse**, which was destroyed by an American mortar shell during the Spanish-American War but later restored.

San Juan Cemetery ㉛, considered by many to be the most picturesque resting place for old bones in the world, sits on a broad, grassy hummock of land tucked between El Morro's walls and the pounding surf. The cemetery's

Map on pages 116–7

The lovely rounded garitas, or sentry boxes, that line the walls of San Juan's forts serve as Puerto Rico's official symbol. But be warned: they are very secluded, and as the city is short on public restrooms, they are occasionally quite malodorous.

BELOW: San Juan Cemetery glimpsed through El Morro's stone walls.

Map on pages 116–7

highlight is a tiny, 19th-century circular chapel, set among the bleached-white gravestones. Abutting El Morro's grounds, the **Casa Blanca** ❸❷ (open Tues–Sat 9am–noon, 1–4pm; entrance fee) is the oldest house in Puerto Rico, having been built for Ponce de León in 1521. Used in the years preceding the construction of La Fortaleza as a shelter against the attacks of savage Carib tribes, it was owned by the conquistador's family until the late 18th century and is now a museum of 16th- and 17th-century family life, with an interesting ethnographic section. The nearby **Casa Rosa** ❸❸ (also referred to as Casa Rosada) is a lovely pink building overlooking the bay and serves as a day-care center for government employees' children.

Irish playwright Oscar Wilde immortalized La Perla in his study of slum life, La Vida.

La Perla

A glance down the beachfront from El Morro will show one of the most bizarre and colorful coastal cityscapes imaginable. One- and two-story shacks, seemingly piled one on top of another, crowd the coastline all the way from El Morro to San Cristóbal, running along the battlements which formerly connected the two castles. This is **La Perla** ❸❹, the so-called "world's prettiest slum." Set against the backdrop of an aquamarine Atlantic, it looks at first glance delightful, but even the toughest of San Juan residents will warn tourists against drugs, violence and a general lawlessness which are rampant in this otherwise charming neighborhood. Along Norzagaray Street, the **Museo de Arte e Historia de San Juan** ❸❺ (open Mon–Fri 8am–4pm; free) beckons visitors for a look at the way the city was way back when.

Though overshadowed by its more famous neighbor to the west, **El Castillo de San Cristóbal** ❸❻ (open daily 9am–5pm; entrance fee) makes as fascinating a trip as El Morro. What El Morro achieved with brute force, San Cristóbal achieved with much more subtlety. Sitting 150 ft (45 meters) above the ocean waves, it reflects the best of 17th-century military architectural thought, and has a fascinating network of tunnels that was used both for transporting artillery and for ambushing luckless invaders.

The fort was completed in 1678 as a means of staving off land attacks on San Juan, like the English one under Cumberland, made to capture El Morro in 1595. But the fort as it is known today is the product of the acumen of two Irishmen, "Wild Geese" who had fled from the Orange monarchy and were in the employ of the Spanish army.

Alejandro O'Reilly and Tomas O'Daly designed a system of battlements and sub-forts that ensured that no one could take El Castillo San Cristóbal without taking all of its ramparts first. No one ever did. The first shot of the Spanish-American War was fired from San Cristóbal's walls.

Frequent guided tours explain how San Cristóbal's unique system of defense worked, and also point out some of the fort's big attractions, like the "**Devil's Sentry Box,**" a *garita* at the end of a long tunnel that runs to the waterline. Views from the battlements are outstandingly spectacular, particularly in the direction *sanjuaneros* describe as "towards Puerto Rico": Condado, Hato Rey and El Yunque. ❏

BELOW: view of La Perla and El Morro from San Cristóbal. **RIGHT:** Puerto Rico's most famous silhouette: El Morro fort in Old San Juan.

METROPOLITAN SAN JUAN

Condado, Ocean Park and Isla Verde have fine beaches,
Santurce is a genuine marketplace, Hato Rey is a major
finance center, and Bayamón has a maverick quality

Map,
page 140

I
t's easy to try to relegate **Puerta de Tierra** ❶ to the status of a sort of verdant buffer zone between San Juan's body and its soul, separating as it does the brawn of Santurce from the historical grandeur and romance of Old San Juan. Puerta de Tierra means "gateway of land," but Puerta de Tierra is a gateway in more ways than just the narrow literal sense.

San Juan

Beachfront capitol

Commanding a fabulous view of beach and water, straddled by Puerta de Tierra's two main thoroughfares, **El Capitolio** ❷, Puerto Rico's Capitol building, serves as the centerpiece to the whole peninsula. Constructed between 1925 and 1929, El Capitolio is a grand, white classical structure resembling the Capitol building in Washington, on a rather smaller scale and with wonderful ocean views. The large rotunda features four corner sections done in Venetian mosaic with gold, silver and bronze, depicting some of the most important events in Puerto Rico's history. In the very center of the dome is a lovely stained-glass rendering of Puerto Rico's seal. Near the main entrance is the original Constitution of Puerto Rico, signed in 1952 and brought back to the island in 1992 after spending nearly five years in a Washington restoration laboratory.

Nearby are a number of buildings which, though less imposing, are no less beautiful. The ornate **Casa de España** ❸, just down the hill toward Old San Juan from El Capitolio, is a blue-tiled, four-towered edifice built in 1935 and paid for by the Spanish expatriate community. Once a popular gathering spot for local men, it now has a restaurant and is the site of cultural events. Of interest inside are the tiled painting of Don Quixote and the Salon de Los Espejos (Mirror Room) with its painted wooden ceiling.

Down Avenida Ponce de León is the lovely **Archives and General Library of Puerto Rico** (open by appointment). Pedestals and pilasters support a graceful pediment and throw a skeleton of white against a lovely sun-washed yellow. Now run by the Institute of Puerto Rican Culture, the General Library lives up to the standards the Institute has set for its other buildings, with tessellation of red stone, delicate chandeliers and fine furniture. There's also a small chapel on the first floor. If this seems out of place in a library, it is because the building, constructed in 1877 as the last major Spanish architectural effort on the island, was originally designed as a hospital.

Another landmark along the boulevard is the **Ateneo Puertorriqueño** ❹, which promotes cultural activity through conferences, lectures, films and the like. Next door is the **Carnegie Library**, established by the Carnegie Foundation and now run by the

PRECEDING PAGES:
the bright lights of
San Juan and
Condado. **LEFT:** El
Capitolio, Puerta de
Tierra. **BELOW:**
relaxing in Muñoz
Rivera Park.

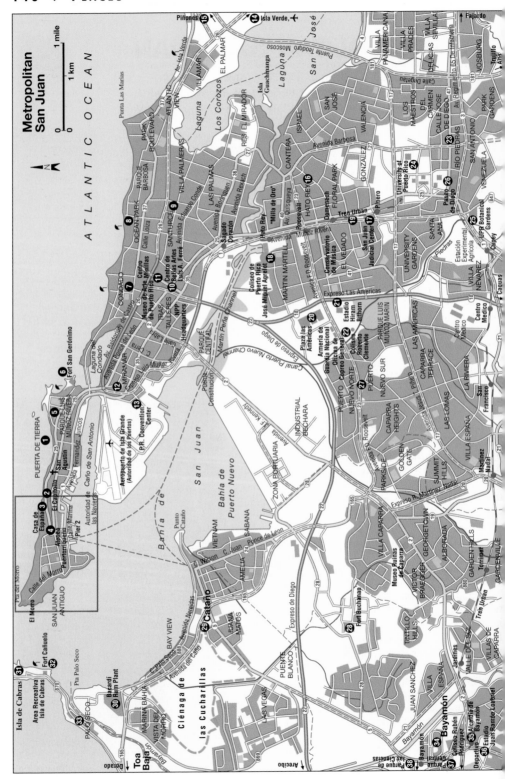

Metropolitan
San Juan

Map, page 140

Department of Education. Further east, **Parque Luis Muñoz Rivera ➎** was dedicated by Nobel Peace Prizewinner and former Costa Rican president, Oscar Arias. The **Caribe Hilton** (*see Travel Tips page 263*) sits on several acres of beautifully landscaped grass and sand, overlooking a little beach-lined cove that stretches to Condado. The hotel played an important role in the industrialization of the island, as the many companies that set up shop from the 1950s onwards used the Caribe Hilton as an initial base for their executives. The Caribe Hilton also has a historical asset in **Fort San Gerónimo ➏**, a small but crucial element of the old Spanish fortifications which stymied a British invasion of the region in 1797. The military museum inside (not always open so call the hotel first, tel: 721-0303) is entertaining and worthwhile. Within view of the Hilton stands the Art Deco **Normandie Hotel**, which first opened in 1942 and was designed to resemble the famous French ocean liner of the same name.

Condado

Condado ➐ in Spanish means "county," and many Puerto Ricans still refer to the glittering strip of land between the Condado lagoon and the Atlantic Ocean as "*the* Condado." If the appellation is meant to convey anything rustic about this part of town, it grossly misses the mark. A trip across the Puente San Gerónimo from Puerta de Tierra takes one out of history and into the tourist zone where gambling, dining, drinking and dancing are the main activities of the evening. **Ashford Avenue**, Condado's main thoroughfare, looks as though it is desperately trying to run for election as the sixth borough of New York City, or perhaps as an annex of Miami Beach. In a large measure, it succeeds. Its lengthy oceanfront is lined with chic boutiques, banks, restaurants and – most conspicuously – hotels.

Hotels are, of course, of varying quality in Condado, but the town's lodgings seldom dip far below the "luxury" rating. The casinos aren't exclusive; non-hotel patrons are welcome at the tables. Restaurants, both hotel-affiliated and otherwise, tend to be of good quality. However, there's a price to pay for quality in Condado, and it is a high one. Some of the restaurants in town are almost legendary – for both their food and their prices – but they are definitely worth it for the experience. The Condado area is constantly changing; old hotels are being knocked down and replaced by newer, bigger, more modern ones, or a public park. The venerable Condado Beach Hotel, constructed by the Vanderbilt family in 1919, is currently under renovation along with La Concha hotel.

To go to the beach in Condado implies more than taking the sun and riding the waves. People-watching is the chief popular pastime, and there is certainly a fine variety of types to watch, enjoying the warm, unpolluted water and the gentle waves. The Condado beaches are mostly pockets of sand tucked behind the major hotels and, although all beaches are public – none of the beachfront is privately owned – they are less accessible. The big hotels aren't going to go out of their way to show anyone the easy route to the beach, but the determined visitor, of course, will usually find the way. El Escambrón, next to the Normandie, is a family-oriented exception.

The Condado beaches are said to be the best in the city. Snorkeling is good, and watersports equipment can be hired. But it is not advisable to walk along the beaches at night.

BELOW: playing in the sun on Condado Beach.

Ocean Park

Heading east on Ashford Avenue, past the Marriott Hotel and the Radisson Ambassador, you approach **Ocean Park** , the most popular beach in the area, where sunbathers, dogs, kiteboarders, children and beautiful people coexist in happy harmony. From here, the high-rises give way to residential houses, and the beaches become less crowded. This is one of the more scenic of San Juan's beachfront panoramas, with views stretching from the palm-lined point at Boca de Cangrejos to the bright white high-rise wall of Ashford Avenue's hotels.

After a swim and a wander along one of the longest and most varied stretches of beaches on Puerto Rico's north coast, you may like to retire to **Kasalta**, an oasis of fine (and reasonably priced) native and Spanish cuisine in a desert of kitsch. In this famous cafeteria, which is also a bakery and delicatessen, you'll find all the San Juan newspapers, a range of Puerto Rican delicacies unmatched anywhere on the island and a fresh cup of local coffee that will electrify you.

Hot stuff: spicy Caribbean sauces are a good buy and a tasty – albeit temporary – reminder of a trip to Puerto Rico.

South of Condado

A knot of highways and main roads, **Santurce** ❾ connects the more touristy and more picturesque areas of the metropolis. It can't claim a seacoast; in fact, one could almost define the area as the set of neighborhoods one encounters moving south from more fashionable Condado and Ocean Park. It hasn't the history of Old San Juan, having been founded only about a century ago as a fashionable suburb. But Santurce does have its own appeal, making it well worth a visit.

Santurce is considered by most to be the heart of San Juan, and not just in the sense that it's the source of the city's main traffic arteries, but it survives as a true marketplace. The quaintest manifestation of this ethic is in the **Plaza del Mercado**

BELOW: shooting pool in Condado.

on Calle Canals, where vendors sell fruits and vegetables and on Friday evenings the neighboring streets come alive with music and dancing.

While many *sanjuaneros* come to work in Santurce, a surprising proportion come to eat, too, at the many elegant restaurants, and the appealing little *fondas*, as low on price as they are on pretentiousness. The arts thrive in Santurce as well, and the construction in 1981 of the attractive **Centro de Bellas Artes Luis A. Ferré ⓓ**, at the corner of *avenidas* Ponce de Léon and de Diego, has brought the neighborhood a share in San Juan's cultural wealth with a 1,800-seat Festival Hall, 760-seat Drama Hall and 210-seat Experimental Theater.

Further along Avenida de Diego is the US$60 million-plus, state-of-the-art **Museo de Arte de Puerto Rico ⓫** (open Tues–Sat 10am–5pm, Wed until 8pm, Sun 11am–6pm; entrance fee; tel: 977-6277 ext. 2230/2261 for guided tours), which traces the history of Puerto Rican art from José Campeche to the present. The façade of the former hospital has been retained and its graceful columns are echoed in the modern construction behind. The museum has a lovely sculpture garden, a fine collection of prints, and revolving exhibitions featuring international and local artists. The restaurant, **Pikayo**, is one of the city's best, offering exotic creole cuisine, but it is an expensive treat. *(See Travel Tips page 271.)*

On the western edge of Santurce, closest to Old San Juan, is **Miramar ⓬**, one of the most appealing suburbs in the metropolitan area, now that the red-light district has been cleaned up, with lovely tree-lined avenues of pretty modern residences. Miramar's crowning jewel is the **Puerto Rico Convention Center ⓭** (tel: 787-641 7722), inaugurated in 2005. Within the 600,000 sq-ft (55,742 sq-meter) state-of-the-art center is a large exhibition space with a modern wave-shaped roof, and a hotel is in the works.

Map, page 140

TIP

If you fancy seeing an art-house film while in Puerto Rico, your best bet is in Santurce. Try the Metro 1, 2, 3; or the Fine Arts Cinema – all on Avenida Ponce de León.

BELOW: contemporary art at the Museo de Arte de Puerto Rico.

Airport beach

Almost everyone arrives in Puerto Rico at Luis Muñoz Marín International Airport in **Isla Verde** . Technically part of the municipality of Carolina, this San Juan suburb takes on a look of affluence that few areas as close to such booming noise, annoying traffic snarls and transient lifestyle possess – big, chalk-white blocks of high-income apartment houses choke one of the most beautiful beachfronts on the island, giving Isla Verde one of the most Miami-Beachesque aspects this side of… well, Miami Beach. Isla Verde is very rich, but a bit dull. The usual airport businesses – car-rental agencies, vinyl cocktail lounges and the like – have overrun the place, and suburbs separate the area from the historical charms of the older parts of San Juan, while water separates it from the allure of Piñones. An array of fine hotels just west of the airport include the Wyndham El San Juan, the Ritz-Carlton and the Inter-Continental San Juan Resort. Along with these giants stand Embassy Suites, Hampton Inn and some smaller hostels. Along Avenida Isla Verde, the many low-priced guest houses, restaurants, fast-food emporiums, the cock-fighting arena and garish stores give the area a honkytonk look.

The golden sandy beach at Isla Verde stretches for over a mile to the north of the airport. To the east are the lovely coral reefs at **Boca de Cangrejos**, and farther on the surf is formidable, especially in winter, rolling into the area known as **Piñones** ⓖ, a popular hangout for young locals, especially on weekends, when a twisting road along 5 miles (8 km) of beaches becomes the site of an ongoing party, and roadside kiosks sell raw oysters, seasoned pork and coco frío. On this wild piece of coastline, hotels have not yet begun to encroach on and replace the natural mangrove forest where visitors can go for a 6-mile (10-km) bicycle ride *(see page 155)*.

In the narrow strip of land beyond Isla Verde, between the sea and the airport, is Avenida Boca de Cangrejos, where many quioscos *– semi-permanent shacks – sell barbecued specialties including fish and cod and plantain fritters.*

BELOW: San Juan's Isla Verde Beach.

Hato Rey

It's odd that, in so many of the great cities of the world, financial brawn and Bohemian asceticism have shared the same neighborhoods. Opposites attract: New York's arty districts of Tribeca and Soho rub shoulders with Wall Street; the City of London is surrounded by universities and galleries. San Juan follows this rule to an unusual degree. Here, **Hato Rey** ⑯, the undisputed business and high-finance capital of the Caribbean, abuts – and often intermingles with – **Río Piedras**, the home of the University of Puerto Rico.

Map, page 140

The Golden Mile

Most of the money in the Antilles is filtered through a group of institutions clustered on a section of Expreso Luis Muñoz Rivera in Hato Rey known as **The Golden Mile**. Though Operation Bootstrap certainly contributed to Puerto Rico's importance as a financial center, the recent emergence of Hato Rey as a mecca for banks and corporations owes a great deal to a long-standing Puerto Rican commitment to banking.

Everyone who visits San Juan should head down to Hato Rey, if only to see the intriguing modern architecture. Particularly interesting is the **Banco de Santander Building** with its reflecting plate-glass arching from an austere concrete shaft. Hato Rey is also home to the headquarters of **Banco Popular de Puerto Rico**, which is the island's oldest and largest bank. Law and order is carried out at the **San Juan Judicial Center** ⑰, where visitors may want to witness a criminal court case – Puerto Rican style.

Enrique Adsuar González, a respected commentator on local custom, has mentioned that the sight of Hato Rey businessmen walking the streets in Wall

BELOW: The Golden Mile – Hato Rey's financial district.

Street-cut woollen winter suits in 90-degree weather is one of the great ironies of contemporary Puerto Rican life.

Hato Rey has also become something of a culinary capital, if in a modest and basic way. One can't expect gourmet food in restaurants which cater solely to men who will lose their jobs if they go for an extra course, but solid Puerto Rican fare is to be had here for prices one wouldn't mind paying in the Cordillera.

The district's majestic 18,000-seat **Coliseo de Puerto Rico José Miguel Agrelot** ⓱ (open Mon–Fri 10am–5pm; tel: 877-265 4736), which opened in 2004, hosts a wide variety of major sports and entertainment events – everything from a Rolling Stones concert to pro sports events.

Puerto Rico's first mass-transit light-rail system, the US$2-billion **Urban Train** or *Tren Urbano* ⓲ (daily 5.30am–11.30pm; tel: 787-729 8714, 866-900 1284) has a direct service to the Coliseo de Puerto Rico from any of its 15 stations. The 10-mile (16-km) train connects the areas of Santurce, Hato Rey, Río Piedras, Guaynabo and Bayamón and is an inexpensive and fun way to get around the metropolitan area. The entire route, from the first stop at Sagrado Corazón University in Santurce to the edge of Bayamón's town center, takes about half an hour. The trains run every 8 minutes during rush hour and every 12 minutes other times. Following the Sagrado Corazón stop, the train makes three stops in Hato Rey, the first in front of the Coliseo de Puerto Rico. There are also six stops in Río Piedras, including one at the University of Puerto Rico *(see opposite)*, and another at Paseo de Diego, a great place for bargain shopping.

A mile west of the business district on Route 23 (Avenida Franklin Delano Roosevelt) are some of Puerto Rico's more adventurous recent structures. The first, on the north side of the highway, is **Plaza Las Américas** ⓴ (open Mon–Sat

The largest J.C. Penney in the world is located in Plaza Las Américas; it has 350,000 sq. ft (32,500 sq. meters) of shopping space.

BELOW: Hato Rey's Estadio Hiram Bithorn, named after one of many Puerto Rican baseball greats.

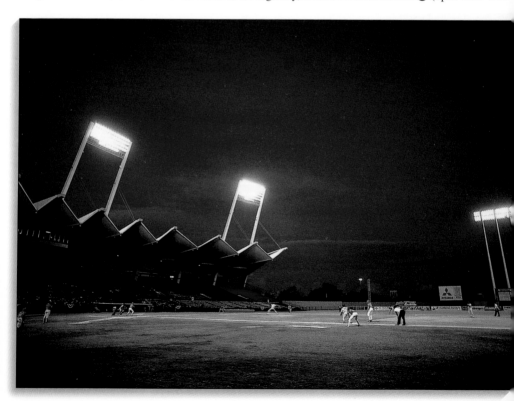

9am–9pm, Sun 11am–5pm), the largest shopping mall in the Caribbean. Locals flock here to stroll amid its fountains and flowered walks and to buy everything from *guayaberas* (traditional Puerto Rican shirts) to guava juice. The mega shopping center now includes Macy's, Brookstone and Borders Bookstore. Across the highway to the south is the **Estadio Hiram Bithorn ㉑**, an odd, hyper-modern stadium, which is the site for a variety of sporting and cultural events – including the start of the baseball season in November each year. Neighboring **Coliseo Roberto Clemente ㉒** also hosts a number of major events, sporting and otherwise.

Río Piedras

Perhaps Hato Rey maintains its humanity due only to the humanizing influence of the university town of **Río Piedras ㉓** to the south. Within the shortest of walks, concrete and plate-glass give way to cobbled paths and flower gardens. With 25,000 students and distinguished faculty from all parts of the world, the **University of Puerto Rico** (UPR) ㉔ is certainly unique in the American university community. Among those who've taught here have been Juan Ramón Jiménez, Pablo Casals and Arturo Morales Carrión. At the intellectual heart of the university on Avenida Ponce de Léon is the **Museo de Historia**, **Antropologia y Arte** (open Mon–Fri 9am–4.30pm, Wed and Thur until 8.30pm; free guided tours by appointment; tel: 764 0000 ext. 2452). Important exhibits include Francisco Oller's masterpiece *El Velorio* (The Wake) and the only Egyptian collection in the Caribbean. Renovation work at the museum began in 2003.

The octagonal clock-tower, which soars out of the palms at one side of the campus, has become something of a symbol for Río Piedras.

The highlight of any visit to Río Piedras must be the **Botanical Gardens ㉕** at

Map, page 140

More than 700 cruise ships arrive every year at the Port of San Juan, the busiest ocean terminal in the West Indies.

LEFT: the Botanical Gardens.
BELOW: the university clocktower.

UPR's Agricultural Experimental Station, a mile south of the university and reached by following the signs after turning off at the intersection of Avenida Muñoz Rivera and Route 847. Hundreds of varieties of tropical and semi-tropical plants, including many from Australia and Africa, make up this extensive park. The gardens comprise 200 acres (80 hectares) and it's hard to imagine a botanical garden landscaped as imaginatively or as subtly as this one. Ponds, lilies, ferns and ubiquitous *yautía* compete for attention with an exceptional orchid garden.

Río Piedras is not, however, all ivory towers and ivied lanes. Its **Paseo de Diego** 🔞 is the largest pedestrian market in San Juan, with all the haggling, gesticulation and frenzy of an Arab *souk*.

Heading west on Avenida Franklin Delano Roosevelt, past Plaza Las Américas, stop at La Ceiba in **Puerto Nuevo** 🔞, a bakery or *panaderia* offering coffee, sandwiches, pastries and delicacies imported from Spain. Further up the road, **Fort Buchanan** 🔞 billets elements of the US Army, which hosts a number of community activities during the year, including Pee Wee Football.

Cataño

Crossing from Old San Juan on the Cataño Ferry allows excellent views of windswept San Juan Bay. **Cataño** 🔞 itself is by no means a picturesque town, but it does have a beachfront area and unrivaled views of the old city. It also has rum. In the most remote corners of the world, people know the name Bacardi. That they automatically associate it with Puerto Rico is all the more surprising, considering that Bacardi isn't the island's only rum, or even its best. Yet few tourists visit Puerto Rico without making a pilgrimage to the sprawling **Bacardi Rum Plant** 🔞 (open Mon–Sat 8.30am–4.30pm; closed Sun and pub. hols; free),

TIP

If you're planning on taking a tour of the Bacardi distillery, try to go there on a weekday when the bottling line is in production.

BELOW: bottling rum at Bacardi.

"LEGEND OF THE BAT"

The next time you pick up a bottle of Bacardi rum, take note of the bat on the label. When Don Facundo Bacardí experimented with the rum-making process in his tiny shed in Cuba back in the 1800s, colonies of fruit bats hung over his head and watched the proceedings with interest. The wine merchant and importer ended up inventing a whole new process, distilled his very first bottle of rum and never looked back. For the Bacardí family, the bat became a symbol of good luck, prosperity and tradition – and was made the Bacardi corporate symbol in 1862. Business was so good that Don Facundo quickly expanded it; by 1936 the family had decided to open a distillery in Puerto Rico.

In 1959, Fidel Castro came to power in Cuba. Shortly after, the Communists confiscated the family's extensive holdings – worth an estimated $76 million at the time – and the Bacardís were forced to shift production to Puerto Rico, Bermuda, the Bahamas and elsewhere. Today, Bacardi is truly a global empire, with plants in more than a dozen countries. Through a web of companies that include Bacardi Corporation, Bacardi & Company, Bacardi Limited and half a dozen others, the empire now accounts for 75 percent of US, and 50 percent of all the world's, rum consumption.

five minutes west on Route 165. From the distillery – which has a capacity of 100,000 gallons a day and is the largest rum distillery in the world – you are taken by trolley to the Bacardi family museum, and finally to the visitors' pavilion in the spacious grounds with a view across the bay, where complimentary *piña coladas* are waiting.

Map, page 140

Seafood center

Just north of Cataño, at the end of a pine-flecked spit of land, is **Isla de Cabras** ③, now a recreational area and hangout for local fishermen. The island originally housed the long-range artillery of **Fort Cañuelo** ㉜, built in 1608. In later centuries it served as a leper colony. Cabras also boasts a beautiful – but unswimmable – beach. Hedonists should head further west on Route 165 to **Punta Salinas**, which is flanked by two pretty beaches.

South of Cabras and bathed in the warm aroma of Bacardi's molasses, **Palo Seco** ㉝ offers an almost unbroken string of seafood restaurants, parallel to the ocean, many named after local pirate Roberto Cofresí.

Cowboy town

To the south of Cataño is **Bayamón** ㉞, whose inhabitants are referred to as *vaqueros* or "cowboys." This is due to a sort of maverick quality that has put the city in friendly opposition to others on the island. Founded in 1509 by a group of settlers led by Ponce de León, Bayamón labors under the stereotype of a sort of glorified shopping mall. It is a place where the antiquated *fincas* and plantations of an older Puerto Rico are set in sharp juxtaposition to some of the most innovative civic architecture.

Bayamón has been fastidious about retaining its regional customs and cuisine. Along almost every road leading into the city are *bayamoneses,* food vendors selling roast chicken, bread, and the most legendary of all local treats – the *chicharrón,* deep-fried pork rinds or crackling in cholestrol-hiking, molar-cracking hunks. (Male visitors should know that *chicharrón* has a connotation which makes it inadvisable to ask a local woman if she'd like a taste.)

The first sight of Bayamón is the eight-story **Alcaldía de Bayamón** ㉟, which spans five lanes of highway. Built in 1978 of concrete, glass and steel, it is the only building so suspended in the Caribbean.

Across the highway is the **Estadio Juan Ramón Loubriel** ㊱, an attractive baseball stadium. Nearby, the **Parque Central** ㊲ is also dedicated to recreation, with historical and cultural displays and in the placid **Paseo Barbosa**, numerous shops are ranged about the restored 19th-century house of Barbosa.

Bayamón native Francisco Oller was Puerto Rico's greatest artist; his work is at the **Museo Francisco Oller** in the Old Alcaldía at Calle Degetau, 2 (open Mon–Fri 9am–4pm; free). And not far from here, on Route 167, is the **Parque de las Ciencias** ㊳ (open Wed–Fri 9am–4pm, weekends and pub. hols 10am–6pm; entrance fee). Much more than just a science museum, this is a major complex of seven themed museums and a zoo. ❏

Every December the Bacardi Artisans Fair is held on the distillery grounds; more than 125 Puerto Rican artisans exhibit and sell the best of their work, and much other family-style entertainment is on offer.

BELOW: antique locomotive in Bayamón's Parque Central.

RUM: HOLDING ITS OWN IN THE SPIRITS WORLD

As Puerto Rico is the world's leading producer of rum, it's no surprise that's the national drink – but few realize its versatility and broad range of flavors

It's Christopher Columbus who can be thanked for the fine Caribbean rums today, because he happened to bring some sugar cane with him on his second voyage to the New World in 1493. It wasn't long before large cane plantations sprang up to meet the growing world demand for sugar. But the Spanish settlers discovered that sugar wasn't the only profitable substance produced from cane when they found that its by-product, molasses, fermented naturally.

Not satisfied with the flavor and proof of this "molasses wine" (which Puerto Ricans used to enjoy as a beverage called *aguardiente* or *madilla*), the Spaniards distilled it, filtering out impurities and increasing the concentration of alcohol. Rum was born.

There are four essential steps in the making of rum: fermentation, distillation, aging and blending. Aging is most commonly done in used bourbon barrels made of white American oak. Puerto Rican law states that rum must age untouched for at least one year; there are, in fact, rigid standards for every step of the rum-making process.

Puerto Rican rum is distinguished from other Caribbean rums by its light body and smooth flavor. Its premium-aged rum competes admirably in the upper end of the spirits world and is said to have a broader range of flavors than single malt Scotch.

▷ A DRINK OF MANY COLORS

Rum can be a light, dry white (a suitable replacement for gin or vodka in cocktails), smooth amber (often mixed with cola and hot drinks), or mellow gold ("on the rocks").

△ RUM GARDEN

The island is full of inviting places to relax and sample the national drink in some of its many guises. Tired of *piña coladas*? Then try the planter's punch.

▷ MODERN METHODS

Stainless-steel stills are said to produce the cleanest rum and are the most widely used. Premium-age rums are distilled in copper to bring out more aroma and flavor.

THE ROLLS-ROYCE OF RUMS?

PUERTO RICAN RUM

If you think rum is only good for fancy cocktails, think again. Gold, premium-aged rums can, at the very least, be a suitable substitute for whiskey: consumed straight or on the rocks. At their best, gold – or *añejos* – rums rank right up there with the finest Cognac. There is more than one *añejo* out there, of course – Bacardi has its "Gold Reserve"; Serralles has "El Dorado". But many rum connoisseurs point to Ron del Barrilito, who *only* makes premium-aged rums, as a real leader in the field with its unblended three-year-old Two-Star and blended six- to 10-year-old Three-Star – both coming in at 86 percent proof. Only 10 minutes away from the ultra-modern Bacardi facility in San Juan, Barrilito rum is produced on a 200-year-old family farm called Hacienda Santa Ana. Instead of using white American oak bourbon barrels for aging like most rums, Pedro Fernández – who developed Ron del Barrilito – used only sherry casks, and this practice continues to this day. So put away those paper umbrellas and get out your snifter: these are rums to be savored.

▽ COCKTAIL, ANYONE?

Any Puerto Rican bartender worth his salt has some sort of favorite rum concoction up his sleeve; rum is amazingly versatile.

△ SWEET SUCCESS

Spanish settlers planted sugar cane on the island in 1515, later discovering how to turn a sugar by-product, molasses, into rum.

▷ CARIBBEAN CLASSIC

Reputedly invented in Puerto Rico, the *piña colada* remains a favorite rum libation. It's made with cream of coconut, white rum and pineapple juice.

THE NORTHEAST

Loíza is a center of authentic African culture, El Yunque is a protected rainforest, Luquillo is arguably the island's finest beach, and Icacos is the most popular cay

Map, page 156

San Juan

I f someone arriving in Puerto Rico with the inexcusable intention of spending only a few days here were to hire a guide and ask to be shown as much as possible of the island, he or she would be driven directly east from San Juan. It is not that the northeastern corner of the island contains all the island's attractions; that would be impossible. It is only that the variety of landscapes and societies – none of them farther than 45 minutes from San Juan – is astonishing. The ease with which one can move from one landscape to another, which bears no resemblance to the previous one, will make even the crassest traveler feel that he or she is cheating.

Nowhere are the island's contrasts more shocking than on Route 187 just east of San Juan. Here, the highway that links the metropolis with the Caribbean's most modern international airport passes over a bridge and heads for **Boca de Cangrejos** ("Crabmouth") ❶, as exotic a spot as one will find within 20 minutes of any major city in the world. Perhaps at first appearance it is Puerto Rico at its most typically Latin American (read "Third World"), but the ricketiness is deceptive. The flocks of sheep and herds of cows in the area belong to the residents of nearby settlements around the *municipio* of Loíza. The shacks on the beach are not residences by any stretch of the imagination, rather seaside food emporia. Boca de Cangrejos is where *sanjuaneros* retreat for a *coco frío* – ice-cold coconut milk, which is served in its own shell.

Grove diggers

Long beaches under luxuriant pine groves are what draw visitors to Boca de Cangrejos. Surfers are the most devoted of such partisans, and can be seen riding the waves at the part called **Aviones** (Airplanes) for the flights from Isla Verde that roar over all day.

It's advisable to stay away from **Piñones** ❷ when the beach is deserted, which seldom happens. A 6-mile (10-km) bike trail goes from end to end and is extremely popular, especially because most of the seaside route is dotted with kiosks serving cold drinks. Bikes can be rented in Boca de Cangrejos.

Piñones grows more eerie, rustic and beautiful as one moves east. At its farthest point from San Juan is **Vacia Talega Beach** ❸, a breathtaking finger of rock capped by palms and carved into strange formations by eons of surf.

Beyond the swamps

Few towns in Puerto Rico balance natural beauty and cultural achievement as gracefully or as charmingly as Loíza Aldea. Just 6 miles (10 km) east of metropolitan San Juan, predominantly Afro-Puerto Rican **Loíza** ❹ (pop. 32,500) has maintained its separateness from the

PRECEDING PAGES: setting moon over El Yunque. **LEFT:** La Mina Falls, El Yunque. **BELOW:** mask maker in Loíza.

Fifty varieties of fern, more than 20 kinds of orchid and some 240 types of tree are just some of the fantastic flora to be found in El Yunque

capital thanks to a cluster of natural barriers. Puerto Rico's largest mangrove swamp, the massive and mysterious woodland of **Torrecilla Baja ❺**, sits smack between the two communities, and can be traversed via the coastal Route 187, which goes through Piñones and crosses the **Río Grande de Loíza ❻**, the island's widest, roughest and only navigable river.

Loíza is arguably among the purest centers of true African culture in the Western world. It was settled in the 16th century by black slaves sent by the Spanish crown to mine a rich gold deposit in the area. When the gold ran out they became cane-cutters and, when slavery was abolished in 1873, many black residents turned to this agricultural economy.

They learned Spanish and became Catholics, but in the subsequent fusion of African culture with Spanish and Indian, the African certainly won out – although the town's Church of St Patrick/Holy Spirit is the oldest in continuous use on the island, dating from 1670. Such influence is most visible during the Fiesta de Santiago Apostól, when the people of Loíza gather to praise Saint James, patron of the town. The week-long celebration commences each July 25, when citizens dress in ceremonial costumes strikingly and significantly similar to those of the Yoruba tribe of West Africa, from whom many Puerto Ricans are descended. Participants include masqueraders, ghouls and *viejos* (old men), and the making of costumes for the ceremonial rites is ordered by a social hierarchy which is quite alien to Latin America.

The most distinctive festival attire, however, belongs to the *vejigantes*, most of them young men, who dress in garish costumes and parade through the streets. Their religious purpose is generally taken to be that of frightening the lapsed back into the Christian faith, though they can be just as much a source

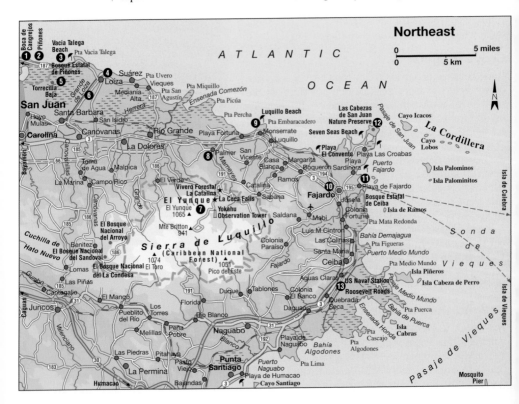

Map, page 156

of celebration and mirth. Most true *vejigante* masks are made from coconuts or other gourds carved into grimaces like those of the most sinister jack-o'-lanterns. At times aluminum foil is used to make a mask's teeth look even more eerie.

El Yunque rainforest

As you continue east, a turn-off at the town of Palmer points toward El Yunque, the rainforest that attracts many visitors to the island.

The only tropical rainforest in the USDA National Forest system, and the only part of Puerto Rico administered by the US Department of Agriculture, the **Caribbean National Forest**, known to practically everybody as **El Yunque ❼** – named after the good Taíno spirit Yukiyú – is home to all the mystery and wonder that comes in the color green. These 28,000 acres (11,000 hectares) of bucking mountain at the highest part of the Sierra de Luquillo offer one of the island's most extreme climates, and the most extreme of its ecosystems as well.

Showers and towers

To begin with, there is the rain. The massive, low-lying, purplish-black clouds one sees moving across the Atlantic onto Puerto Rico's northeast coast dump most of their cargo when they hit the northern flank of the Sierra de Luquillo, with the result that this is far and away the rainiest section of the island.

El Yunque gets upward of 240 inches (600 cm) of rain annually – put in more alarming terms, this is 100 billion gallons per year. However, rain does not bother the hundreds of different animal species that make El Yunque their home, among them 26 endemic to the island. Puerto Rico's most familiar animals are here, like the mellifluous tree frog known as the *coquí*. And

Literally millions of the tiny coquí tree frogs – which have become somewhat of a Puerto Rican "symbol" – make El Yunque their home. They are nocturnal and endemic to the island; their distinctive cry of "koh-KEE" gave them their name.

BELOW: mist settles into the rainforest.

TIP

It is wise to allow at least a day to fully appreciate El Yunque. If you're planning on hiking, the staff at the Catalina Service Center (tel: 888-1880/1810) can provide hiking information and, with notice, can help plan overnight treks into the forest.

more exotic ones are here as well, like the colorful but endangered Puerto Rican parrot, and the rare Puerto Rican boa, the island's largest snake, which can grow up to 7 ft (2 meters) long.

Looking out at all the palm trees, ferns and other plant life crowding the road, it's hard to believe that Hurricane Hugo nearly wiped out this paradise on September 18, 1989. The storm's 200-mph (320-kph) winds left a path of destruction extending from the eastern fringes of San Juan to the offshore islands of Vieques and Culebra. Yet Hugo may have done El Yunque a favor. Ecologists say that the hurricane has removed the canopy of darkness created by taller trees, giving smaller plant life a chance to flourish.

Driving rain

However alluring the upper reaches of El Yunque, most people will see it only by automobile. The most popular and varied route leads south from the town of **Palmer ❽**, known in Spanish as Mameyes, along Route 191. Palmer is a tiny, haunting town, one which seems all the more so for its striking contrast to the 45-minute drive from San Juan, which carries you through glittering, modern industrial and commercial landscapes. Nonetheless, Palmer is admirably uncommercialized and untouristy for a park entrance.

Route 191 used to lead straight through the forest to Naguabo, but a landslide which damaged roads on the southern edge of the forest about 20 years ago has never been cleared; a gate now blocks access to the damaged part of the road at Km 13.5. But despite the damage, and despite the fact that Puerto Rico's hiking enthusiasts will tell you that you have to get up *into* the woods to appreciate them, Route 191 provides a sterling introduction to the forest.

BELOW: the El Portal Rainforest Center is very informative.

Another good introduction – which really should be a required pre-hike stop – is provided at the new **El Portal Rainforest Center** (open daily) within the forest. Here, visitors can learn about the unique beauty and history of El Yunque and the forest environment through interpretive displays, discussions and a 15-minute documentary film. Patios provide a place to relax and admire the superb view.

Map, page 156

Attractive falls

Rising gradually, Route 191 hits one of El Yunque's premier attractions at a bend in the road not far into the forest. **La Coca Falls**, at Km 8.2, is a blurry cascade of ice-gray river rushing down a wall of beautiful moss-covered stones. Though the forest service claims most of the water in El Yunque to be perfect- ly potable, and although you'll almost certainly see people drinking from the stream, do exercise caution here, as anywhere in the mountains, because Puerto Rico has a number of river snails which produce *"schisto" (schistosoma)*, a bacterium causing the highly dangerous liver disease bilharzia.

El Yunque's second great waterfall, **La Mina**, is just off the road a mile (2 km) ahead. Unfortunately, it's invisible from Route 191 and can be reached most easily from the Palo Colorado Recreation Site at Km 12. On your way there, you will pass the **Palma de Sierra Visitors' Center**, which also houses a food concession.

The island's road network traverses a surprising amount of rugged terrain.

Hoofing it through the highlands

The landslides on Route 191 have left El Yunque much less accessible by car. Of the many hiking attractions of the place, a few are especially recommended.

BELOW: forester enjoys a breather in the rainforest.

THE MANY FACES OF THE FOREST

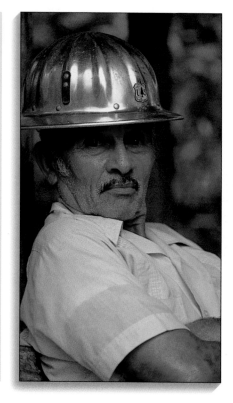

One would think that a forest is full of pretty much the same types of tree, but in fact a place like El Yunque – with an intensity characteristic of Puerto Rico's sub-climates – offers a startling diversity of vegetation and "forest types." Most widespread is the Tabonuco forest, which ranges around the warmer, drier parts of El Yunque at altitudes of under 2,000 ft (600 meters). Higher up is the Colorado forest, which is mossy and more humid than the Tabonuco. Although taking up less than a fifth of El Yunque's territory, the reserve's palm forest is the "rainforest" that gives the area its reputation. Perhaps this is because its beauty is so unexpected and almost unnatural; perhaps it's because Route 191, which most tourists take through El Yunque, never gets above 2,500 ft (760 meters), where the palm forest stops.

Sierra palms, which account for most of the sub-climate's vegetation, can grow in very slippery and unstable soil. Thus they can be found in the most dramatic locations: half-submerged in river beds or jutting from cliffsides. Areas above the palm forest are even more bizarre and fascinating. This cloud forest with moss-covered dwarf trees represents less than 1,000 acres (400 hectares) and gets the full brunt of the island's sometimes intense weather.

Mountain flora adds a touch of color in the rainforest.

The **Tradewinds National Recreation Trail** connects with El Toro to form the island's longest nature trail, at about 4 miles (6.5 km). Commencing a few hundred yards beyond the gate on Route 191, it tends to be rather a trail out of the forest, bypassing all of El Yunque's "big" attractions, but it does have the advantage of going through all the major ecosystems and vegetation types of the forest. The **Big Tree Trail**, leaving from the first parking lot along Route 191, gives a good bird's-eye view of La Mina Falls before meeting the road again at the Palo Colorado Recreation Area.

Perhaps most spectacular of all is the **El Yunque Trail**, which you may access from **Caimitillo Trail** (Route 191 Km 12) for three of the most spectacular vistas in the forest. To get to **Los Picachos Lookout Tower**, continue along El Yunque Trail. When you get to the junction with the Mount Britton Trail, a left will take you to Mount Britton Tower. A right turn will keep you on El Yunque Trail where you will encounter another right which will bring you to Los Picachos Trail. A left turn just before reaching Los Picachos leads you to the lookout tower at **Pico El Yunque** and the fabulous vistas at the remote **El Yunque Rock**.

The best beach

While it's true that there's plenty to see in Puerto Rico's northeast, few visitors get to see any of the area's attractions without first making at least a day's detour to what many consider is the island's finest beach. Shimmering **Luquillo** ❾ is just 35 minutes east of San Juan on either Route 66 or Route 3, which, in travelers' terms, is about the same time it would take to get to lovely but arduous El Yunque, or Fajardo's mob scene *(see opposite)*, and about half the time it would take to get to Humacao. *(See page 167.)* The only liability of a trip to palm-fringed Luquillo is that it can get very crowded, especially at weekends.

Mountains to the sea

Even those not terribly enthusiastic about beaches will find it hard to ignore Luquillo's appeal. This beautiful, bleached-white town is tucked cozily between dark Atlantic waters and Puerto Rico's most imposing mountain chain, the Sierra de Luquillo, from which the town draws its name. There are few more dramatic sights on the island than that of the white-caps of the shoreline glistening in summer sunlight while the peaks of the El Yunque rainforest just inland are suffused in purple thunder clouds. Occasionally, some of the rain intended for the forest does fall on Luquillo, and there are times when the beach is under heavy cloud cover.

On the eastern end of the beach is Mar Sin Barreras (sea without barriers), a park specially constructed for people with physical impairments. Personnel are on hand to help the disabled visitors enjoy one of Puerto Rico's best strands.

Luquillo is also the premier beachside food emporium in Puerto Rico; a seemingly endless string of *friquitines*, or kiosks sells delectably rich local seafood specialties along with a variety of alcoholic and soft drinks.

Two-faced town

To some, the town of **Fajardo** , the next sizeable destination beyond Luquillo, is merely an overcluttered dockfront town, ranking third behind Brindisi in Italy, and Hyannis in Massachusetts, in the "Grim Ferry Ports of the World" rating. To others it is an eminently glamorous resort, a charming community, gateway to a handful of fabulous islands and home to some of the finest sailing in the Caribbean.

The first major town along Puerto Rico's northeast coast, Fajardo remains a mecca for yachting enthusiasts. Originally a small fishing and agricultural village, in the late 1700s it became a popular supply port for many pirate and contraband vessels. The town itself, a hodge-podge of clothing, furniture, and video stores, will appear somewhat unprepossessing to most visitors compared with the area's natural attractions – the calm, clear waters and cays and coral reefs of Vieques Sound. **Playa de Fajardo** , a waterfront community at the east end of the town, is the docking-place for the ferries headed to Culebra, Vieques and a small island marina nearby. Next to the ferry terminal is the pink stucco **US Post Office/ Customs House** and one of Fajardo's few hotels.

Just north of Fajardo, two condominium high-rises, architectural anomalies here, loom over the small fishing village of **Playa Sardinera**. Hundreds of fancy motorboats and yachts of all descriptions crowd the two waterfront marinas nearby. Local fishermen line the beach in the middle of the village with boats and tents; they supply the half-dozen expensive seafood restaurants in the town.

A road over the hill passes a comfortable guesthouse and the lavish **El Conquistador Resort & Country Club**. With 918 rooms and more than

Don't let the Puerto Rican nickname for the residents of Fajardo – cariduros, meaning "the hard-faced ones" – put you off; the people here are very friendly.

BELOW: many trails criss-cross El Yunque.

TIP

A tour of Las Cabezas de San Juan is well worthwhile. There are four each day (three in the morning and one in the afternoon) and there is an admission charge of US$7 for adults and US$4 for children.

BELOW: a local hazard! Iguanas frequent the El Conquistador golf course.

2,000 employees, El Conquistador is one of Puerto Rico's largest resorts. It's also one of the most expensive. First built in the 1960s, the resort was abandoned at one point and later turned into a Maharishi university that soon went bankrupt. Today it is spread among five distinct themed areas, with Moorish and Spanish architecture featured throughout. Guests can even take a ferry to Palomino Island, not far offshore, where the hotel maintains its own private beach and grill.

The road continues on to **Playa Soroco**, a long, narrow stretch of crisp white-sand beach whose clean, shallow waters make it a favorite among locals. At the leftmost point of Soroco, a track leads to **Playa Escondido**, an isolated beach stretching for miles.

Nearby, right off Route 987, on Seven Seas Beach and Campground (tel: 863 8180) is the **Las Cabezas de San Juan Nature Preserve** ⑫ (open to groups Wed–Thur, to general public Fri–Sun only by reservation; entrance fee; tel: 722 5882, or 860-2560 on weekends), an environmental paradise that encompasses 316 acres (128 hectares) of some of the Caribbean's most stunning landscape. Admission to the preserve is by guided tour only *(see left)*. Considering the preserve's natural beauty, it's surprising that so few tourists spend time here. One can observe nearly all of Puerto Rico's natural habitats – coral reefs, thalassia beds, sandy and rocky beaches, lagoons, a dry forest and a mangrove forest.

Another important attraction at Cabezas de San Juan is the lighthouse, known simply as "El Faro." Built in 1880, this pristine white neo-classical structure with black trim is one of only two operational lighthouses on the island. The view from Las Cabezas de San Juan is head-spinning. As you look back toward the heart of Puerto Rico, El Yunque towers over the island. In the

other direction a chain of cays ranges like enticing stepping stones to the islands of Culebra and Saint Thomas.

The dozens of cays and islands off Fajardo provide Puerto Rico's best boating. A protective reef stretching from Cabezas de San Juan to Culebra and beyond keeps the waters calm, while swift Atlantic tradewinds create perfect sailing conditions. Charter a yacht from one of Fajardo's marinas, such as Puerto del Rey Marine, and spend the day sailing, sunbathing and snorkeling.

Map, page 156

Popular cays

Icacos, the largest and most popular cay, offers a narrow stretch of bone-white beach, making it a great spot for picnicking or even camping. Two rows of wooden posts from an abandoned dock march into the water, and, just beyond, a coral underworld descends to the sandy bottom 20 ft (6 meters) below, providing all the action: elkhorn, staghorn, brain, star and other corals host legions of underwater plant and animal life.

Other popular cays, somewhat less readily accessible, include **Culebrita**, **Cayos Lobos** (wolves), **Diablo** (devil), **Palominos** (doves) and **Palominitos** (take a wild guess). These and many smaller cays are ripe for underwater exploration among coral, caverns and tunnels.

Just south of Fajardo is **Roosevelt Roads** ⓭, an area formerly leased by the military for one of the largest naval bases in the world. Occupying about a quarter of Puerto Rico's eastern coastline this was the headquarters of the US Caribbean Naval Forces and a reserve training base. The land will be turned over to the Puerto Rican government, following an environmental clean-up. The nearest town to Roosevelt Roads is **Ceiba**, founded in 1838. ❏

BELOW: pretty plaza in Fajardo.

THE SOUTHEAST

*Palmas del Mar is a busy resort, Cayo Santiago is strictly for
the monkeys, there are quiet beaches near Punta Tuna,
and towns such as Patillas and Arroyo are down to earth*

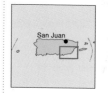

The southeastern section of Puerto Rico – thought by many to be one of the
prettiest parts of the island – has the interesting characteristic of having
some of the most heavily developed, as well as some of the least developed,
parts of the country. It is largely residential and quiet, blessed by the pleasant
Caribbean tradewinds that blow steadily in this region all year, stabilizing the
weather. During the "rainy" season, from about May to September, the southeast may get some 9 inches (23 cm) of rain a month, while during the December to April "dry" season, monthly rainfall averages 3 to 5 inches (7 to 12 cm).

A major town in the region is **Humacao ❶**, which, although a first-rate
industrial center, does have its charms. Previously subsisting off agriculture,
Humacao now aspires to being a first-rate resort town, which it is on the way to
achieving; several tourist resorts, golf courses and beaches are among its attractions. The restored **Casa Roig Museum** (open Wed–Fri and Sun 10am–4pm;
free), the former home of a wealthy sugar-cane landowner, is worth a visit if you
are stopping in the town. It was designed by Antonin Nechodemo, a protegé –
some say plagiarist – of Frank Lloyd Wright. Only a 45-minute drive from San
Juan via Route 30, Humacao is within 2 miles (3 km) of some of the most dazzling beachfront that Vieques Sound has to offer. Add to that its convenience as
a starting-point for excursions in the southeast, and it
earns its standing as a serious holiday resort.

The best way to begin a beach tour of this part of
the island is to head north to **Playa Humacao ❷**,
probably the best-equipped public beach on the island.
It boasts not only miles of bright sand, and a handful
of offshore cays, but also a veritable arcade of lockers,
refreshment stands and other amenities. The beach
benefits from its size, drawing heavily enough from
local and tourist groups alike to ensure that there's
always something going on, if only a pick-up volleyball game: join in.

Halfway down the eastern coast and a 10-minute
drive south from Humacao is **Palmas del Mar ❸**,
Puerto Rico's largest vacation resort. The self-
appointed "New American Riviera," this 2,700-acre
(1,100-hectare) holiday heaven comprises just about
everything but a monorail: 20 tennis courts ("Is there
a court available?" "No, sir, not 'til Thursday."), two
gorgeous beachfront golf courses, riding stables, fine
beaches, deep-sea fishing, 18 restaurants, numerous
bars, a casino, a marina and so on.

Monkey business

A little less than a mile off the coast of Playa
Humacao lies a 39-acre (16-hectare) island that few
people have had the opportunity to visit. This place,
Cayo Santiago ❹, is home to approximately 700

PRECEDING PAGES:
colorful resident at
a Puerto Rican
resort.
LEFT: horsing
around at the
seaside.
BELOW: enjoying
golf at Palmas
del Mar.

rhesus monkeys. With a grant from Columbia University, the animals were brought from India to Puerto Rico in 1938 for research into primate behavior. Never before had such a social troupe of monkeys been transported into the Western world and placed in semi-natural conditions. Despite the comfortable climate and undisturbed environment of Cayo Santiago, many experts remained skeptical on the question of whether the primates could survive and breed.

For two years, tuberculosis scourged the colony. Then, during World War II, grant money ran out and the monkeys faced the threat of starvation. Townspeople from Playa de Humacao helped the colony by regularly taking bananas, coconuts and other foods out to the island for the duration of the war.

Today, the island is administered by the University of Puerto Rico, and scientists from the Caribbean Primate Research Center there spend many, many hours studying the behavioral patterns of these fascinating creatures.

Due to the ongoing research and possible health hazards (and the fact that rhesus monkeys have large canine teeth and at times can be very aggressive), visitors are not allowed on the island. However, there are various sightseeing boats that can take visitors relatively close to the island, where they can snorkel and get a closer glimpse of the frisky primates (with the help of binoculars in most cases). Check at the Palmas del Mar marina.

Brilliant red-blossomed flame trees dot the south-eastern countryside.

Sugar-cane center

From Humacao to **Yabucoa** ❺ (a native Indian term meaning "Place of the Yuca Trees"), rolling hills, semi-tropical forests, sugar-cane fields and cow pastures highlight an exceedingly pleasant drive. Just before reaching Yabucoa – also known as "The Sugar Town" – Route 3 passes the **Roig Sugar Mill**, a

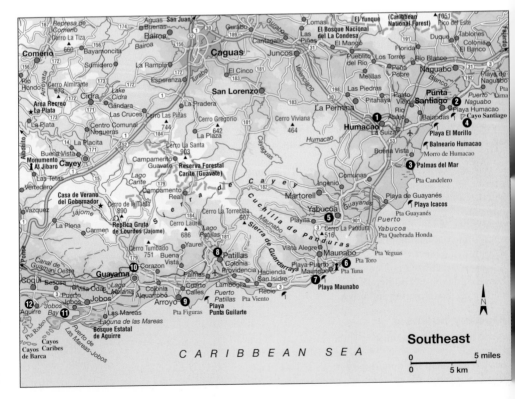

Southeast

rusty piece of antiquity, one of the few survivors of the southeast's agricultural economy that unfortunately has gone belly-up. Also of interest in the area is **Hacienda Lucia**, an old sugar plantation.

Yabucoa marks the beginning of an industrial circuit that continues southwestward. Taking advantage of low-wage labor and liberal tax laws, oil refineries, pharmaceutical companies, textile manufacturers and industrial chemical plants border the smaller towns all the way down the coast.

Leaving Yabucoa, Route 30 to Route 901 takes you on a scenic drive southward (part of the Ruta Panoramica) through arid coastal headlands which form part of the Cuchilla de Pandura mountains.

Map, page 168

Ghost beach

A few miles away from town along the **Balneario Lucia** shore, abandoned seafood restaurants indicate that, at one point, this spot was believed to have potential as a popular bathing retreat. Now, it's a ghost beach; few bother with it. Rows of planted coconut palm trees grow in awkwardly misshapen directions along the beach. The trunks of these trees are wrapped with sheet metal, apparently to prevent rats from climbing them.

The rats, seemingly, have joy-riding in mind. According to a native writer: "When there are no such bands, rats with a penchant for primitive piloting climb the trunks, nibble a hole in the coconuts, lap out the milk, crawl through the hole into the nut, gnaw off the stem and sit inside the shell as it makes its break-neck descent to the ground…"

Route 901 curves upward into a series of hills overlooking rugged shoreline and an expanse of the Caribbean Sea, with the island of Vieques in the distance.

The Festival del Azúcar *(Sugar Festival) is held in Yabucoa each May – one of half a dozen festivals held in the town throughout the year.*

BELOW: hazy day at Punta Tuna.

Map,
page 168

*Samuel Morse,
inventor of the Morse
code, visited Arroyo
in 1848 and later
personally installed
the local telegraph
line. The town's main
street, Calle Morse,
is named in his
honor.*

BELOW: catching
some rays in
Guayama.
RIGHT: tuning up for
a big performance.

Down to Punta Tuna

The road descends the hills to **Punta Tuna** ❻, where one of Puerto Rico's two active lighthouses stands. Built in the 1890s by Spain, the lighthouse is now run by the US Coast Guard. Adjacent to Punta Tuna, a little-known beach ranks among the nicest on the southeastern coast.

Farther down the road, on the opposite side of Punta Tuna, another good beach arches for nearly a mile around tiny **Puerto Maunabo** ❼. Pack a picnic in the morning before setting out from Yabucoa and have a lunch break on one of these lovely beaches; camping is also allowed here.

The Ruta Panoramica continues past the town of Maunabo and winds up a narrow road past cliffside houses and damp verdure over the Cuchilla de Pandura and back to Yabucoa.

Unspoilt corner

At first glance nothing much has happened in the southeastern corner of Puerto Rico since the sugar-cane industry died. But in its isolation, it has acquired a patina of genteel respectability. Coming here is like visiting a venerable maiden aunt who may not have bought anything new in years, but quietly maintains the fine pieces she's had forever.

Patillas ❽ is known as the Emerald of the South for its rolling green hills and agricultural base. "Patilla" is a word for watermelon and reflects the fruit basket reputation of this town. Today, remarkably enough, vineyards dot the landscape, as a number of Patillan farms, like Hacienda Córcega, have planted grapes from North America and are producing wine. **Carite Forest** and **Charco Azul** natural pool are two other attractions of the area.

Samuel Morse installed the first telegraph line in Puerto Rico in **Arroyo** ❾ in 1859 and the **Old Customs House Museum** (open Mon–Fri 9am–4pm; closed for lunch; free) holds memorabilia of the event. From here, train buffs can ride the only working train in Puerto Rico (until the Tren Urbano starts up in 2004). **Tren del Sur de Arroyo** (open daily in summer 9am–4pm, winter Mon–Fri 8am–4.30pm, Sat–Sun 9am–5pm; ticket fee) takes visitors back and forth to **Guayama** ❿ in transformed cane wagons on an hour-long trip along old sugar rails through cane fields and across two rivers.

Guayama has one of Puerto Rico's best-preserved and truly lovely plazas, and the church of **St Anthony of Padua** beside it is the only neo-romantic church on the island. A clock painted on the right tower points to 11.30, the exact time the church was "baptized." The Art Deco cinema still shows first-run films, while **Casa Cautiño**'s façade is a riot of embellishments called neo-classical creole. The house of a wealthy 19th-century family, it is now a museum (open Tues–Sat 9am–4.30pm, Sun 10am–4.30pm; entrance fee).

Jobos Bay ⓫, one of the finest protected shallow-water areas on the island, is close by. Popular with ichthyologists (fish enthusiasts) and ornithologists, the reserve has several species of rare Puerto Rican birds, and fish are well-served by the bay's healthy quantity of micro-organisms. ❑

THE NORTH

*Dorado has upscale attractions, Playa de Vega Baja is a popular
beach, Arecibo has a renowned observatory, and San Sebastián
is a good base for exploring the remarkable karst country*

Map,
pages
176–7

San Juan

Driving west from San Juan on Route 2, as the landscape opens up a bit and
the first hills begin to rise, first-time visitors may begin to feel they have
left the metropolis and are about to penetrate Puerto Rico's fabled countryside. That is, until you hit sprawling, congested Bayamón; then you begin to
wonder if the big cities will ever stop. They stop in **Dorado ❶**, 10 miles (16 km)
west of San Juan, the first town which can claim to be out from under its shadow.

Dorado's a pleasant, quiet, unassuming little town. You'll miss it if you stay
on the highway, and may have to look twice for it even if you take the detour
on Route 165, which leaves Route 2 and runs north across emerald marshlands
before looping back to it.

The hospitable hamlet of **Toa Baja ❷** signals the turn-off. If Dorado is unassuming, Toa Baja is positively diffident, though it is full of charms which
belie the quiet. Dividing Toa Baja from Dorado itself is the sluggish **Río de la
Plata**, whose grassy banks and meandering course would remind you of some
of the more timeless parts of rural England were it not for the clayey river bed
which has turned the stream's waters a rugged brick red.

Dorado follows Route 165 loosely on both sides. No cross streets slow traffic enough to draw attention to the small main plaza by the roadside, and the
town's businesses are admirably free of gaudy bill-
boards and other "Welcome to..." bric-a-brac. "Urban"
Dorado is just clean, slow-paced and friendly, and a
disproportionate number of its business establishments – bakeries, bars, juice stands – have cama-
raderie as their *raison d'être*.

Of particular interest here are the historical Catholic
church and **La Casa del Rey**, a former Spanish garrison. Both were built in 1823, the year the town was
founded; the latter was restored in 1978 by the Institute of Puerto Rican Culture and is now a museum.

But Dorado is not all culture. Its beaches are inviting and easily accessible via the *guaguas* (buses) that
leave from near the town plaza. A mile northwest of
town, through a spinney of mangroves and a bone-
white graveyard on Route 693, is the irresistibly
lovely beach at **Playa Dorado-Sardinera**, and also
nearby is **El Ojo Del Buey** (The Ox's Eye), a seaside
recreational area that takes its name from a large rock
bearing an amazing resemblance to the head of an ox.

In May of 2006 Dorado's fabled luxury hotel, the
Hyatt Dorado Beach, closed its doors. Its sister hotel,
the Hyatt Cerromar, was shuttered in 2004, and converted into timeshare units. The 297-room Dorado
Beach hotel, built on the site of a grapefruit plantation,
originally opened its doors in 1958 as one of Lau-
rance Rockefeller's Rockresorts. In its heyday the
hotel, once owned by Clara Livingston, Puerto Rico's

PRECEDING PAGES:
motocross racing in
San Sebastián.
LEFT: Caribbean
sunset.
BELOW: cheerful
northerner.

first woman pilot and head of the Air Civil Defense, welcomed celebrities and dignitaries from around the world. The 900-acre (365-hectare) property is to be converted into the kind of upscale vacation apartments, for which Dorado has become well known. Dorado Beach's four championship golf courses, at one time administered by Juan "Chichi" Rodriguez, remain open for business to club members and guests.

Popular beachfront

Further west, a fast, 35-minute drive from San Juan on Routes 2 and 686, **Playa de Vega Baja** ❸ is one of the most popular of San Juan's metropolitan beachfronts, and is dotted with cabins belonging to the local residents. It benefits not only from spectacular juxtapositions of sand and sea, but also from lush and unusual surrounding countryside. The beach itself draws most attention for its weird and haunting rock formations, which are actually a string of coral islands running parallel to the seashore for 2,500 ft (760 meters), from the palm-lined cove of **Boca del Cibuco** to craggy **Punta Puerto Nuevo**. This odd, almost unique formation has sheltered most of the beach, while causing its western end to resemble at times a sort of preternaturally large jacuzzi.

The nearby town of **Vega Baja** has grown into a fairly modern and uniform Puerto Rican municipality. The town does have a sense of humor about its reputation as something of a hokey place. An official town bulletin offers not only the usual information on town history and famous residents but also a tongue-in-cheek roster of *Personajes típicos de Vega Baja*. These include the tallest man, the drunk, the beggar and the basketball fan. A town that can parody itself so remorselessly deserves a visit, but not so much as the

Pineapples are just one of the many agricultural products of the fertile north; they're often sold at roadside kiosks.

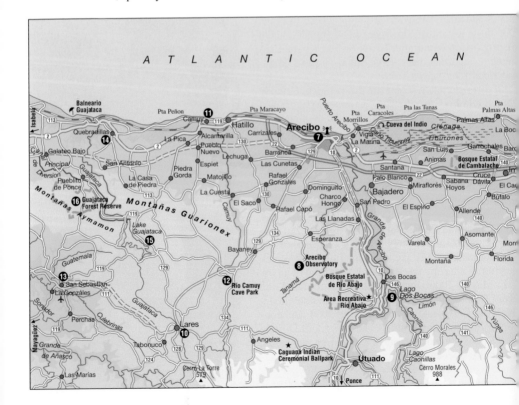

surrounding countryside does. Vega Baja sits in the middle of the fertile coastal flatlands west of San Juan. Visitors will be rewarded with long vistas over canefields and marshes, and an array of deciduous foliage: most impressive in an island full of tropical trees.

Further west along the coast, and accessible by Route 686, which runs near the bottom of it, is **Playa Tortuguero**, the largest and most palm-lined of the beaches. Half a mile inland, **Laguna Tortuguero** ④, while not officially a nature reserve, provides a haven for bird life.

Continuing west, the **Manatí** ⑤ area has produced most of the island's pineapple products. Here Puerto Rico's famous Lotus pineapple juice is canned under the supervision of the Land Administration. Vendors offer fresh pineapples along the road (Route 2). The sweet, Spanish Red variety goes into the 100 percent juice. No water is added. A short drive from town takes you to **Playa Mar Chiquita** ⑥, an unusual beach in that the surf comes pounding through the high rocks to produce a most dramatic effect. The rocks enclose an oval lagoon that provides excellent swimming.

Arecibo

There are prettier cities on this island, but few are prettier to approach than **Arecibo** ⑦. Route 2 takes a tortuous turn 48 miles (77 km) west of San Juan and reveals the second capital city of Puerto Rico's north coast, backed by the blue Atlantic. Directly to the south of Arecibo lies karst country, with typical landscapes of pine and mahogany in the Río Abajo forest.

The western end of the expressway (PR 22) affords another dramatic perspective of the island's north coast, this one just west of Arecibo in Hatillo.

Map, pages 176–7

The nickname for those who live in Vega Baja is "melao-melao," meaning "molasses-molasses," because of the large quantities of molasses produced here.

BELOW: swimmers brave the Atlantic at Playa de Vega Baja.

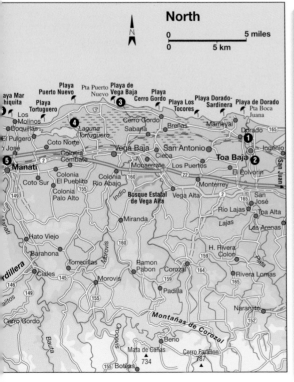

Travelers are treated to a spectacular, unobstructed view of the Atlantic Ocean's crashing waves, fronted by acres of palm trees. This is Puerto Rico unspoiled. Navigation via the expressway obliges you to double-back east to reach the town of Arecibo. However, it is not an unpleasant trip: Route 2 is packed with shopping malls and fast-food outlets, but in just a few miles you return to the town's historic area, all the while enjoying glimpses of the ocean to the north.

The coastal road, Route 681, is the road the expressway left behind. It meanders, meaning you won't get to Arecibo quickly, but you will enjoy the view from the cliffs. The drive runs from Palmas Altas through Islote, past Desvio Valdés and to Punta Caracoles (Seashell Point), site of **La Cueva del Indio** (Indian Cave), where you can walk to a hole in the cliff for a look at some (supposedly) pre-Columbian drawings.

The lighthouse and beyond

Further ahead, off Route 655 to your right at Punta Morrillos, is the **Arecibo Lighthouse and Historical Park** (open weekdays and holidays 9am–6pm; Sun 10am–7pm; tel: 787-817 1936, 880 7540; parking fee). The excursion is both fun and educational for children and adults alike. An expansive deck with a children's play area accompanies a restored museum that includes replicas of a Taíno Indian village, Christopher Columbus's ships and African slave quarters. A pirate's cave and a pirate's ship, along with a mini zoo, complete the facilities, along with the lighthouse itself, which was the last one built by the Spaniards in 1898.

The reality of Arecibo is a bit more worldly than you would assume from its externally Arcadian aspect. It is one of the oldest Puerto Rican towns, and since

TIP

An interesting detour from Arecibo is to take the coast road (Route 681) past Mar Chiquita to another headland, Punta Caracoles, on which is the Cueva del Indio (Indian Cave). A short walk leads to the hole in the cliff, inside which are some (supposedly) pre-Columbian drawings.

BELOW: limestone rocks by the Indian caves near Arecibo.

its foundation in the 16th century has enjoyed one of the highest levels of prosperity on the island.

Operation Bootstrap, the project which was designed by Muñoz Marín and the US Congress to boost Puerto Rico into the industrial world, and Section 936, the American legislation that offered tax incentives to companies investing in Puerto Rico, accelerated Arecibo's advance in the business world. Puerto Rico makes more pharmaceutical products than any other place in the world *(see page 48)*, and Arecibo is a hub for the island's pharmaceutical manufacturing industry.

Map, pages 176–7

Oil for the wheels of life

Arecibo was a leader in the art of manufacturing products that have eased the country along the troubled road of life long before the pharmaceutical boom. The town still produces agricultural machinery, clothing, plastics, paper and sporting goods. Ronrico, one of the greatest rums on the island (which is itself the rum capital of the world), was once the major industry in the town, and Arecibo is proud of its legacy from the island's rum trade.

Arecibo's name comes from a local Indian chief called Jamaica Aracibo.

Salubrious surroundings

For a town in its situation, Arecibo is center to a surprising variety of terrain. It forms a semi-peninsula pointing northeastward at the delta of two rivers: the **Río Grande de Arecibo** and the **Canal Perdomo**. The roads from San Juan hug the shoreline here, giving pleasant views of the city from afar. Those roads were put here for a reason: to the east recede swamps of unmeasured depth and gloom. Be warned that the surrounding area is chock-a-block with irritating mosquitoes in the wet season.

BELOW: Arecibo, one of the oldest, and most prosperous, towns in Puerto Rico.

The century-old Punta Morillos lighthouse in Arecibo is now restored as a museum focusing on the city's heritage. For more details call the Puerto Rico Tourism Company on 1-800-866-7827 or 721-6363.

BELOW: Arecibo's attractive Plaza Luis Muñoz Rivera.

Arecibo itself disappoints some tourists who use the city as a way-station on their indefatigable search for all that is mundane and tacky on the island. It takes an intelligent and observant traveler to realize that Arecibo is one of the finer and more livable-in cities, not only on the island but also anywhere in the Caribbean. Its streets are broad, its citizens relatively well-off, and its shopping district has far more variety than one might expect from a city of only 100,000 inhabitants.

Moreover, Arecibo has cafés and theaters – not as commonplace as one might think in Puerto Rico – and its oldest building, a distinctive wooden structure, dates from 1884. **Calle Alejandro Salicrup**, at the tip of the semi-peninsular wedge, is one of the best thoroughfares on which to see such timbered architecture, which is as unique to Arecibo as the southwestern townhouse style is to San Germán. In a somewhat different vein, the **San Felipe Cathedral**, between calles José de Diego and Gonzalo Marín, has an unusual cupola and is the second largest cathedral built by the Spaniards in Puerto Rico.

The **Alcaldía** (town hall), tucked in at the intersection of calles José de Diego, Romero-Barceló and Juarregui, is among the prettier offices in Puerto Rico, and its inhabitants are among the friendliest and most receptive. Nearby at No. 7 Gonzalo Marín is **Casa Ulanga** (tel: 787-880 6079, 878 8044), Arecibo's cultural center. Built in 1854 by Spaniard Francisco Ulanga, Casa Ulanga was the city's first three-story building. Over time it served as a center for banking and business with stints as a jail, courthouse and town hall.

Formerly the Plaza Mayor, now the **Plaza Luis Muñoz Rivera**, this is another of Puerto Rico's pretty plazas, with a cathedral facing over an idiosyncratically landscaped park surrounded by wrought-iron railings and multicolored Spanish

colonial architecture. The plaza has undergone an astounding number of trans-formations in the past 100 years. In the mid-1890s, it was burnt to ashes during a fire that consumed much of the city. In 1899, a hurricane and the ensuing surf, which was not far short of a tidal wave, pounded it into disrepair.

Arecibo was one of the first of the Puerto Rican cities to jump off the Span-ish imperial bandwagon and to honor its own native heroes. The monument in memory of Queen Isabella II of Spain, which for so long stood in the middle of the plaza, was replaced in 1927 with an obelisk honoring local hero and politi-cian Luis Muñoz Marín.

The waterfront drive is quite lovely, with views of the lighthouse and the Atlantic coast, although the *malecón* (boardwalk) is somewhat sad. The **Museo de Arte e Historia** (open Mon–Sat 9am–4.30 pm; free) on calles Juan Rosado and Santiago Iglesias, is a former transportation center, and displays old post-cards of early Arecibo. Built in 1919, it was once used as a warehouse to store rum, and was painstakingly restored and reinaugurated in 2006.

The radar/radio-telescope at the Arecibo Observatory is equal in size to 13 football fields.

Star attraction

Anyone who has ever taken sixth-grade science should have some familiarity with Arecibo. On one of those big, full-page spreads that fill up space in astron-omy textbooks, the **Arecibo Observatory ❽** is generally featured prominently. A complicated trip 20 miles (32 km) south of the town of Arecibo into the karst country will bring you to this mammoth complex. From downtown Arecibo, fol-low de Diego to Route 129. Bear left on Route 651 and follow it for the 4 miles (6 km) before it becomes 635. Travel about the same distance until you come to a T-intersection, at which you will turn right (onto Route 626) and travel a few

BELOW: fresh fruit on display at the market.

Arecibo Observatory

Hidden among the mountains of north-western Puerto Rico, where the stars shine undimmed by city lights, sits the most sensitive radio telescope on Earth.

The Arecibo Ionospheric Observatory is so huge that you can spot it from a jumbo jet at 33,000 ft (10,000 meters). Yet on the ground, first-time visitors need a detailed road map to find its guarded entrance.

Located at the end of winding Route 625, in the heart of Puerto Rico's karst country, the observatory has been the focus of numer-ous astronomical breakthroughs over the years, ranging from Alexander Wolszcan's 1992 discovery of planets outside our own solar system to NASA's $100-million Search for Extra-Terrestrial Intelligence.

In 1993, the Arecibo "dish" gained world prominence when two American astronomers, Russell A. Hulse and Joseph H. Taylor Jr, won the Nobel Prize for Physics for work done using the Arecibo facility.

The observatory owes its existence large-ly to Puerto Rico's political status as a United States Commonwealth and to the island's geographic position 17° north of the equa-tor. That makes it ideal for the observation of planets, quasars, pulsars and other cosmic phenomena. The telescope is so sensitive that it can listen to emissions from places 13 billion light years away.

The Arecibo Observatory is funded by an annual $7.5 million grant from the National Science Foundation, though its day-to-day affairs are managed by Cornell University of Ithaca, New York. The observatory counts 140 full-time employees among its staff, and has hosted more than 200 visiting scientists from countries as diverse as Argentina, Bul-garia, Brazil and Russia. No military experi-ments of any kind are conducted here, and, despite the presence of security guards, there's nothing secretive about this place.

The "dish" itself, suspended over a huge natural sinkhole, is by far the largest of its kind in the world. Spanning 1,000 ft (300 meters) in diameter, it covers 20 acres (8 hectares) and is composed of nearly 40,000 perforated aluminum mesh panels, each measuring 3 ft by 6 ft (1 by 2 meters). A 900-ton platform is suspended 425 ft (130 meters) over the dish by 12 cables strung from three reinforced concrete towers.

Underneath the dish lies a jungle of ferns, orchids and begonias. In fact, until recently tourists could get only as far as a viewing platform high above the site. The dish itself is off-limits, and visitors were limited to a five-minute audio tape describing the facility and a display area explaining the telescope's construction together with some current sci-entific results. However, this situation was remedied when Cornell University built a $2-million visitors' center (open Wed–Fri 12–4pm, weekends and most holidays 9am–4pm; open to students and groups Wed–Fri from 10am), including a 120-seat auditorium, a 4,000-sq. ft (370-sq. meter) scientific museum, a gift shop, and a trail leading to a viewing platform from which the telescope can be seen at close range.

The observatory can be seen in the movies *Contact*, in which Jodie Foster plays an astronomer seeking extraterrestrial life, and *Goldeneye*, the James Bond movie. ❑

hundred yards before making a left turn onto 625, at the end of which is the renowned observatory. *(For further details of this, one of the most important research observatories in the Americas, see the panel on the facing page.)*

Map, pages 176–7

The karst country

Puerto Rico is one of those places blessed to an almost unfair extent with an enormous variety of beautiful landscape. But such places are legion, and what do you give in Puerto Rico to the tourist who has everything? The answer is not hard to find: the dark green sector of the island's northwest where the land rises in regular green-and-white hillocks and appears to be boiling – the intriguing area known as the karst country.

Limestone sink holes

Karst is the name for one of the world's oddest rock formations and can occur only under the most fortuitous circumstances. Some geologists claim there are only two other places on earth where rock formations resemble those of Puerto Rico: one just across the Mona Passage in the Dominican Republic, and one in the former Yugoslavia.

Karst is formed when water sinks into limestone and erodes larger and larger basins, known as "sinkholes." Many erosions create many sinkholes, until one is left with peaks of land only where the land has not sunk with the erosion of limestone: these are *mogotes*, or karstic hillocks, which resemble each other in size and shape to a striking extent, given the randomness of the process that created them. All this leads you to realize that the highest point on the highest *mogote* in the karst country is certainly below the level which the

LEFT: the dish at the Arecibo Observatory is hidden in a natural sinkhole. **BELOW:** a valley amid the karstic hills near Arecibo.

limestone ground held in earlier days when the first drop of rain opened the first sinkhole.

It's hard to say where the karst country begins. Some say at Manatí, though there are two hills not 10 minutes' drive west of San Juan which look suspiciously karstic. From Manatí, they carry on as far west as Isabela, and are at their most spectacular a short drive (5 miles/8 km) south of the major cities of Puerto Rico's northwest.

It's just as hard to say wherein their appeal lies. Part of it must be in the odd symmetry of the things – despite the fact that it is the holes, not the hills, which have undergone the change over eons.

These hills are impressive mountains only 100 ft (30 meters) high – they are probably the grandest landscape within which humans can feel a sense of scale. They encompass a startling variety within their regularity; certain *mogotes* can look like the Arizona desert tucked in for bed in the Black Forest.

Cars to karst

Arecibo is the capital of the karst country, and some fine drives can begin from there. The easiest to undertake is certainly Route 10 south to **Lago Dos Bocas** . Taking Route 129 southwest to Lares is a pleasant jaunt, which never lets you stray into the Cordillera, as the Route 10 trip is prone to do; the 129 is flanked by *colmados* (grocery stores).

If you like karst a lot, though, head west on Route 2, turn left on Route 119, and follow the road to **Lake Guajataca** for perhaps the finest views of the water and limestone that made the whole unfathomable but evocative landscape possible.

Make it a point, if at all possible, of getting out to the karst country. The

TIP

If you have the time, take advantage of the 2-hour free launch trips on Lago dos Bocas provided four times a day (7am, 10am, 2pm and 5pm) by the Public Works Department.

BELOW: Lake Caonillas, one of many nestled into the hills of the north.

THE KARSTIC FORESTS

Puerto Rico's Department of Natural Resources has recognized the beauty and fragility of its unique karstic landscape. It has created four national forests in which it is protected: **Cambalache** (east of Arecibo, with plantations of eucalyptus, teak and mahoe trees), **Guajataca** (west of Arecibo, offering some 25 miles/40 km of hiking trails), **Río Abajo** (south of Arecibo, and home to 223 plant and 175 wildlife species; 70 trails criss-cross its 5,780 acres/2,300 hectares), and **Vega Alta** (west of Toa Baja).

Not all the karst country is limited to these forests; in fact, they are woefully small, comprising only about 4,000 acres (1,600 hectares) in total, with Río Abajo accounting for over half of these. All are ripe for hiking, yet the trails in the karst country never seem as crowded as those up El Yunque and other Puerto Rican mountains. Perhaps this is owing to the dangers involved with this sort of landscape. Sinkholes are not like potholes, but they can come as unexpectedly, especially in heavy brush.

Get a trail map from the visitors' center at whatever reserve you try. Otherwise, *The Other Puerto Rico* by Kathryn Robinson offers helpful advice, and one read of it will convince you that there's nowhere in Puerto Rico that's not worth risking a little danger to see.

unique beauty is staggering, and is worth a visit by itself. Even more, though, the sight of karst will add another dimension to this tropical paradise too often labeled as a place for a "beach vacation."

Map, pages 176–7

Frontier town

If this tiny island has a frontier town, surely **Lares ❿** must be it. It sits at the western edge of the Cordillera Central's main cluster of peaks, and rests at the southernmost spur of the karst country. Lares is as far from the sea as you can get in Puerto Rico, and to its west a placid corridor of plains runs just to the north of the hills of La Cadena and south of Route 111 and the sleepy Río Culebrinas.

Like many of the towns in this area, where plains meet uplands to produce eerily spectacular vistas, Lares is as scenic to approach as it is to leave. Arriving from the south on either Route 124 or Route 128, the traveler is greeted by a tiny, toylike and close-packed community perched on a gentle rise across a valley and shadowed by rugged twin karstic *mogotes*. Emerging from the east on Route 111 from the karstic clusters of the Río Abajo Forest Reserve, you are hit by surprise at Lares' anomalous urbanity.

Puerto Ricans pride themselves on their friendliness and warmth.

The town itself exudes much of the toylike ambience which you may well have perceived from afar. It's an attenuated cluster of little businesses, bars and shops snaking along two main one-way streets that run in opposite directions. In the central **Plaza de la Revolución** stands an imposing 19th-century Spanish colonial church, whose pale pastel façade and gracefully arched roof give it something of a Middle Eastern look.

If Lares has a stern side, pride rather than inhospitableness is its source. For as the scene of the "Grito de Lares," Puerto Rico's glorious and ill-fated revolt

BELOW: coffee and banana farm near Lares.

against Spanish colonial rule, the town is generally considered to be the birthplace of modern Puerto Rican political consciousness.

The Grito de Lares

The "Grito de Lares" ("Shout of Lares") was not merely a Puerto Rican historical event; its roots lay in the serious political grievances that were to sweep Spain's Caribbean colonies in the mid-19th century and result, some decades later, in their ultimate loss.

When, in 1867, native Puerto Rican guards demonstrated in protest at discrepancies between their own salaries and those of Spanish guards, many liberals were expelled from the island, including Ramón Emeterio Betances, a distinguished physician and certainly the most prominent voice in Puerto Rican politics at the time. He went to New York, Santo Domingo and Saint Thomas, where he rallied support for abolition and self-determination.

On September 23, 1868, hundreds of Emeterio Betances' followers seized Lares and began to march on nearby San Sebastián. There they were met by Spanish forces, and easily routed. Though Emeterio Betances was merely exiled to France, and the revolution came to nought, the "Grito de Lares" led Puerto Ricans to think differently of their land and their aspirations for it, and the spirit of that September day lives on – not only in the streets of Lares but also in the hearts and on the tongues of Puerto Ricans throughout the island.

Speleology

Also significant, but in a rather different way, is the unspectacular town of **Camuy ⓫**, just far enough west of Arecibo and just far enough north of Route

A plaque that commemorates the 1868 revolution in Lares.

BELOW: flower shop brings a splash of bright color to Lares.

Map, pages 176–7

2, to appear almost untouched by the life of modern Puerto Rico. What appeal Camuy has is more primordial – a bewildering maze of one-way streets that will never accommodate automobiles; a lifestyle tranquil to the point of torpor; a few vestiges of an older era, like shops that sell salves and incense for the appeasement of various saints; and, most primordial of all, one of the largest cave systems in the Western world.

Most easily reached by driving due south on Route 129, the cave system is actually a series of karstic sinkholes connected by the 350-ft (106-meter) deep **Río Camuy**, which burrows underground through soft limestone for much of its course from the Cordillera to the Atlantic. The largest of these entrances has been developed as a tourist attraction, with inducements of the "fun for the whole family" variety.

The **Río Camuy Cave Park** ⓬ (open Wed–Sun, pub. hols 8am–4pm last trip at 3.45pm), which is managed by the Puerto Rico Land Administration, contains one of the most massive cave networks in the Western hemisphere. This 268-acre (106-hectare) complex includes three crater-like sinkholes and one cave. The Taínos considered these formations sacred; their artifacts have been found throughout the area. The park's main attraction is the 170-ft (52-meter) high and 695-ft (210-meter) long **Cueva Clara**, which is specially lit, and accessible only by trolley and in guided groups.

The cave is home to a unique species of fish that is completely blind. The entrance looks like a cathedral façade, with a broad row of toothy stalactites descending from the bushy hillside. Visitors will notice that inside the cave's overhang, the light becomes bluish, and a weird silence descends, broken only by the constant chirp of bats hanging from the ceiling and minute distant

The part of Río Camuy that runs underground forms the second-largest subterranean river in the world.

BELOW: the impressive Río Camuy caves.

echoes. Could they be the far-off sounds of water dripping through yet undiscovered passages? It is indeed. Dozens of river cave systems lie beneath the spectacular karst landscape.

Leaving the cave park, you have two excellent choices for lunch not far away. The **Restaurante Las Cavernas** and the **Restaurante El Taíno**, both located along Route 129, pride themselves on traditional Puerto Rican cuisine, bilingual waiters, a family atmosphere and fairly reasonable prices. At Las Cavernas, the house specialty is *arroz con guinea* (rice with guinea hen), served on a large plate with beans, and *amarillos* (fried bananas) for dessert.

And even more caves...

If you're an avid spelunker, there's still more for you to see: close to Río Camuy is the privately owned **Cueva de Camuy** (open daily 9am–5pm, Sun to 8pm; entrance fee) on Route 486. Although smaller and less interesting, it too has guided tours as well as family-centered activities that include a swimming pool and waterslide, amusements, a café, ponies and go-karts.

Day-long caving and rappelling (abseiling down sinkholes) trips can be organized through Aventuras Tierra Adentro (tel: 766 0470), which include floating down underground rivers solely by the light of headlamps. Some 2,000 caves have been discovered in the karst region. They provide homes for 13 species of bat, the tiny *coquí*, the *guavá* (an arachnid), crickets and other species.

More caves are to be found near the town of **Hatillo**, on the north coast just east of Camuy, which produces most of the milk consumed on the island. But Hatillo's biggest attraction is in late December, when one of the most popular mask festivals in Puerto Rico is held here. Hundreds of people from around

TIP

If you're thinking of taking some photographs in the caves, bring a tripod along for the best results.

BELOW: ready for cruising: Lares man and his customized 1960s' Chevy.

the island gather at the town's main square to enjoy the colorful festivities, which see locals dressing up with masks to enact King Herod's soldiers running after newborn boys with murder on their minds.

Map, pages 176–7

San Sebastián and back to the coast

Of all the prosperous provincial towns of Puerto Rico's northwest, **San Sebastián** ⓭ stands out both as the most representative of the region and in the most noticeable contrast to the gloomy villages of the Cordillera Central which lie to the south and east.

Perhaps this is because it is the first of the towns which is truly out of the highlands and secure in its footing as part of the low-lying northwest. Perhaps too it has something to do with the cornucopia of food products which come from the region, for this is the heart of many of the island's oldest and most traditional food industries.

San Sebastián is surrounded by green and moist rolling grassland, and stood as one of Puerto Rico's sugar-boom towns in the cane industry's heyday. Now the area is given over to scattered dairy farming and various agricultural pursuits which used to be associated with other parts of the island.

Tobacco grows in many of the valleys, and coffee plants, once the preserve of Yauco and other towns in the island's arid southwest, can be seen growing on local hillsides.

With close to 40,000 residents, most of them living in the shady main streets that cluster about a lovely plaza, San Sebastián has more of an urban ambience than most of the northwest. The weekly Friday bazaar at Plaza Agropecuaria is a big attraction in town, as is the Hammock Festival in July.

BELOW: the plaza in San Sebastián.

Map, pages 176–7

Outside of the town, **Puente El Barandillo** is a hanging bridge over Río Guatemala on Route 446, it is a great spot from which to begin exploring the karst region. There's also the famous **Pozo del Virgen**, a well that is a religious shrine which attracts thousands of devout Catholics every year. To the north, Lake Guajataca has nature walks and a couple of *paradores* (country inns), as well as excellent fishing. And any drive into the countryside will invariably lead to scenic delights.

Surprising town

Perhaps the single most stunning view in all of Puerto Rico is the approach to **Quebradillas** ⓮ heading west from Arecibo on Route 2. As you drive up a hill that curves to the left you will see deep-blue sea and then a breathtaking coastline of cliffs and rolling sea. Make the approach slowly. On your right is a *miradero* (look-out point) where you can stop to take some incredible pictures. A little further on, your first right will take you down towards the beach and a collection of creole restaurants as well as an old tunnel.

Quebradillas itself adds to the appealing oddities you expect from the towns west of Arecibo – spiritualist herb shops, narrow streets and houses sloping towards the waterline – with some geological oddities that make it a town well worth going out of your way for.

A short drive or walk northwest of town, **Playa Guajataca**, described paradoxically by the local people as a "nice, dangerous beach," is to be taken with extreme care. Deep waters, white sands and raging surf make it a highly attractive proposition for surfers and bathers, but highly dangerous for the average swimmer, virtually anyone incapable of swimming the English Channel. Even expert swimmers and surfers should exercise serious caution.

The **Río Guajataca** is another spot that is as beautiful as it is forbidding, and pocked with a cave system which, although not completely charted, appears to be quite as extensive and awesome as that of the caves at Camuy.

Lakeside *paradores*

Nearby **Lake Guajataca** ⓯, 7 miles (11 km) south on Route 113, is man-made, as are the rest of Puerto Rico's lakes, but offers a splendid natural retreat, with two *paradores*, Vistamar and El Guajataca, both situated on the coast, serving as convenient bases for hikes – the well-marked trails are easily conquered by even the not-so-fit – into the rolling **Aymamon Mountains** in the **Guajataca Forest Reserve** ⓰, located just to the west.

Both *paradores* are very good: El Guajataca's rooms open onto the Atlantic Ocean, and the dinners – blending creole and international dishes – are remarkable; Vistamar, one of Puerto Rico's largest *paradores*, features beautiful gardens and the opportunity to fish in a green waters of the nearby river.

The lake itself is stocked with freshwater fish, and small electric boats are available for rental. You can climb the observation tower here and see no other man-made structure for miles. ❑

BELOW: geese await their fate at the Friday bazaar in San Sebastián.
RIGHT: view of dammed Lago dos Bocas.

THE WEST

Aguada and Aguadilla are attractive seaside centers, Rincón has spectacular surf, Mayagüez mixes history and a world-class university, and San Germán is the island's second-oldest town

Map, page 196

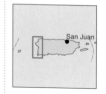

I t's not exactly the wild frontier, but Puerto Rico's west coast is an action-packed collection of surfing, snorkeling, diving, windsurfing and kiteboarding beaches bordered by intriguing towns ranging from gracefully colonial to beach blanket bingo. When *sanjuaneros* need a break from the busy metropolitan area, they plan a weekend on the west coast. God's Own Waterpark is as far as you can get from the heat and stress of bustling San Juan without crossing the sea. Just two to three hours from the capital by car, towns like Isabela, Aguadilla, Rincón and Cabo Rojo offer a variety of adventure options, but also a serenity that Puerto Ricans flock to year round.

Isabela ❶, along the north coast, is an amalgam of all the charms of this corner of Puerto Rico, with a cluster of brilliant, whitewashed houses tumbling down the hills to some of the island's most renowned surfing and swimming beaches. The city, like many Puerto Rican towns in the face of multiple factory closings, continues to soldier on, but is looking to tourism to fill the gap. Fortunately for Isabela, small farms still abound, providing much of the produce available at local markets. Isabela is also known for *queso de hoja* (leaf cheese), a delicious small-production white cheese that pulls apart in leaves and can be bought at local *panaderías* (bakeries) or at roadside stands. You may feel the occasional tremor here – Isabela is located on the Milwaukee Trench – but full-scale earthquakes are rare occurrences.

Breeding and beaches

Horse enthusiasts should not miss **Arenales ❷** to the southwest, where a number of the fine *pasofino* stables have made Isabela a renowned equine breeding center. Most visitors to Isabela, however, come to ride waves, not steeds, and **Jobos Beach ❸**, just west of town on Route 466, is the place they head for. Beautiful cliffs frame many of the beaches. One of these is home to **El Pozo de Jacinto ❹**, a spurting well where waves meet cliff. The story goes that Jacinto was a farmer who had a favorite cow. He tied himself to the cow with a rope while he was pasturing his herd around the cliffs so he wouldn't lose her. Said bovine got too close to the edge and tumbled into the sea, taking poor, hapless Jacinto with him. Today, locals stand at the edge of the cliff and shout "*Jacinto! Dame la vaca!*" (Give me the cow!) as the spray comes up. It is said to bring good luck.

Nearby, **Shacks Beach** is an all-purpose destination; diving, snorkeling and swimming among underwater caves are favorite activities, while windsurfers and kiteboarders from around the world skim across the waves with their colorful sails and riders gallop horses along the beautiful sand.

PRECEDING PAGES: colorful *yolas* at Aguadilla. **LEFT:** pensive Puerto Rican. **BELOW:** Jobos Beach near Isabela.

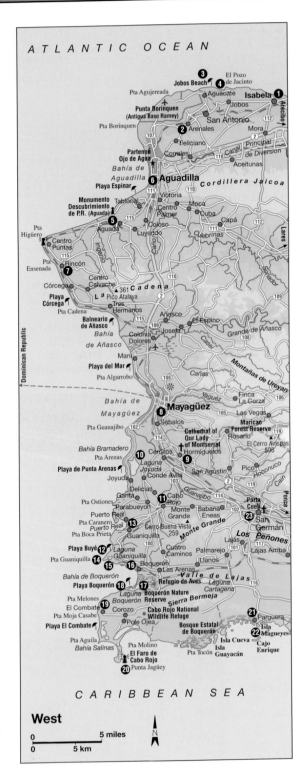

Rival resorts

The two lovely seaside towns of **Aguada ❺** and **Aguadilla ❻** have a running rivalry over the exact spot of Columbus's first landing on Puerto Rico in 1493. **Parque de Colón**, a mile northwest of Aguada on Route 441, dead center of **Playa Espinar**, a 2,500-ft (760-meter) stretch of golden beach, is Aguada's monument to its Columbus claim. Aguadilla's believed site is at **Parque El Parterre**, where a freshwater spring seems to give historical backing to the belief that Columbus and his sailors stopped here for refreshment on their second voyage of discovery to the West Indies.

Aguadilla, the home of **Ramey Airforce Base**, is the more prosperous of the towns. The base is no longer in service, but **Rafael Hernández Airport** is operated from there and has the longest runway, at 11,000 ft (3,350 meters), in the Caribbean. The airport is mainly used for domestic flights but direct flights from Canada, North America and Europe are increasing and it is hoped they will bring more tourism and more prosperity to the region (*see page 262.*) In the meantime, the Coast Guard and National Guard offices are still based there.

The town's windswept, palm tree-studded, 18-hole golf course is the cheapest on the island, and there are a dozen pretty little beaches tucked among the coves that form Aguadilla's northwest border. **Crashboat Beach** (Route 2 to Route 107 to Route 458) is one of the best-known and serviced; it is frequented by ebullient locals at the weekends, when you can go for a look at how Puerto Ricans celebrate the natural gifts of their island.

International waves

Rincón ❼, southwest of Aguadilla, has become an escape destination for locals and visitors over the past 10 years. A peninsula that becomes the western-most point of the island and is separated from the rest of Puerto Rico by green mountains, Rincón's relative isolation makes it seem like an island unto itself. And its community, made up of farmers and fishermen who have lived there for generations and tow-headed gringos there for the surf and the ecology, creates a friendly, if schizophrenic, environment more like the tiny islands of the Eastern Caribbean than bustling Puerto Rico. *Rincón* means corner in Spanish and is an apt moniker for the town, but it actually got its name from a Spanish aristocrat called Rincón who deeded this hill-side village to the laborers who worked for him. That generosity of spirit is evident in the unhurried smiles of the inhabitants.

Rincón beaches

Visitors mostly come for the beaches. The Atlantic north side of the point is the Caribbean's stellar surf strip. The south side is a dead-flat bathing beach with excellent snorkeling, particularly at Steps. The coral and the colorful small fish that live off it are particularly fine. Winter tends to be high season, because of the waves and whales *(see page 200)*, but more and more families and couples are coming in the low season for the romantic sunsets, photo opportunities at the **Punta Higuero lighthouse** – recently restored and set in a charming strolling park overlooking the sea and Domes beach – and lower off-season prices.

Favorite activities include horseback riding, drives over the mountains to photograph panoramic views and collecting sea glass on Sandy Beach. Because of the numerous tourists, this is as good a place as any to try authentic creole food as the waiting staff are likely to speak English very well. And if you are there in the month of June, the dozens of lush mango trees that line the south end of Route 115 will be dropping ripe fruit all over the road. Pull over and harvest some; they are free for the taking and delicious.

Map, page 196

Whale-watchers are becoming increasingly attracted to the Rincón shores; a bit further out is a wintering place for humpback whales. (See page 200.)

BELOW: airborne in the Aguadillan surf.

Mayagüez – looking forward

Known as *La Sultana del Oeste* (The Sultaness of the West), **Mayagüez** 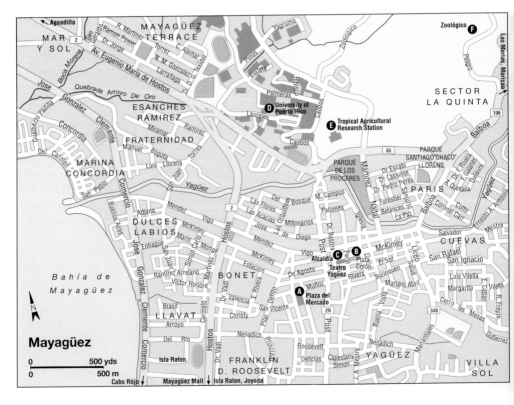 *(see map below)*, a one-time colonial gem, is undergoing a transformation. The third-largest city in Puerto Rico, its port once flourished and its tuna-canning factories provided as many as 8,000 jobs until the mid 1980s. Dolphin-safe tuna-fishing regulations, instituted since the 1990s, reduced the amount of tuna that needed canning, and when Section 936 of the US tax code began to reduce the benefits of running a factory in Puerto Rico, StarKist International and Bumble Bee began to pull out. It has been a devastating blow. Today Bumble Bee retains just a small presence, employing around 600 workers and there is not a whole lot of industry going on to replace the lost jobs.

But Mayagüez has survived devastating blows before. The earthquake of 1918 practically swallowed up the town; a fire took out the imposing Teatro Yaguez in 1919; and then Hurricane San Cipriano almost blew away the city and all the surrounding farms in 1932.

Today the town is benefitting from a multi-million dollar investment program by the central government that will provide much needed infrastructure in time to host a major sporting event: the Central American-Caribbean Games in 2010. An apartment complex is being constructed to provide housing for athletes during the games, which will be sold off after the competition. It is hoped that the development will strengthen the city as a tourism hub and complement the role of Mayagüez's port, home to **Ferries del Caribe**, a passenger ferry that links Puerto Rico to the Dominican Republic.

Juxtaposed among Mayagüez's modern structures are architectural treasures that happily coexist. Wooden homes with gingerbread trim dating back to the

A big attraction in Rincón has nothing to do with the surf: the Horned Dorset Primavera Hotel (see page 266) *here is considered one of the best hotels in the whole of the Caribbean (tel: 823-4030).*

1800s, which somehow survived the disasters, and colonial mansions are part of the mixed up cityscape.

The **Plaza del Mercado** Ⓐ (market square) is one of the most active and traditional around, despite modernization. Once an open-air covered market filled with the sounds of chickens and roosters, it is now positively deluxe, with air conditioning and no more livestock. Although much of the exotic fruits and vegetables come from the Dominican Republic and Costa Rica, you can still buy *productos del país* (local products) such as bananas, plantains and the prized, small, round, yellow Mayagüez mangoes. Mayagüez is also famous for its *brazo gitanos*, a jelly-roll style cake, and the family-made Sangria de Fido.

Ladies of Barcelona

And Mayagüez continues to battle decay valiantly, slowly but surely. The central **Plaza Colón** Ⓑ has been restored. Under the enormous shade trees a large statue commemorates Christopher Columbus. He is surrounded by a court of 16 aristocratic bronze ladies brought from Barcelona. He is also often surrounded by transvestites; Mayagüez is well known for its coterie of exclusive cross-dressers who have made Plaza Colón their weekend evening catwalk for the past 50 years.

Around the plaza, the restored Corinthian **Alcaldía** (town hall) Ⓒ is an experience in filigree. Just opposite, the long-suffering cathedral of **Nuestra Señora de la Candelaria** underwent a multi-million dollar restoration, completed in 2003, which was paid for by generous parishioners who raised funds through extra collections; even the two towers that fell in the 1918 earthquake were finally replaced.

Maps:
City 198
Area 196

UPR's Mayagüez campus is a major engineering recruiting center for NASA and other US Government intelligence and military agencies.

BELOW: sprawling modern Mayagüez.

Making Waves and Watching Whales

Precisely when the northeastern United States gets battered by nasty, winter weather, northwestern Puerto Rico becomes heaven on earth for the Hang Ten set and whale watchers. The cold fronts blowing southeast from Canada may drop unwelcome snow and ice on New England, but those same weather systems push wind toward the Caribbean. That wind ruffles the Atlantic into waves – big waves – that hit the northwest corner of Puerto Rico and produce the Caribbean's best surf.

The first town on the island to become a surf Mecca was Rincón, a pointy peninsula at the very western tip of the island which hosted its first World Amateur Surfing Competition in 1968. This tropical corner of America was rapidly colonized by surfers, who began opening campsites and bunk-bed accommodations for fellow wave seekers.

Rincón has continued evolving into a guesthouse and resort town where surfers are still the main – but not the only – avid repeat guests. Several high-end resorts, including The Horned Dorset Primavera, Puerto Rico's only Relais & Chateaux property, pamper the wealthy, while beach bungalows cater to the proletariat.

Tourists from the north are not the only ones escaping winter in Rincón. Humpback whales are regular visitors January through March, calving and frolicking in the warm waters. While there is at least one tour operator taking whale watchers out on boats to get close to the magnificent mammals, most locals prefer not to disturb the animals and limit themselves to lookout towers along Road 115, afternoon observations with binoculars at the Punta Higuero lighthouse and random sightings along Sandy Beach.

North of Rincón, the towns of Aguadilla and Isabela are following the surf town's lead. They also have superior surf locations and now more enterprising surfers and hoteliers are opening up businesses to service the growing interest in watersports.

Among the best northwestern surf spots are Tres Palmas (the heaviest spot in the Caribbean), Domes (next to a closed nuclear facility and the lighthouse) and Sandy Beach (beginners) in Rincón; Hawaiian-style Table Rock in Aguada; Gas Chambers, Wilderness and Pressure Point in Aguadilla; and world-famous Jobos (heavily territorial), left-breaking Golondrines and Sálsipuedes (which means get out if you can) and not-so-Secret Spot in Isabela. Do lock your car and leave nothing attractive inside; these are often isolated places and break-ins do happen.

And all of the towns are playing up their year-round aquatic attributes: windsurfing and kiteboarding are world-class and attract adventurous Europeans who don't mind very simple amenities. Reefs just offshore create tranquil pools for swimming, snorkeling and diving, perfect for beginners – manatees are frequently spotted – while expert divers can scuba in the underwater karst caves. Although there are evermore upscale hotels and restaurants popping up, Puerto Rico's northwest remains a more rugged destination with rough winding roads and deserted beaches with few, if any, amenities. ❑

Around the corner from the plaza, the historic **Teatro Yaguez** has also been totally restored, as part of a project that was completed in 2004; its colorful dome is a beloved Mayagüez landmark. And the surrounding small businesses – the mom and pop shops of downtown Mayagüez continue to bustle, even with intense shopping mall competition – are taking their cue from the restoration and painting and smartening up their own historic buildings.

Natural sciences

The **University of Puerto Rico Mayagüez ⓓ** campus on Route 108 is an engineering and agricultural powerhouse that draws students from neighboring islands and Latin American countries. The campus is hilly and green and has some notable buildings, as well as a noisy flock of emerald green parrots. The adjoining **Tropical Agricultural Research Station ⓔ** (open Mon–Fri 7am–4pm; free), run by the US Department of Agriculture, offers wonderful grounds for strolling and learning about the many tropical trees and plants brought here from around the world.

Across the street **Parque de los Proceres** (Patriots Park) is a riverside park with walkways and fountains and new gazebos popular with families and early morning walkers. And on the northeastern outskirts of the city is the **Zoológico ⓕ** (open Wed–Sun 8.30am–4pm; entrance and parking fee), the island's premier collection of animals that roam freely in an environment as close to their natural habitat as possible.

The Taíno Indians had numerous settlements in the Mayagüez area. It is no wonder. With the many streams and rivers crisscrossing their way toward the sea, it is a fertile plain. While the years of tuna canning have left Mayagüez bay

Maps:
City 198
Area 196

TIP

While in Mayagüez, try the local gastronomic specialty: traditional *mofongo* stuffed with shrimps. (*See page 79*.)

BELOW: Plaza Colón and the Alcaldía, Mayagüez.
LEFT: humpback whales are seasonal visitors.

The Spanish influence is evident throughout Puerto Rico – even in the little touches.

BELOW: a favorite (and serious) Puerto Rican pastime: dominoes.

in need of a clean-up, nearby **Joyuda**, a strip of seaside restaurants a few miles south of Mayagüez, does have some shoreline suitable for swimming. However, most visitors prefer to limit themselves to a rustic, slap-up seafood meal overlooking tiny **Isla Ratón** (Rat Island).

Head for the hills

Just 5 miles (8 km) south of Mayagüez, inland off Route 2, is the tiny *municipio* of **Hormigueros** ❾. This is a city with the slow pace of the northwest and the layout of a Cordillera town, with narrow winding streets and one of the finests cathedrals on the island. The cathedral of **Our Lady of Montserrat** is at once awesome and unassuming. Bone-white towers of varying dimensions rise to silver domes, topped with austere white crucifixes of wood. Its hilltop position gives the impression that it is soaring into the sky and it makes a very useful landmark for finding your way around. The red brick stairs up to the cathedral are a work-out, but the view from the top is worth it.

Current public works, including brick paving, are making Hormigueros a tiny treasure, certainly worth a stop as you travel between the bigger towns along Route 2.

Heading back toward the coast via Cerrillos you'll reach **Laguna Joyuda** ❿, a mangrove swamp that is a sanctuary for native birds. Mangroves, in addition to being the nursery for all the delicious crustaceans and fish served in the local restaurants, are hotbeds for semi-tropical bird life, and this 300-acre (120 hectare) expanse is one of the most populated. Herons, martins and pelicans, including the lovely maroon pelican, make their home here, and the lagoon itself is full of fish. On moonless nights, it is reputed to be

phosphorescent, due to a concentration of the marine organism dinoflagellate *Pyrodinium bahamense*.

Map, page 196

To the point

Washed by coral-studded Caribbean waters, bathed in dry tropical heat year-round and sculpted into an odd network of cliffs, lagoons, promontories and swamps by fickle surf and tides, the district of **Cabo Rojo ⑪**, to the south, shows Puerto Rico's landscape at its most alluring. Stretching along 18 miles (29 km) of coast from Mayagüez, this region is among the most remote on the island; whether approaching from Ponce or Mayagüez, you notice the landscape becoming drier and more hummocky, the population more sparse and the scenery more beautiful.

But for those to whom the name "Cabo Rojo" has become synonymous with isolated retreats and breathtaking vistas, the town of Cabo Rojo comes as a bit of a disappointment. But it's worth exploring the place to see the sewing factories that are open on to the street, the shoe-repair shops and variety stores that are reminiscent of the 1950s.

The infamous Puerto Rican buccaneer Roberto Cofresí made Cabo Rojo his base during his 19th-century raids on European merchant ships.

A battery of beaches

When it comes to picking a favorite beach along the Cabo Rojo coastline, there are plenty to choose from, but mention **Playa Buyé ⑫** to a Puerto Rican and you are sure to receive a nostalgic sigh for an answer. The houses in tiny Buyé, just southwest of Cabo Rojo town on Route 307, come up close to the water's edge, and there is something magical about its half moon curved beach that inspires love. At the other end is **Puerto Real ⑬**, perhaps the last authentic fishing village in the region. Stroll around for more nameless hidden beaches. The landscape changes with shocking suddenness just south of Buyé, as the cliffs of **Punta Guaniquilla ⑭** give way to the swamps and mangroves of tiny **Laguna Guaniquilla ⑮**.

The cliffs and lagoon are best reached by making the ¾-mile (1-km) walk south out of Buyé or by taking the dirt road that leads out of the tiny settlement of **Boca Prieta**.

BELOW: Playa Boquerón, one of the island's finest beaches.

And more beaches

Just 7 miles (11 km) south of the town of Cabo Rojo on Routes 4 and 101, lies **Boquerón ⑯**, a one-time fishing port turned recreational beach town. It is blessed with a mangrove forest which shelters some of Puerto Rico's loveliest birds – the Laguna Rincón and surrounding forests have been designated a bird sanctuary as one of three parts of the **Boquerón Nature Reserve ⑰**. But what really brings visitors to the town is the 3-mile (5-km) long curving bay whose placid coral-flecked waters and sands backed by a palm grove make **Playa Boquerón ⑱** almost without question the finest beach on the island. In a place like Puerto Rico, where regional rivalries are intense, the fact that even Luquillo residents concede that this beach is the best is significant. However, Boquerón at the weekends is often a frenzied, crowded and noisy place and it is impossible to get into the small town at

BELOW: jetty spans
white sand and
turquoise waters at
El Combate beach.

night because of the wild revelries. To enjoy its wooden shacks, fried snacks and tranquil waters in peace, go on a weekday.

At the end of Route 301, a circuitous 6 miles (10 km) south of Boquerón, **El Combate ⓵** is another remarkable stretch of beach along the Cabo Rojo coastline with few services and a park in the sand ambiance, which provides a perfect setting for concerts and festivals. The salt flats at the dirt-road end of Route 301 give a view into Puerto Rico's past which continues as you hike over the promontory to reach **El Faro de Cabo Rojo**, one of the island's historic lighthouses, which overlooks another of the island's beautiful crescent beaches. **Punta Jagüey ⓶**, a kidney-shaped rock outcrop, supporting the lighthouse, is connected to the land by a narrow isthmus which is flanked by two lovely bays – **Bahia Salínas** and **Bahia Sucia**, also called **La Playuela**.

Herons and eelgrass

Here too is a nature reserve of grand proportions; both the peninsula and the surrounding waters are protected as part of the same Boquerón system that embraces Laguna Rincón. But there is more to Punta Jagüey than herons and eelgrass. **Cabo Rojo Lighthouse** is a breathtaking specimen of Spanish colonial architecture, with a low-lying, pale-sided main building and squat, hexagonal light-tower. It perches atop dun-colored cliffs at the very extremity of the peninsula and commands views of almost 300 degrees of the Caribbean.

The lighthouse is at its most awe-inspiring when given a faint blush of color by either sunrise or sunset. However, it's more likely that you'll see the latter, as many excursions to Cabo Rojo are conceived as day trips and somehow carry on into the evening.

Around the southwest corner

Parguera , on the southern coast, leads a dual life as a quiet coastal town and – on summer nights and weekends – a party town alive with young *sanjuaneros* and thrill-seeking tourists. This is not to say the place is spoiled; it serves the useful function of diverting the crowds from the area's more delicate attractions.

Boats ply the waters between the village and the bay with reassuring frequency. For a few dollars, you'll most likely get an hour in the flying Caribbean spindrift and one of the rare opportunities Puerto Rico affords to make use of a warm sweater. Leaving the docks, cruises run through the yachts and fishing boats of Parguera's poorly sheltered harbor and past a tiny chain of islets whose focus is **Isla Magueyes** ②, home to a large colony of lizards.

As cruise boats enter the bay, their wakes turn an eerie pale green. Captains invite the passengers to trail their hands over the gunwales and into the water to produce odd, remarkable patterns. A bucket is generally brought on board for the curious to play with, and in cupped palms the water breaks into shapes resembling splattering mercury. The phosphorescence is produced by billions of micro-organisms which belong to the family of dinoflagellates known as *Pyrodinium bahamense*. Try to see this unique phenomenon on a cloudy night with a light breeze, when no other light sources muddle the brilliance of the waters, and wavelets make ever-changing patterns on the surface. Unfortunately, in recent years the effect has been reduced owing to pollution.

San Germán

Seeds of colonization in the New World have not always brought culture, but they have generally created overpopulation, and the large cities of the Americas,

Map,
page 196

BELOW: a lively night in Parguera.

with their millions of citizens, were generally in place if only as minor outposts more than a couple of centuries ago. **San Germán** ㉓, with a population of 30,000, is a different sort of locale – it is one of those major 16th-century towns, which has been blessed by never having been too thoroughly dragged into the squalid rat race of the modern world. Although old, it has never grown into a sprawling urban center.

San Germán – Puerto Rico's second-oldest town – is a diamond in an emerald setting, a pearly-white town tucked into an uncharacteristically lush and verdant section inland from the south and west coastlines, about halfway between Ponce and Mayagüez on pretty Route 119.

Founded in 1510 by the second wave of Spanish colonists, San Germán was San Juan's only rival for prominence on the island until the 19th century. Forces invading or retreating from San Juan, notably the English, French and Dutch, often stopped here to arm themselves or lick their wounds. In the 19th century it became one of Puerto Rico's great coffee towns, with magnates building some of the truly unique homes on the island.

Today, San Germán owes its prominence and cultural vibrancy to the Inter-American University, which has 8,000 students and well-tended grounds, and the diligence with which it has preserved some of the earliest European architectural works to survive in the Western hemisphere.

Heaven's gate

The **Porta Coeli Church** (open Wed–Sun 8.30am–noon and 1–4.15pm; free) is San Germán's – and arguably Puerto Rico's – greatest architectural inheritance. Founded in 1606, it is the oldest church under the United States' flag. It is also

TIP

When planning a trip to San Germán, take note that, as it is a university town, it can be difficult to get cheap accommodation in term time.

BELOW: picturesque main street in San Germán.

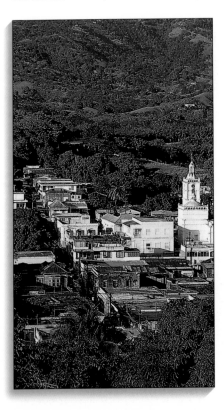

THE ART OF JOSÉ CAMPECHE

It is no surprise that the work of José Campeche adorns San Germán's Porta Coeli, one of Puerto Rico's most architecturally important churches. Many of the island's churches – as well as the cathedral in Old San Juan – feature paintings by Campeche, Puerto Rico's first native painter and its first artistic genius. He was born José de Rivafrecha y Jordán in 1751; his father, Tomás Rivafrecha y Campeche, was a black freeman and his mother, María Jordán y Márques, was a Spaniard from the Canary Islands. Campeche, like his brothers, learned about art and painting through Tomás, who was a master gilder and carver, a painter and an ornamentalist.

But José excelled at more than art: he was also a professional musician, sculptor, surveyor and decorator, and an architect. Well-educated and a devoted Catholic, he was considered a gentleman. He was fortunate to live after Puerto Rico's towns and cities were established: before that, not much emphasis had been given to the arts. Through his approximately 400 paintings of religious themes and historical events, and portraits of politicians and local landed gentry, he gained a reputation as "the most gifted of Latin American rococo artists." Campeche died in 1809 and is buried in San Juan Cathedral.

one of only a few buildings in the New World constructed in the Gothic architectural style. It is one of the great glories of Spanish colonization that the conquest came about early enough to ensure that this neo-medieval style, which peppers all the countries of Europe with some of the greatest monuments to man's artistry, could also flourish in the New World.

Map, page 196

Porta coeli means "heaven's gate" and, indeed, the church portals are of great importance to its artistry. A squat little whitewashed building standing at the top of a broad, spreading stairway of scrabbly brick and mortar, its large doors are of beautiful *ausubo*, a once-common Puerto Rican hardwood.

Inside, the pews and altar are all original, with embellishments. The altarpiece was painted by the first great Puerto Rican artist, José Campeche (*see panel opposite*), in the late 18th century, a fact that would indicate the church was fairly well established as a historical landmark even by then. Today the church is a small religious museum containing some ancient *santos*. (*See page 83.*) Porta Coeli overlooks one of the most beautifully landscaped plazas in Puerto Rico, with terraced benches and beautifully groomed trees.

One of the many santos displayed in the Porta Coeli Church, now a museum.

Name that church

San Germán, like Ponce, is a two-plaza town, and its second, the **Plaza Francisco Mariano Quiñones**, is no less impressive than that overlooked by Porta Coeli, with the same lovely walks, period lamplights and marvelous topiary. But it also has a church to rival Porta Coeli in appeal, if not in age. The church of **San Germán de Auxerre** commemorates the French saint who is the town's patron. Its steeple does not face the plaza directly but has its façade on a nearby side street. While less important than much of San Germán in historical terms, it dominates the town, and is particularly impressive when viewed from the surrounding hills on a bright and sunny day.

BELOW: the second of San Germán's pretty plazas: Mariano Quiñones.

Ancient homes

San Germán's oldest attractions – the two churches, in particular – have always captured the attention of visitors, but there is much more: 249 noteworthy sites, to be exact. (San Germán is one of only two Puerto Rican cities – the other is San Juan – to be included in the National Register of Historic Places.) But few have stopped to examine the general layout and ambiance of this ancient town with the rigor and delight that tourists have always brought to San Juan and Ponce. Marvelous haciendas of the late 19th-century coffee barons are abundant, and demonstrate a style which, while it can be seen throughout the southwest – in Yauco, for example – is as much San Germán's own as Porta Coeli.

These houses must be entered to be appreciated, as much of their charm lies in the way in which the interior spaces are divided. Beautiful *mediopunto* carvings – delicate lacy half-screens of snaking wood – create conceptual divisions between rooms without actually putting up substantial physical barriers. Some of them are astounding harbingers of art nouveau, as are the simple and sinuous stencilings which grace the walls of many of the houses.   ❏

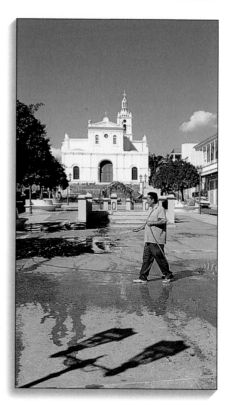

PUERTO RICO'S FANTASTIC FLORA

One would expect luxuriant flora on a tropical island, but Puerto Rico's exceeds all expectations, and much of it is protected in forest reserves

Everything grows in Puerto Rico – and in abundance. This lush, green island produces a vast array of flora which ranges from myriad varieties of orchid to a cornucopia of trees, many of them bearing fruit.

Puerto Rico's flora is as colorful as the many other aspects of the country. Visitors will at once notice the exotic splashes of bougainvillea that adorn homes, businesses and even bridges. Gardenias and jasmine fill the air with their fragrance, while pink oleander and red hibiscus dot the countryside and towns. Bamboo, mahogany and *Lignum vitae*, the hardest wood in the world, are cultivated for local use as well as export.

The 200-acre (80-hectare) Botanical Gardens in Río Piedras *(see page 147)* is a particularly good place to see much of the island's tropical plantlife in one location. Along similar lines, the Tropical Agricultural Research Station in Mayagüez *(see page 201)* has one of the largest collections of tropical and semi-tropical plants in the world.

Although various hurricanes have taken their toll, Puerto Rico also provides ample locales to explore the island's flora in its natural state, including the Caribbean National Forest – better known as El Yunque *(see pages 157–60)*. There are also well-kept hiking trails in the Guánica Forest Reserve, which is known for its birdlife as well as for its endangered plant species. Puerto Rico's wild karst country *(see pages 183–4)* can also be discovered via the trails running through that area's four national forests.

(see page 147), (see page 201), (see pages 157–60), (see pages 183–4)

▷ **DELICATE BLOOMS**
The Caribbean National Forest (El Yunque) is home to 240 species of tropical trees, flowers and wildlife, including more than 20 kinds of orchid.

▷ **LUSH RAINFOREST**
More than 100 billion gallons of rain falls annually in El Yunque, creating an environment in which bromeliads, palms and ferns like these thrive.

△ **LOCAL EXOTICA**
The island's beautiful flora isn't limited to reserves – in nearly every garden and around every corner are brilliant tropical blossoms.

FRUITS OF A FERTILE LAND

It would probably come as no surprise to a Puerto Rican if a planted toothpick took root, so fertile is the soil. Fruit-bearing trees are a prime example: oranges, limes, mangos, papaya and guava grow wild on the island, although many fruits – and vegetables – are also cultivated. The country's most unusual fruit has to be the weird, head-sized breadfruit, which islanders prepare in a number of ways, but most commonly as *tostones* – fried green breadfruit slices – that accompany many main courses. More familiar to visitors is the banana, which grows in abundance here, alongside its close relative, the plantain, which cannot be eaten raw. You'll see plantains on menus everywhere, most commonly in the form of appetizer *tostones* or fried up in *mofongo*, a particular island favorite.

△ **TOP GARDENS**
The University of Puerto Rico's Botanical Gardens at Río Piedras are considered to be one of the best in the Caribbean.

◁ **FLAMING BEAUTY**
Bright red blossoms of the flamboyant tree, or poinciana, light up the Puerto Rican countryside in June and July.

▷ **DRY FOREST FLORA**
Guánica Forest, west of Ponce, is a dry and dusty region unexpectedly brimming with beauty. Some 750 plant and tree species grow here – 48 of them endangered and 16 indigenous.

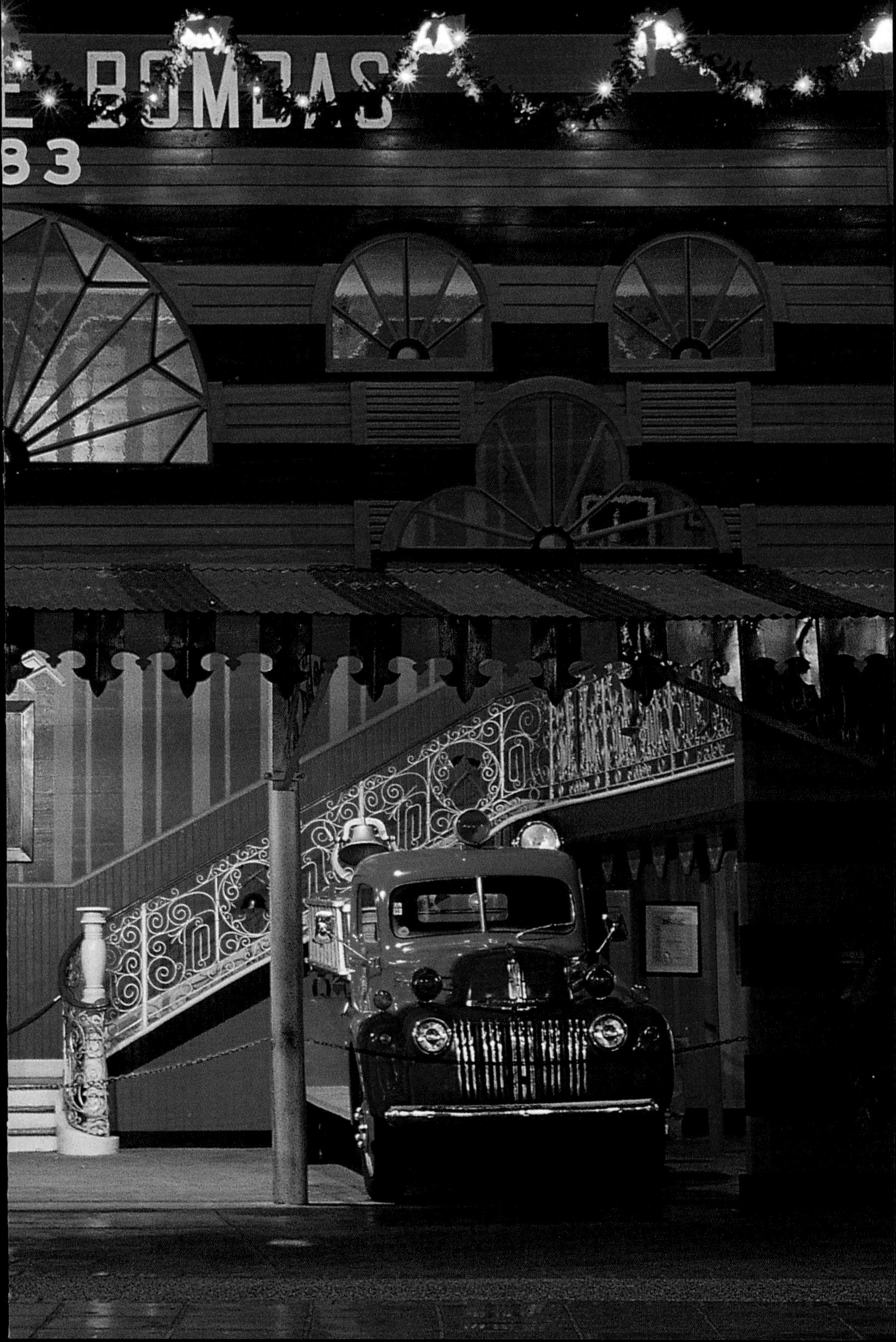
E BOMBAS
83

THE SOUTH

Salinas is known for its fish restaurants, Coamo for its springs, and Ponce is rich in history. Guayanilla is a good base point and birdwatchers and snorkelers head for the Guánica Forest Reserve

Map, page 215

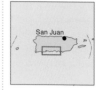

San Juan

The completion of Expreso Las Américas or the Autopista Luis A. Ferré between San Juan and Ponce in 1975 created a bridge between the traditionally separated north and south of the island. The toll road, which winds through mountains and valleys, is low on development and high on scenery. As you cross into the south and descend from the central mountain range, you'll discover more arid, sweeping vistas that recall South Africa more than the Caribbean opening out before you.

This bridge may bring many more visitors from the metropolitan area, but it hasn't changed the locals much. The *ponceños*, the inhabitants of the south coast's largest city, are still as proud as ever of their charming, marble-lined streets and their intimate city center that harks back to a more gracious age.

And the farmers and fishermen in the outlying areas have equal pride in the landscape. Here you will find the remains of a once-flourishing sugar-cane industry. The now quiet *centrales* (cane processing plants) are surrounded by the wood and glass homes of the American managers who lived there and by the smaller homes of the laborers whose descendants still paint and plant.

Eastern allure

Salinas ❶ is a lip-smacking destination, famed across the island for its seafood restaurants, which can be found tucked behind a beautiful bay edged with mangroves. This small town, crisscrossed by narrow roads, is considered the birthplace of *mojo isleo*, the sautéed onion, pepper and tomato sauce that all Puerto Ricans love to smear on their fish.

Salinas is also home to the **Albergue Olímpico Germán Rieckehoff** (Olympic Training Center; open daily 6am–10pm; entrance fee) where so many of Puerto Rico's world-class athletes come to train before international events. Automotive sports are also big in this area and the **Puerto Rico International Speedway** on Route 3, Km 155.2, is one of the largest (open Wed 5pm–12am, Sat 4pm–12am, some Sundays).

South of Salinas is **Aguirre**, the site of a former sugar mill where many of the old buildings still stand. A nine-hole public golf course, built here in 1926, is claimed to be the oldest one on the island (tel: 853-4052). Aguirre is framed by the **Jobos Bay Estuarine Reserve** (Visitor Center on Road 705 open Mon–Fri 7.30am–4pm, Sat–Sun 9am–3pm, closed for lunch; entrance fee; calling ahead is recommended, tel: 853-4617), a research site encompassing mangrove forests, a series of cays and salt flats, where you can rent a kayak, birdwatch and hike.

Driving around the area, you will come across seafood kiosks such as La Casa del Pastelillo, a water-

PRECEDING PAGES: Ponce's celebrated Parque de Bombas. **LEFT:** Salinas Beach. **BELOW:** Puerto Ricans have practiced hammock-weaving for many centuries.

front deck with hammocks and seafood-stuffed pastries of every description. If you see an inviting beach, ask around first before stopping for a dip, as some parts along here have dangerous currents.

Bathing beauty

Moving westward across the mountains from Aibonito *(see page 236)* further inland, Road 14 goes directly to **Coamo ❷**. Its thermal springs – known to the Taíno Indians, who considered them sacred – were discovered by the Spanish in 1571 and the city itself was founded in 1579, making it one of the oldest cities in Puerto Rico. Some say that the springs are the Fountain of Youth that Ponce de León was looking so hard for. In the early part of the 20th century, the springs (located at the end of Road 546) grew into a major Caribbean resort and attracted an international clientele. After World War II, however, the resort fell into decay.

Today, a new resort stands on the ruins of the old one and once again visitors join locals in taking to the waters at the pool, staying at the atmospheric Parador Baños de Coamo whose foundations date from 1848 *(see page 266)*. Top international runners flock to the town in early February to take part in the San Blás Half Marathon. There is an adjacent golf course, Coamo Springs, which could be developed in the future to include a condo-hotel on the site as well.

In the **Museo de Coamo** (call 825-1150 ext. 206 for opening times) on José Quinto Street, several rooms are furnished with antiques to re-create a typical (and prosperous) 19th-century household.

Continuing west you reach the town officially called **Juana Díaz ❸**, but also known as *La Ciudad del Río Jacaguas* (City of Jacaguas River), *La Ciudad del Poeta* (City of the Poet – Luis Llorens Torres) and Ciudad del Maví (City

TIP

While in Salinas, kids will probably enjoy spending some time at the Albergue Olímpico Germán Rieckehoff, the Puerto Rican Olympic athletes' training facilities. Attractions here include a mini-mall, a botanical garden, the Puerto Rican Museum of Sports, a water park, and a playground (tel: 824-2607).

BELOW: side-stepping on one of Puerto Rico's fine *pasofino* horses.

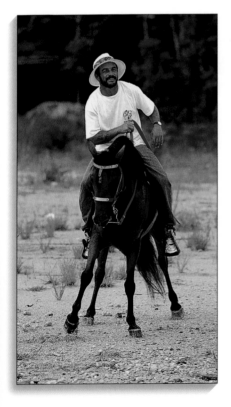

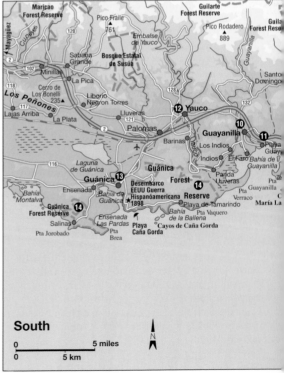

South

0 _____ 5 miles

0 _____ 5 km

of Maví, a fermented bark drink). Quiet for most of the year, Juana Díaz comes to life on the Feast of the Epiphany or Three Kings Day on January 6, when an enormous street festival celebrates the African, Taíno and European roots of modern-day Puerto Rico.

Maps:
City 216
Area 215

Ponce and its environs

The honors for most fabulous city in Puerto Rico is a theme that *sanjuaneros* and *ponceños* have fierce and passionate arguments about. But even the *capitalinos* from the northern coast admit to what *ponceños* proudly claim as the sobriquet of their city. That **Ponce ❹** is indeed *"La Perla del Sur"* or "The Pearl of the South."

Perhaps the most surprising thing is that Ponce, Puerto Rico's second-largest city, actually *is* a pearl of sorts. Though not so distant in the imagination of travelers as Mayagüez, it's still far enough away from the San Juan/Dorado/Palmas del Mar circuit to seem to belong to another place entirely.

However, Ponce is an easy 90-minute drive from San Juan – take Expressway 52 from San Juan all the way there – and so there's very little excuse for not heading south to see what all these southerners are bragging about.

Bloody big business: cock-fighting, while distasteful to many, is a popular sport in Puerto Rico, particularly in Salinas.

Hot stuff

To begin with, Ponce has the best weather on the island. It's located in what ecologists call a "rain shadow"; the afternoon storms which beleaguer the north coast are stopped dead by the peaks of the Cordillera Central. You can see the rain from Ponce – it's in those purple clouds pulsing above the hills 10 miles (16 km) north – but you're not going to feel any of it.

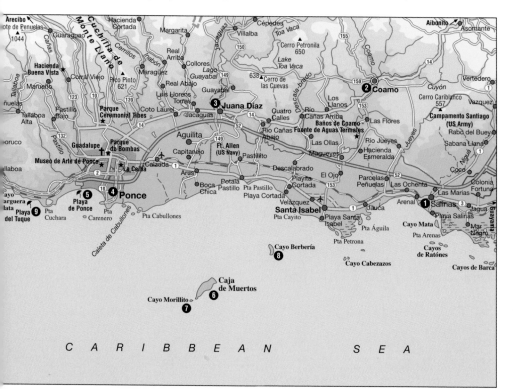

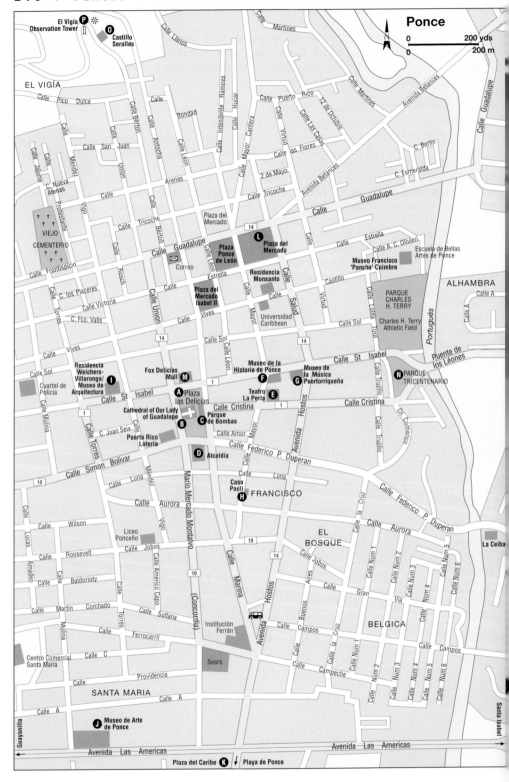

Ponce

0   200 yds
0   200 m

El Vigía **P** ☼
Observation Tower
O Castillo
Serralles

EL VIGÍA

Calle Pico Dulce

Calle Bertoli

Calle San Juan

Calle Antocha

Calle León

Calle Mayor Cantera

Calle Intendente Ramírez

Calle Huicar

Calle Martínes

Calle Llanos

Calle Puerto Rico

Calle Virtud

Calle Las Casas

12 de Octubre

Calle Martínes

Avenida Betances

Avenida Betances

Calle Guadalupe

C. Berlín

C. Esmeralda

Bondad

Calle Méndez

Calle Jalome

C. Nueva
Atenas

Vigo Protestante

Calle

Calle

Arenas

2 de Mayo

Calle Tricoche

Calle las Flores

VIEJO
CEMENTERIO

Calle Frontispicio

Calle Tricoche

Calle Bertoli

Calle Guadalupe

Calle León

Plaza del
Mercado

14

L

Plaza del
Mercado

Estrella

Calle A. C. Olivieri

Museo Francisco
'Pancho' Coimbre

Escuela de Bellas
Artes de Ponce

ALHAMBRA

Calle A

Correo

Plaza
Ponce
de León

Calle Ios Placeres

Calle Victoria

C. Fco. Valls

Calle Torres

Calle Rosch

Calle Union

Estrella

Plaza del
Mercado
Isabel II

Residencia
Monsanto

Calle Salud

Calle Castillo

Calle Virtud

Calle Lolita Tizol

Calle Portugués

PARQUE
CHARLES
H. TERRY

Charles H. Terry
Athletic Field

Calle A

Puente de
los Léones

Vives

Universidad
Caribbean

Calle Sol

Calle Vives

Calle Sol

Calle Sol

Calle León

Calle Sol

14

Calle St   Isabel

Museo de la
Historia de Ponce

F

Museo de
la Música
Puertorriqueña

G

N PARQUE
TRICENTENARIO

Calle Trujillo

Cn. Comercia

Residencia
Weichers-
Villaronga/
Museo de
Arquitectura

I

Fox Delicias
Mall

M

A Plaza
las Delicias

Teatro
La Perla

E

Cuartel de
Policía

Calle Sol

Calle St   Isabel

Cathedral of Our Lady
of Guadalupe

B

Parque
de Bombas

C

Calle Cristina

Hostos

Calle Cristina

Calle Molina

Calle Torres

C. Juan Seix

Puerto Rico
Lotería

Calle Amor

D Alcaldía

Calle Federico P. Duperan

Avenida

Calle Federico P. Duperan

La Ceiba

Calle Simón Bolívar

10

Méndez

Calle Luna

Calle Luna

Casa
Paoli

H

FRANCISCO

Calle la Cruz

Calle Aurora

Calle Aurora

10

Calle Wilson

Calle Vigo

Mario Mercado Montalvo

Calle Marina

Calle

(Concordia)

EL
BOSQUE

Calle Jobos

Liceo
Ponceño

Calle Jobos

14

Calle Aires

Calle Gran

Calle Via

Calle Num 1

Calle Num 2

Calle Num 3

Calle Num 4

Calle Num 5

Calle Num 6

Calle Roosevelt

Calle Lucas

Calle Amadeo

Calle Baldorioty

Calle Americo Capo

Calle Sultana

10

Hostos

Calle Buenos

Calle Campos

BELGICA

Calle Martín Corchado

Molina

Calle

Calle Torres

Calle Ferrocarril

Institución
Ferrán

Calle Campos

Calle la Cruz

Calle Campeche

Calle Num 2

Calle Num 3

Calle Num 4

Calle Num 5

Calle Num 6

Calle Campos

Centro Comercial
Santa María

Calle C

Calle Providencia

Sears

SANTA MARIA

Calle A

Calle Á

Guayanilla

J Museo de Arte
de Ponce

Avenida   Las   Américas

Avenida   Las   Américas

Santa Isabel

Plaza del Caribe **K** ↓ / Playa de Ponce

Maps:
City 216
Area 215

The landscape surrounding the city is a typical southwestern palette of tumbling grasslands, parched to gold by the Caribbean sun, against purple and lavender skies. This is no Atlantic coast – although a place as far south as Ponce can take on that ocean's hostile cobalt aspect – as a look from the hills above the town will demonstrate. Especially from El Vigía (*see page 221*), the view across Ponce shows the coral and white of the town's stately houses, the turquoise waters of its Caribbean harbor and the stripes of green mangrove and travertine coral formations of the archipelago surrounding the isle of Caja de Muertos.

The inland port

Ponce proper – and if there's a proper city in Puerto Rico, it's Ponce – is perhaps the archetype of a strangely Puerto Rican sort of city: a bustling port with an enviable natural harbor which has nonetheless developed around a city center some distance inland. A left turn off the *autopista* will take you, not to the center of a busy waterfront town, but to the interesting outpost at **Playa de Ponce 5** – a collection of old brick warehouses and more modern storage areas – and the wharf at **Muelle de Ponce**. On evenings and weekends, **La Guancha Board Walk** is a popular gathering place, where there are plenty of seafood restaurants, shops, an open-air stage and a massive playground.

To get into the heart of Ponce, continue in a northwesterly direction on Road 133 as it passes over the sluggish Río Portugues and becomes **Calle F.P. Duperan**, the main commercial street, also known as Calle Comercio. If you are coming from San Juan, leave the *autopista* at the Ponce/Road 1 exit and head into the historical district, which has earned Ponce the epithet Museum City (*see page 222*), where you can take advantage of the trolley system.

"Ponce is one of the oldest towns on the island... It is located on a big plain covered with trees... 115 houses form an irregular square. The parish church [Guadalupe], which is small and deteriorated, is on one side; 5,038 souls live here."

– HISTORIAN IÑIGO ABBAD Y LASIERRA, 1784

BELOW: view of Ponce from El Vigía.

Here, you'll see the results of the $450-million "Ponce en Marcha" program, begun in 1986 by former Puerto Rican Governor Rafael Hernández Colón, himself a *ponceño*. The massive beautification effort resulted in the burying of unsightly phone and electric cables, the repaving of streets, and the renovation of nearly every structure in the downtown district. Hernández Colón is no longer governor, and the program has recently run out of money, but its astounding success was enough to turn Ponce into one of the Caribbean's most beautiful cities. Its image was further boosted in 1993 when Ponce hosted the 17th Central American and Caribbean Games.

There is a continual raging academic controversy about how Ponce (pronounced Pon-tsé) got its name – some say it's from the first governor of the island, Ponce de León; others argue that it was taken from his great-grandson.

A square deal

At the end of Calle Duperan is the cluster of architectural beauties which gives Ponce its reputation as being one of the most Spanish of Puerto Rican cities. Here the magnificent **Plaza las Delicias Ⓐ**, lush and beautifully landscaped, sits pounded by sunlight amid a pinwheel of centuries-old streets. Huge fig trees stand in lozenge-shaped topiary, and large, shady islands of grass are punctuated by dramatic fountains. Broad paths of rose-colored granite weave through the squares, bordered by slender old lamp-posts which make the plaza both attractive and accessible in the evening.

Plaza las Delicias is dominated by the cathedral of **Our Lady of Guadalupe Ⓑ** (open daily with limited hours so call first, tel: 842-0134) named for the patron saint of Ponce. It's a pretty, low, pinkish structure, reminiscent in its colors and rounded turrets of San Juan Cathedral. Though not as old as San Juan's, having been begun in the late 17th century, Ponce's cathedral makes ample use of the reflected sunlight from the plaza. Its silvery twin towers – a

BELOW: the ornate Casa Armstrong-Poventud.

FANTASY FIRE STATION

What must be the oddest – and certainly most whimsical – fire station ever built, Ponce's Parque de Bombas was originally erected as an exhibit for the 1882 Trade Fair. It was one of two structures built in Arabic architectural style for the fair; the other, known as the Quiosco Arabe, was destroyed in 1914, although a glassed-in scale model of it can be viewed in the Industry Room at the Museo de la Historia de Ponce. The Parque de Bombas was put into use as a fire station the year after the fair, and it remained the headquarters of the Ponce Fire Corps for over a century, until 1989. The following year the remarkable red-and-black wooden structure was restored and reopened as a museum featuring fire-department memorabilia. The old fire-fighting equipment on display includes antique fire trucks and hand-pulled tanks, which needed the movement of rushing to the scene of a fire to build up the pressure. The exhibits in the upstairs museum also detail fire-fighting techniques of the late 19th century and provide interesting information on the Great Fire of 1906. With its playful collection of poles, sideboards, crenellations and cornices, the Parque de Bombas is a gaudy and riotous building with a playful, truly *ponceño* spirit – and has come to symbolize Ponce itself.

characteristically Puerto Rican touch in religious architecture – are shaped like little hydrants, and glow oddly at midday. This gives the building a bright and inviting look, against which the eerie stillness of its lofty interior creates a shocking contrast.

A museum tour

Our Lady of Guadalupe may hold the religious high ground, but the fancy-looking red-and-black striped building behind it cuts more ice with the tourist crowd. This is the **Parque de Bombas** ❻ (open daily 10am–6pm; closed Tues; free), Ponce's unmissable Victorian fire station and perhaps the most photographed building in all of Puerto Rico (*see panel opposite*). The **Alcaldía** ❶, diagonally across the plaza from the two buildings, has a pleasant hacienda feel to it and contrasts in a lively way with its two more renowned neighbors. Across from the fire station, King Cream ice-cream shop sells some of the island's best homemade ice cream. Delicious flavors to try are coconut, mango or almond.

About a block away from the cathedral, at the corner of *calles* Cristina and Mayor, is the stately **Teatro La Perla** ❸, where plays are performed by local theater companies. On occasion, productions shown in San Juan go on the road to Ponce. Built in 1864 but partially destroyed in the 1918 earthquake, it is also the home of Ponce's annual Luis Torres Nadal Theater Festival.

Around the corner on Calle Isabel, history comes to life at the **Museo de la Historia de Ponce** ❺ (open weekdays 10am–5pm, Sat 10am–8.30pm, Sun 11.30am–7pm; closed Tues; tel: 844-7071). A fascinating feature outside is a 1,500-lb (680-kg) marble bathtub, built by Samuel B. Morse, inventor of the telegraph. (*See page 170.*) The museum was inaugurated on December 12, 1992 – Ponce's 300th anniversary – and is considered Puerto Rico's best civic museum. Two hours here and you'll emerge an expert on all aspects of Ponce's history: economic, political, racial, medical, educational and industrial. This is also the starting point for a walking (or trolley) tour of the historical area. (*See page 222.*)

Close by on the corner of *calles* Isabel and Salud is the **Museo de la Música Puertorriqueña** ❻ (open Wed–Sun 9am–4.30pm; entrance fee), where you can see the instruments and history of the island's music, which has evolved from African, European and native traditions, and watch videos of it in action.

On Calle Mayor, at No. 14, **Casa Paoli** ❶ (open Wed–Fri 2–5pm, Sat 11am–3pm closed Sun; tel: 840-4115) is the home of the renowned tenor Antonio Paoli (1871–1946) heralded as the 'King of Tenors' in the early 1900s in competition with Enrico Caruso.

About four blocks westward from the History Museum stands the pink confection of the **Residencia Weichers-Villaronga/Museo de Arquitectura de Ponce** ❶ (open Wed–Sun 9am–4.30pm; free). This beautiful home was built by the architect Alfredo Weichers for himself in 1912 and illustrates life at around that time when Ponce was in its heyday.

The jewel in the city's crown is the **Museo de Arte de Ponce** ❶ (open daily 10am–5pm; entrance fee; guided tours in English and Spanish; tel: 848-0505) further south in Avenida Las Américas, across from

An island license plate: públicos – the cars and minibuses providing low-cost public transport – have the letters "P" or "PD" following the numbers.

BELOW: Ponce Cathedral.

Maps:
City 216
Area 215

The El Vigía Observation Tower, or Cruz del Vigía (Virgin's Cross), is a 100-ft (30-meter) structure with lateral arms measuring 70 ft (21 meters) long.

BELOW: Plaza del Mercado, full of many surprises.

the Catholic University. Mostly dedicated to Western art, with contemporary and classical works, the museum houses more than 1,000 paintings and 400 sculptures and has three gardens. The Italian Baroque School and 19th-century pre-Raphaelite paintings are among its greatest strengths. However, Lord Frederick Leighton's *Flaming June* (1894) is its most treasured work of art, which has become iconic on the island, inspiring local theater and dance performers.

Shopping experiences

Continuing south on the road to Playa de Ponce, shopaholics may wish to experience Ponce's **Plaza del Caribe Ⓚ**, a vast shopping center rivalling San Juan's Plaza Las Américas, where you can purchase anything from a Sony TV to a $1,000 frock. Children especially love its full-scale carousel. The more traditional shopper may prefer the buzz of the finest market in town, in the **Plaza del Mercado Ⓛ**, which spreads across several blocks north of the Plaza las Delicias. Here, merchants haggle with customers over anything that can be worn, ogled or eaten, in an ambiance as charged with excitement as any market in San Juan. Back opposite the Plaza las Delicias, the **Fox Delicias Mall Ⓜ**, is a shopping mall which was a functioning movie theater from 1931 to 1980.

There are plenty of peaceful perambulations to be made around Plaza las Delicias. **Calle Cristina** and **Calle Mayor** are particularly renowned for the wrought-iron grilles and balcony work which evoke in Ponce, as in San Juan, the spirit of European cities. Even the highly commercialized Calle Duperan has a number of quaint shops and a shady marketplace. Also worth a visit is the **Parque Tricentenario Ⓝ** and the Puente de los Léones, called the Lion Bridge because of its twin lions, at the eastern end of Calle Isabel.

The people and the city

Ponceños have always been a breed apart from other Puerto Ricans. Their insularity and haughtiness are legendary, and some Puerto Ricans claim that even the dialect here differs slightly from that spoken on the rest of the island. They're also racially different: you'll see more people of African descent here than anywhere else on the island save Loíza Aldea, because Ponce's prominence as a port antedates slavery. As a result, a great deal of African and other regional customs live on in the city. Every February, at the Festival of Our Lady of Guadalupe, *ponceños* parade around the city in weird, spiked horror-masks made of local gourds. The tradition actually derives from medieval Spain, but it's unquestionable that such a transoceanic transplant required a soil as culturally fertile as Ponce's in which to take root.

A walk on the nice side

There's no better way to take in all the beauty and diversity of this city than to stroll north of Plaza las Delicias for several hundred yards to **El Vigía**. This hilly neighborhood is so beloved of the *ponceños* that you'll surely be directed to the place if you show the slightest interest in the city. From the winding road to the top you can see the mansions of Ponce's great families, the roofs of its 17th- and 18th-century townhouses and the turquoise glint of the Caribbean below, which does more than any questions of demography, government or economics to shape the daily lives of the proud inhabitants. The most important of these mansions is the magnificent **Castillo Serralles O** (open Tues–Sun 9.30am–5.30pm; entrance fee), located right next to the huge, 100-ft (30-meter) high cross-shaped **El Vigía Observation Tower P**.

Maps:
City 216
Area 215

In March every year, the largest artisans' fair on the south coast is held in Ponce. In addition to some wonderful handiwork, this regional craft fair features folklore shows, plentiful Puerto Rican food and a children's folk-music contest.

LEFT:
Castillo Serrallés.
BELOW: a shopper's delight, the Fox Delicias Mall.

A Museum City

Ponce is not only filled with museums. The town itself is a museum. While the city center bustles with real people going about their real business, it is also a living museum of unusual architecture that has been well preserved and, these days, celebrated on a national scale.

This town, established in the late 1600s, was first populated by Spanish farmers and ranchers. Spanish policies of encouraging immigration to boost coffee and sugar-cane production in the 1800s brought adventurers from Spain, particularly Catalunya. As *ponceños* became more wealthy, they began to visit Europe bringing back architectural trends that they applied to their own homes. The result is an almost whimsical blend of neoclassical, Spanish revival, creole and even Moorish styles that change from house to house and block to block.

It is such a wonder that the US National Endowment for the Humanities and Puerto Rican Foundations for the Humanities have designated 45 sites singled out for their architectural beauty and historical importance. Of course you can just wander around on your own, but with a deposit of $20, you can borrow a guidebook for two days to take you through the historical and architectural importance of the city in English and Spanish. The book is available from the Museo de la Historia de Ponce, the first stop on the museum trail. (*See page 219.*)

From there, you can walk or take the free trolleys that leave from Plaza las Delicias. The first stops on the plaza are the Parque de Bombas (*see* Fantasy Fire Station, *page 218*) and the Cathedral of Our Lady of Guadalupe. The neoclassical Museo de la Música Puertorriqueña, which has some magnificent stained-glass panels, is next. You can see Catalan-styled furniture and curious bathroom fixtures at the Residencia Weichers-Villaronga and the precious Moorish-style Dog Plaza (Plaza Ponce de León). Even the home of renowned tenor Antonio Paoli is now a cherished museum.

Further away from the center, but no less important to Ponce or to the Caribbean, is the Museo de Arte de Ponce. Established in 1959 with just 71 paintings, it was the brainchild of *ponceño* founder of the pro-statehood New Progressive Party and former governor Luis A. Ferré who wanted to broaden the understanding of the arts in Puerto Rico and who, in 2003 aged 99, was still one of the island's most vigorous supporters of the arts. Now located in a long, low-slung building designed by American architect Edward Durrell Stone (designer of New York's Museum of Modern Art), the museum holds more than 1,800 registered works in its spacious galleries.

As well as Lord Leighton's *Flaming June*, you can see 14th-century pieces by Luca di Tomm, Leandro Rossano's 16th-century masterpiece *The Flood*, paintings from the Spanish, Flemish, Italian and Dutch schools and gorgeous canvases by Sir Edward Burne-Jones. ❑

Castillo Serralles was formerly the home of Don Juan Serrallés, whose family became rich and powerful during the rum- and sugar-boom years of the early 20th century. The castle itself was designed by architect Don Pedro Adolfo de Castroy Besosa in the Spanish revival style popular throughout the 1930s. The Serrallés family moved in around 1934 and stayed until 1979. In 1986, the city of Ponce bought it from the estate for $500,000 – an unbelievable bargain – and spent the next three years restoring it in painstaking detail.

Among the castle's highlights are a formal dining room with the table set for 12; a vestibule decorated with furniture of the era; an 1865 rum-distilling unit in the central interior patio; and an octagonal fountain with tiles imported from Spain. Even the kitchen is preserved with its original stove and refrigerator made of metal and porcelain. An upstairs terrace offers a spectacular view of Ponce and the Caribbean.

Just outside Ponce are two other interesting sites. The **Tibes Indian Ceremonial Park** (open Tues–Sun 9am–4pm; free) is the first; it is a 15- to 20-minute drive north of the city. An archeological treasure, it features rectangular ballcourts and ceremonial plazas dating from AD 300 to AD 700. The second is **Hacienda Buena Vista** (open Fri–Sun, by reservation; tel: 722-5882; entrance fee), about 7 miles (11 km) north of Ponce on Road 10. This is a restored coffee and corn plantation from the late 19th century, complete with working original machinery, that details every step in the coffee-harvesting process.

Southern isles

It's almost true that it never rains in Ponce, but at times the weather on Puerto Rico's sun-bombarded south coast can get so hot and steamy that you wish that some of those clouds would make it over the Cordillera Central. Fortunately, however, the environs of Ponce offer strategies for cooling off as diverse as they are effective. Nautical enthusiasts head their boats into the breezy waters for a trip to the fascinating rock archipelago that is located 8 miles (13 km) south. You'll need to know someone with a boat, or else find one to charter, in order to get there. Try Ponce Yacht and Fishing Club. *(See page 275.)*

This string of Caribbean islets centers around **Caja de Muertos** (Dead Men's Coffin) ❻. Largest of the islets at 2 miles (3 km) long and 1 mile (1½ km) wide, Caja de Muertos is as popular with birdwatchers and botanists as it is with sailors. This being one of Puerto Rico's driest regions, the majority of Caja de Muertos' flora resembles that of the Guánica Forest Reserve. (*See page 226.*) Some of the more prevalent plant species are certain herbs, some dwarf forests of white mangrove, and loads of bindweed.

Four of the plant species on Caja de Muertos are extinct on the Puerto Rican mainland and classified as endangered. This is also a haven for endangered reptiles; iguanas and wall-lizards abound, and two species of Culebra lizard live here.

In different cays

Caja de Muertos is only one of the three islets that make up the **Caja de Muertos Nature Reserve**. The

Map, page 215

TIP

Although ferries no longer run to Caja de Muertos, Island Ventures offers private daytrips by appointment. Call 842-8546.

LEFT: one of many treasures at the Museo de Arte de Ponce.
BELOW: tying the knot – Puerto Rican style.

others, though far smaller, are no less enticing. **Cayo Morillito ❼**, just a few hundred yards across flat sea, is the smallest, with only a few acres of territory, but is home to more endangered birds than the other two combined. Among these is a variety of gulls, pelicans and sea eagles.

Cayo Berbería ❽, which is the closest of the cays to the mainland at 3 miles (5 km), is blessed with a fauna no less extensive and no less idiosyncratic. Most of the fish – many of them endangered species – for which the southern isles are famous, populate the waters around its shores, and consequently some of them put in an appearance on the menus of the south coast's seafood restaurants.

Guayanilla and Guánica

Some beautiful architectural touches grace the homes of the inhabitants of Yauco.

Though the charms of the rippling, brown-green, semi-arid landscapes of Puerto Rico's southwest are well known to those who love the island, few travelers get this far. Its towns are small, but surrounded by natural preserves that UNESCO has recognized as World Heritage sites.

Road 2 moves westward out of Ponce and hugs the shore for about 2 miles (3 km). It meets the coast of popular **Playa del Tuque ❾** where there is now an enormous water park operating in the summer and an auto racetrack complex that includes excellent and economical family accommodations, just 3 miles (5 km) outside the city. Continue westward and you will find **Balneario Las Cucharas**, a tiny bathing beach more notable for the excellent seafood restaurants that overlook the bay.

BELOW: Yauco, once the "coffee capital."

Another 6 miles (9 km) on is the **Guayanilla ❿** exit. This pretty town was founded in 1833, but its history goes back to one of the Taínos' most important *caciques*, Agüeybana. A mile away, at the mouth of the Río Guayanilla is the

desolate and hushed fishing port at **Playa de Guayanilla** ⓫. And this is where the fun starts. With hundreds of species of wild birds and small creatures, mangrove forest and a beautiful bay formed by Punta Gotay and Punta Verraco, you can spend hours here enjoying the natural beauty of the region.

Map, page 215

The Isle of Java

The attractive town of **Yauco** ⓬ lies 3 miles (5 km) west of Guayanilla on Roads 2 and 127. The latter is probably the more pleasant drive, except when it rains, which on this arid coast is about once every millennium. Anyone with the most cursory experience of driving in the southwest knows that those little oily bushes huddled on the brown hillsides are coffee trees, but few know the pre-eminence that the Yauco area holds as a coffee capital. By the late 19th century, Puerto Rico had developed the most advanced coffee industry in the world. In the coffee houses of late-colonial Europe – in Vienna, London, Paris, and Madrid – Puerto Rican coffee was considered the very best that one could drink. "Yauco" was that coffee's name.

Whatever can be said about its other effects, the 20th-century presence of Americans on the island removed Yauco from this position of pre-eminence, as emphasis on manufacturing and cane production sapped the industry's resources. Fortunately, vestiges of that halcyon era remain – the stately homes of Yauco's coffee barons.

Owing to the variety of sub-climates in the southwest, coffee was a mobile industry, and its gentry and their residences were no less itinerant than their crops. As a result, Yauco shares with San Germán and Mayagüez an architecture that is distinctively Puerto Rican and among the best Spanish-influenced

BELOW: Yauco is known for its outstanding architecture.

Map, page 215

Among the flora found in the Guánica Forest Reserve is the knotted guayacan tree, or lignum vitae *– a wood so hard it was once used to replace metal propeller shafts and ball-bearings.*

BELOW: beach in the Guánica Forest Reserve.
RIGHT: girls show off their national dress in Ponce.

work of its day. Some of these old residences are open to the public; for information on the southwestern style and how to see it, the best source is the **Colegio de Arquitectos**, located in the Casa Rosa in Old San Juan. (*See page 134.*)

Even more fortunate is the fact that Yauco has regained some of its old prominence as a coffee producer and exporter. One of Puerto Rico's most successful brands, Yauco Selecto, is now sold in Japanese gourmet coffee shops for over $20 a pound.

Warships by woodlands

On to **Guánica** ⑬, 5½ miles (9 km) past Yauco on Road 116. About the same size as Guayanilla, but with an understandably more oceanic ambiance, Guánica might be worth visiting even without the historical significance which draws so many travelers and historians. In the mid-summer of 1898, at the height of the Spanish-American War, General Nelson Miles, having had no success in a month-long attempt to break the Spanish defenses around San Juan, landed in Guánica with some troops before traveling on to Ponce. He had come, he said, "to bring you protection, not only to yourselves but to your property, to promote your prosperity, and to bestow upon you the immunities and blessings of the liberal institutions of our government."

Out of this promise came American Puerto Rico, and the degree to which the promise has been kept or breached has defined almost all political arguments on the island for the past century. The commemorative stone placed at the edge of Guánica harbor by the local chapter of the Daughters of the American Revolution is encased in a wrought-iron cage guarded by lock and key – presumably to protect the marker against political vandalism.

The birds of Guánica

Guánica is the ornithological capital of Puerto Rico. Covering 1,570 acres (635 hectares) of subtropical dry forest, the **Guánica Forest Reserve** ⑭ is home to half of Puerto Rico's bird species. Most treasured among these is the highly endangered Puerto Rican whippoorwill (found here in the 1950s, some 80 years after it was thought to be extinct).

This low-lying area also has 48 endangered plant species, 16 of which are endemic to the forest. Well-kept hiking trails and a pleasant beach make the reserve a good respite in a hectic sightseeing schedule. UNESCO has designated the area a World Biosphere Reserve, and it is also part of the US National Forest network.

Some of the best bathing, snorkeling and diving around the island can be found here. **Caña Gorda** is the public beach which acts as a springboard for the popular **Cayos de Caña Gorda** – a string of mangrove cays dotting a large and shallow bay protected by an extensive reef – and Ballenas Beach at the easternmost point of the cays. Small launches leave from a tiny dock on the beach several times a day, costing about $4, or you can rent a kayak and paddle your own way there. The bay area gets extremely crowded and noisy at weekends so try and go during the week. ❏

Between Adjuntas and Monte Guilarte are many small farms, tended by the last of the *jíbaros* (mountain smallholders). This area is one of the few places on the island with such a concentrated population of these legendary people. The Ruta Panoramica passes right through their farmland, and they enjoy the opportunity to talk to travelers in a Spanish that is nasal, twangy and high-pitched.

North of Adjuntas toward **Utuado** ⓳, the Cordillera begins its descent to the coastal plain. But that does not mean the land gets flat. The haystack karstic hills north of Utuado march all the way to the Atlantic.

Land of the Indians

West of Utuado on Route 111, the **Caguana Indian Ceremonial Ballpark** ⓴ (open daily 8.30am–4pm; free) should not be missed. Built by the Taínos nearly a millennium ago, the ballpark includes 10 *bateyes* (ball courts) on which the early Indians played a lacrosse- or *pelota*-like game in a blend of sport and religious ceremony. Overlooking the courts, a small rocky peak has been guarding the park for centuries, and looks as though it will continue to do so for centuries to come. Strange sounds echo back and forth over the landscaped grounds. An owl hoots. A dry leaf rasps across one of the *bateyes*. The Taíno gods Yukiyu and Juracán continue to make their presence felt here.

North of Utuado on Route 10, **Lago Dos Bocas** ㉑ (Two-Mouthed Lake) curves into a U-shape around steep hills. At Km 68, Route 10 skirts the lake shore. From there, a launch service carries passengers back and forth across the lake at the weekends, while restaurants situated by the lake also pick up passengers in their private boats to take them across for lunch.

Land of the baby fish

On the far western edge of the Cordillera, not far from Mayagüez, is **Maricao** ㉒, one of the smallest *municipios* in Puerto Rico. Route 120 approaches the town from the south through the **Maricao Forest Reserve** ㉓ or you can take Route 105 out of downtown Mayagüez. By the roadside in the middle of the forest is a castle-like stone tower, four stories tall, which overlooks the entire western half of the island from 2,600 ft (800 meters). There is also a campground.

Maricao's tiny plaza features a rustic cream-and-brick colored church. Just outside the town is the **Maricao Fish Hatchery** ㉔, where many species of freshwater fish are hatched and raised, then dumped in 26 lakes around the island to replenish their indigenous stocks. On the road to the fish hatchery is a mountainside shrine, a haven of serenity and dignity.

The **Hacienda Juanita** in Maricao is yet another coffee plantation converted into a *parador*, surrounded by groves of oranges, bananas and avocados. Guests are invited to pick their own breakfasts. For the lazy ones, bowls of fragrant fruits are always within reach, and bunches of bananas hang from 150-year-old beams. Some of these beams are hewn from precious *ausubo*, a type of ironwood native to Puerto Rico. This wood, prized for its resistance to rot and termites, was once plentiful, but today it is among the rarest of the world's hardwoods. ❑

Map, pages 232–3

The Los Chorros restaurant at Lago Dos Bocas takes its name from a nearby cave, which can be reached on foot.

BELOW: one of the Cordillera's many lovely *paradores*, the Hacienda Juanita in Maricao.

THE OUTER ISLANDS

Off the east coast of Puerto Rico, Culebra and Vieques beckon with their pristine beaches and wild horses, while untouched Mona, far off the west coast, has unique charms of its own

Map, page 248

San Juan

Six miles (10 km) off the east coast of Puerto Rico lies **Vieques**, with twice the acreage of Manhattan and twice the charm of some islands many times its size. Like Culebra, Vieques belongs geologically to the Virgin Islands, but this is not all that separates it from mainland Puerto Rico. The island has grown in popularity among expatriates, although traditional ways live on. Islanders still refer to crossing the sound as "going to Puerto Rico," and the more formal *Usted* form of second-person address, which is extinct on the mainland, is still heard in everyday conversation here.

Much of Vieques looks like Californian cattle country: dry, rolling hills, scattered lazy herds and flocks of white egrets. But the island also enjoys scores of beaches, a small rainforest, exotic wild flowers and a healthy population of tree frogs, mongooses and horses. A hundred or so beautiful *pasofino* (fine-gaited) horses, descended from 16th-century Spanish steeds, roam wild over the island.

The Taíno Indians who first settled the island called it *Bieques*, or "small island"; Columbus named it *Graciosa* (gracious). English pirates called it "Crab Island" for the still-common land crabs they'd depend on for a tasty dinner. And the Spanish (who built the lighthouse and an unfinished fort) called Vieques and Culebra *las islas inutiles* – the "useless islands" – because neither had gold. The island took a direct hit in September 1989, when Hurricane Hugo passed directly overhead, its 200-mph (320-kph) winds destroying many houses and businesses before moving onto "mainland" Puerto Rico.

For years, the island was beset by protesters demanding the exit of the US Navy, which had a base on the island for more than 50 years. They moved out in 2003 and since then property values in Vieques have more than doubled as the affluent clamor for a piece of what may be the last affordable, unspoiled paradise in the Caribbean.

Tucked into various spots on the island are some first-rate inns and hotels, such as the eco-friendly Hix Island House, built on 13 acres (5.25 hectares) mid-island, and the Inn on the Blue Horizon perched on a bluff overlooking the Caribbean Sea *(see Travel Tips)*.

Isabel Segunda

Vieques is accessible by air from San Juan or by sea from Fajardo (a twice-a-day, 18-mile/29-km journey). Unless you have a tight timetable, the latter is the preferable route, offering an exhilarating excursion through brisk, choppy waters; a distant view of stormy El Yunque; and – with luck – a full double rainbow stretching for miles across blue waters. During high season (December through April) you can also reach Vieques and Culebra via the **Island Hi-Speed Ferry** (Thurs–Sun; tel: 877-899 3993; www.islandhispeed

PRECEDING PAGES: the tiny *coquí,* Puerto Rico's "mascot."
LEFT: Sun Bay Beach, Vieques.
BELOW: slice of life in Isabel Segunda, Vieques's only town.

Both Vieques and Culebra are known for their pristine, uncrowded beaches.

ferry.com), which leaves from Pier 2, the public ferry dock in Old San Juan in the morning. The 40-mph (65-kmph) catamaran skims the coastline from San Juan to Fajardo, providing great views, although the sea can be rough coming out of San Juan Bay. The return trip to San Juan is usually smoother.

Near the ferry landing, **Isabel Segunda ❶**, Vieques's only town, has the staples of any modest Puerto Rican municipality. Many of the island's 9,000 residents live here or nearby. Some work in factories, but unemployment remains relatively high. Agriculture, which has been in decline for many years, may yet become an important source of income. In spite of its problems the town is dotted with trendy restaurants, upscale bakeries and real-estate offices, and the sound of construction is in the air as mansions and small developments are built.

The town has the distinction of having the last fort built by the Spaniards in the New World, **El Fortin Conde de Mirasol**. Although it was never completed, what was there has been well restored and has an excellent historical museum (open Wed–Sun 10am–4pm, other days by appointment; tel: 741-1717; free). There's also an interesting exhibit (and great views) at the **Punta Mulas Lighthouse** (open daily 8am–4.30pm; free) to the north of town.

The place to be

A 10-minute drive across the 25- by 4-mile (40- by 6-km) island, **Esperanza ❷**, a small fishing village, consists of little more than a strip of guesthouses and restaurants overlooking the water. Do not be fooled: this is *the* place to eat well, sleep well, sunbathe and explore. A lovesick French army general turned sugar-plantation owner bought the **Casa del Francés** here in 1910 for his pretty young bride. Word has it that the spoiled girl was impressed with neither the island, the

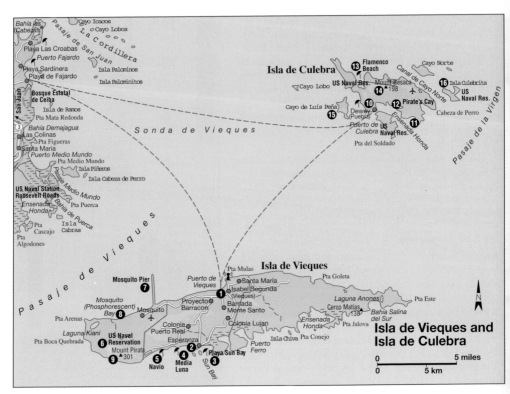

Isla de Vieques and Isla de Culebra

Map, page 248

house, nor even the husband, and promptly fled back to Paris. Today it is a rather dilapidated guesthouse, but still a landmark. Once the only place to stay on the island, Casa del Francés has been eclipsed by a half-dozen ultra-chic or ultra-charming boutique hotels and the Martineau Bay resort. Visit the **Esperanza Archeological Museum** (open daily 11am–3pm; free) for a historical look at pirate and Indian life around these parts. If it's nightlife you're after, try Banana's, Tradewinds and (Saturdays) Cerromar. Saturday nights are especially lively, when pretty much the entire town turn out along the sea front to promenade in their finest, talk and flirt. During the *Fiesta Patronal* (patron saint's festival), which takes place in the last two weeks of July, things really hop.

Just outside Esperanza, **Sun Bay 3** (Sombé to locals) glistens with a popular crescent-shaped beach. Camping is permitted here, as long as campers have the free permit. Beyond Sun Bay, and more secluded, lie **Media Luna 4** and **Navio 5** beaches. Final scenes from Peter Brook's classic 1963 movie *Lord of the Flies* were shot at Navio, a favorite spot for locals. The other good beaches to visit are not far away, within former **US Navy land 6**. In 1941 the navy acquired over 70 percent of Vieques to use for land and sea exercises. As an impediment to development, the navy was partly responsible for the island's charm. Though the inhabitants protested at the military presence, the navy built roads, let cattle owners use navy land and left reserves open for public access to beaches.

Colorful beaches

With characteristic imagination, the navy named three of the island's beaches Red, Blue and Green. Merely getting to these places is a small adventure; rocky approach roads wind through thick seagrape overbrush. **Red** and **Blue** beaches

Vieques has some 40 palm-lined white-sand beaches on its 60-mile (96-km) coastline. It is hoped that the entire stretch of beach will be open to the public now that the US Navy has returned the property to the control of the Puerto Rican government.

BELOW: ponies abound on Vieques.

A gallon of water from Mosquito Bay may contain almost three-quarters of a million tiny (⅟₅₀₀ inch) bioluminescent swimming creatures, which are a type of dinoflagellate called Pyrodinium bahamense.

are ideal for swimming, snorkeling and scuba-diving. Just 75 yds (68 meters) off Blue Beach lies a cay to swim to and explore for helmet shells and coral. The way to **Green Beach** is long, bumpy and tortuous. If you make the trek, stop to see **Mosquito Pier ❼**, a mile-long dock built earlier in the last century when sugar production still flourished.

Vieques has a good number of minor expeditions on which to embark. Ask a local fisherman to take you out at night in a boat to **Phosphorescent** (or **Mosquito**) **Bay ❽**, considered to have the best phosphorescent display in the world. Billions of luminescent microscopic creatures emit a green fluorescence when the water stirs. The best time to come here is on a moonless night, when swimming becomes quite a scintillating experience.

Or climb to the cave atop **Mount Pirata ❾**, where the ancient *cacique* Bieque allegedly hid his tribe's treasure once he realized the conquistadors' murderous intentions. Islanders say the sound of the cave's ceaseless roar attests that the great chief's ghost still rages. And while on the subject of superstitions, on Vieques' north coast near **Roca Cucaracha** (Cockroach Rock) is **Puerto Diablo** (Port Devil), said to be the third point of the notorious Bermuda Triangle.

Pirate's Cay

From Isla Grande Airport, the short flight to isolated **Culebra** to the north of Vieques overlooks dramatic coastline, dozens of varied cays and a turquoise-green Caribbean Sea. Columbus reportedly discovered this island on his second voyage in 1493. The first known inhabitants, the Taíno Indians, sought refuge on Culebra after the Spanish started colonizing the Puerto Rican mainland. Before long, pirates and privateers began to use Culebra's Pirate's Quay as a hid-

BELOW: visit Phosphorescent Bay at night.

Map,
page 248

ing place and supply base before sailing off to raid ships in the Virgin Islands. Infamous corsairs, including the Welshman Sir Henry Morgan, may have buried their treasure on and around Culebra; according to local legend, a road near Punta del Soledado, a bend on Los Vacos Beach, a clump of large trees near Resaca Beach, and a rocky mound at the end of Flamenco Beach might be good spots to start looking for the 17th- and 18th-century fortunes.

By 1880, settlers from Puerto Rico and Vieques were braving severe droughts and swarms of mosquitoes to build a colony which grew tamarind, mango, cashew and coconut trees. Then, a few years after the Spanish-American War of 1898, the US Navy opened facilities on Culebra, making Ensenada Honda its principal Caribbean anchorage. About this time, the island's town moved from what is now Campamento to Dewey. In 1909, one of President Theodore Roosevelt's last executive orders established parts of Culebra as a National Wildlife Refuge, one of the oldest in the US.

Grazing livestock and fishing are the principal activities of Culebra's inhabitants.

By the end of World War II, the US Navy had begun to use Culebra for gunnery and bombing practice. Sea vessels and fighter planes from the United States and its allies pummeled target areas; islanders recall days and nights of constant bomb bursts.

The Culebrans protested bitterly for many years. In 1971, navy personnel and Culebrans exchanged tear gas and Molotov cocktails, for which some islanders were imprisoned. Finally, President Nixon decided that all weapons training on Culebra should be terminated. President Ford's National Security Council reaffirmed the decision, and Culebra was left alone in 1975.

Probably the most important feature of Culebra is its arid climate; with only 35 inches (89 cm) of rain a year, there's always some sunshine here. Its 24

BELOW: music plays an important role in the day-to-day lives of Puerto Ricans.

TIP

To see giant
leatherback turtles
laying their eggs
between April and July
is a truly worthwhile
experience. The best
beaches are Resaca
and Brava;
you may wish to go
with a guide.

islands comprise 7,700 acres (3,100 hectares) of irregular topography and intricate coastline. Most of the terrain is good only for pasture, forest or wildlife. Much of the land is administered by the US Fish and Wildlife Service, which aims to maintain the diverse fauna and flora of the islands. Culebra's cays provide flourishing nesting colonies for a dozen marine bird species, including brown boobies, laughing gulls, sooty terns and Bahama ducks. The brown pelican, an endangered species, can often be spotted in mangrove areas. Rare leatherback turtles nest on many of Culebra's beaches from April through July. Turtle-watchers on Resaca and Brava beaches frequently stay up from 6pm to 6am in order to catch sight of the large, lumbering amphibians delivering and protecting their eggs. Call 1-877-772-6725 to make reservations with a qualified guide.

Because the island has no freshwater streams, sedimentation is low, and Culebra enjoys one of the healthiest coral ecosystems in the Caribbean. Remarkable reefs make for an abundance of fish species and clear water.

More than 2,000 people now live on Culebra, many in pastel-colored houses amid scrubby hills. Roads and front yards abound with jeeps and chickens. Time passes slowly; the atmosphere is one of tranquility and bonhomie.

Main town

The town of **Dewey** ❿ (which locals defiantly call **Puebla**), a 10-minute walk from the airport, covers only several blocks. (Be sure to remember Culebran law – no walking around town without a shirt!) At one end of town, is the Fajardo ferry dock, known as the waterfront. Nearby you will find a dive shop, guesthouses, gift shops, a deli and the highly recommended **Mamacita's Restaurant**.

BELOW: Culebra's
beautiful Flamenco
Beach.

Down the road are two markets, the bank, the post office and, across the bridge, you'll find Dinghy Dock Restaurant & BBQ for a lively bar crowd and American and creole seafood dishes.

Just beyond town is one of the few drawbridges in the Caribbean. Nearby is **Ensenada Honda ⑪** ("Deep Bay"), surrounded by mangrove forests and one of the most secure hurricane harbors in the area, not to mention a nice spot for windsurfing. Smack in the middle of the bay is **Pirate's Cay ⑫**.

Much to the dismay of locals, who prefer to keep tourism to a minimum in Culebra, several boutique hotels have opened here, among them Club Seaborne and Bahia Marina. The central government began work in 2006 on the installation of a modern sewage system for Culebra, which it is hoped will help keep Culebra's waters pristine.

Perfect beach

While on Culebra, make a point of seeing **Flamenco Beach ⑬**. A *público* (bus) can take you there, or you can make the long walk from Dewey. This is the sort of beach you have always heard about – soft white sand, clear blue water and no one to kick sand in your face. A few hundred yards down the beach rest two archaic US Marine Corps tanks. Hikers occasionally find unexploded shells in the vicinity. Another fine beach is **Zoni Beach**, on the island's northeastern edge, some 7 miles (11 km) from Dewey.

Half-a-mile uphill and east of Flamenco Beach stands **Mount Resaca ⑭**, the highest summit on Culebra, with a formidable 360-degree view of cays and some of the Virgin Islands. Resaca hosts a dry subtropical "rock forest" where exotic Caribbean flora thrives amid thousands of large boulders. Last officially

Welcoming smiles come from all ages.

LEFT: non-operational lighthouse on Isla Mona.

Maps, pages 248, 253

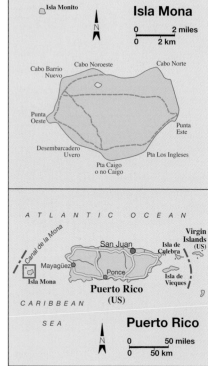

Isla Monito

Isla Mona

N

0   2 miles
0   2 km

Cabo Noroeste

Cabo Barrio Nuevo

Cabo Norte

Punta Oeste

Punta Este

Desembarcadero Uvero

Pta Los Ingleses

Pta Caigo o no Caigo

A T L A N T I C   O C E A N

Canal de la Mona

Virgin Islands (US)

San Juan

Isla de Culebra

Mayagüez

Ponce

Isla Mona

Isla de Vieques

Puerto Rico (US)

C A R I B B E A N

S E A

N

Puerto Rico

0   50 miles
0   50 km

Map, page 253

TIP

If you decide to make the long journey to Mona, make sure to take everything you need (including water); there are no facilities.

BELOW: the unspoiled beauty of Isla Mona. **RIGHT:** enjoying a peaceful island vacation. **FOLLOWING PAGE:** doorway in Old San Juan.

sighted in 1932, the Culebra giant anole, a huge lizard, is still believed to survive in the forested areas of the mountain.

The best way to see Culebra is by packing a picnic and hiring a boat for the day. Do some snorkeling or scuba-diving from the boat as you travel to otherwise inaccessible beaches, lagoons, forests and rocky bluffs on **Cayo de Luis Peña** and the mile-long **Culebrita** . Here you will find the most exuberant wildlife on the island. On Culebrita, you can also see tidal pools and more spectacular, virtually deserted snow-white beaches.

Untouched island

Throughout the Caribbean it is hard not to feel that, however breathtakingly beautiful the landscape may be, it must *really* have been heart-stopping before the European settlers arrived. There are still a few places that the reckless hand of civilization has not reached, though, and one of them, the tiny **Isla Mona**, belongs to Puerto Rico. Stuck 45 miles (72 km) out to sea, in the Mona Passage halfway to the Dominican Republic to the west, this rugged island of 25 sq. miles (65 sq. km) is a haven for some of the oddest and most interesting wildlife in the Antilles.

Mona is protected by the Department of Natural Resources, which also supervises the use of Cabo Rojo and other spots of great scenic beauty on the mainland's west coast. Nobody lives there now, but Mona has had a long history of habitation. Christopher Columbus found Taíno Indians there when he landed on the island, and Spanish settlers visited for many years in hopes of finding habitable and pleasant spots to settle. For centuries it was the stronghold for some of the most notorious of European and Puerto Rican pirates. Only a few naturalists and hermits visit the place now.

The landscape these solitary types have found is reported to be astounding. Except for an isolated lighthouse on a remote promontory, Mona is much as the Taínos left it. Cliffs 200 ft (61 meters) high ring the tiny island, and are laced with a cave network which some say rivals that of the Camuy. Much of the island's ground is covered by small cacti that resemble a miniature version of Arizona's organ-pipe cactus, and tiny barrel cacti are common here as well.

Booby 'trap'

Some of the vegetation on the island is known nowhere else in the world, while the fauna is even more astounding. Here are found the biggest lizards in Puerto Rico, as well as three species of endangered sea turtle. Besides an extensive variety of gull, there lives on Mona a red-footed bird beloved by visitors and known disrespectfully as the "booby."

There are those who would claim that anyone who wished to visit Mona could be called a booby as well. Those hardy souls who are not dissuaded would be best advised to charter a boat or private plane in Mayagüez. Planes can be chartered from San Juan's Isla Grande Airport as well. Official information on hiking trails and on the island's topography is hard to come by, but try writing to the **Departamento de Recursos Naturales** in San Juan. ❑

TRAVEL TIPS

TRANSPORTATION

GETTING THERE AND GETTING AROUND

GETTING THERE

By Air

San Juan's **Luis Muñoz Marín International Airport** (tel: 791-4670/791-3840), just west of the city center in Isla Verde, is one of the largest airports in the Caribbean, serving not only as Puerto Rico's main port of tourist entry but also as a stopping point for most US and European flights to the Virgin Islands, and several other Caribbean islands. The main international carriers serving San Juan include the following:

Air Canada
www.aircanada.com
In Canada and the US, tel: 1-888-247 2262 (toll-free); 514-393 3333
In Australia, tel: 1300-655 767 (toll-free)
In Ireland, tel: 1-679 3958
In New Zealand, tel: 0508-747 767
In South Africa, tel: 21-422 3232
In the UK, tel: 0871-220 1111
American Airlines
www.aa.com
In North America, tel: 800-433 7300 (toll-free)
British Airways
www.britishairways.com
In Australia, tel: 1300-767 177 (toll-free)
In New Zealand, tel: 09-966 9777
In North America, tel: 800-247 9297 (toll-free)
In South Africa, tel: 11-441 8471
In the UK, tel: 0870-850 9850
Continental
www.continental.com
In North America, tel: 800-523 3273; 800-231 0856 (toll-free)
Delta
www.delta.com

In the US, tel: 800-221 1212 (toll-free); 404-765 5000
International, tel: 800-241 4141 (toll-free in the US)
Iberia
www.iberia.com
In Canada and the US, tel: 800-772 4642 (toll-free)
In Ireland tel: 0818-462 000
In the UK, tel: 0870-609 0500
Jet Blue
www.jetblue.com
In Canada and the US, tel: 800-538 2583 (toll-free)
International, tel: 1-801-365 2525
Lufthansa
www.lufthansa.com
In Australia, tel: 1300-655 727 (toll-free)
In Canada, tel: 1-800-563 5954
In Ireland, tel: 84-455 44
In New Zealand, tel: 0800-945-220
In South Africa, tel: 0861-842 538
In the UK, tel: 0870-837 7747
In the US, tel: 800-399 5838/800-645 3880 (toll-free)
Northwest
www.nwa.com
In Australia, tel: 9767-4333; 1300-767 310 (toll-free)
In the UK, tel: 0870-507 4074
In the US, tel: 800-225 2525 (toll-free)
Spirit
www.spiritair.com
In the US, tel: 800-772 7117/800-538-2583 (toll-free)
United
www.ual.com
In North America, tel: 800-864 8331 (toll-free)
In the UK, tel: 0845-844 4777
US Airways
www.usairways.com
In Ireland, tel: 1890-925 065
In the UK, tel: 0845-600 3300
In the US, tel: 800-428 4322/800-622 1015 (toll-free)

Virgin Atlantic
www.virgin-atlantic.com
In Australia, tel: 1300-727-340 (toll-free); 03-9920-3887
In South Africa, tel: 11-340 3400
In the UK, tel: 0870-380 2007
In the US, tel: 800-821 5438 (toll-free)
A free shuttle bus service operates between the airport and most car rental agencies located outside the airport. The service operated by the Metropolitan Bus Authority runs to various parts of the city, 9 miles (14 km) away, for a small charge; you can only take carry-on luggage.
Taxis from the airport operate on a fixed-rate zone system for tourist areas; meter charges apply for journeys to places outside tourist locations.

By Sea

While regular passenger service to Puerto Rico is rare, cruise ships are commonplace. San Juan is the most popular cruise port in the Caribbean, receiving over 1 million visitors annually. Several modern "tourism piers" have been constructed at the harborside in Old San Juan, with the result that most cruise companies plying the South Atlantic make at least an afternoon stop in San Juan.

Specialist Tours

Following is a list of tour companies operating trips to Puerto Rico:
Acampa Nature Adventure Tours
Tel: 706 0695
www.acampapr.com
Specializes in customized trips with guides to waterfalls, caves, rainforests or mountains. Also hiking, camping, rappelling and/or rock climbing in Toro Negro, the Tanamá River in Utuado, El Yunque in Río

Grande, the San Cristóbal Canyon, Mona Island and the Monagas Park in the San Juan metro area. Adventure gear and gadgets on sale.

Aventuras Tierra Adentro
Tel: 766 0470
www.aventuraspr.com
One-day adventures rappelling, rock climbing, zipping down tyroleans, free jumping, rock climbing, body rafting, exploring caves and canyons. Tours depart from San Juan metro area to El Yunque and Río Camuy Cave Park. Pricey but exciting.

Captain Duck Tours
Tel: 447 0077
www.captainduck.com
A 90-minute land and sea tour on an amphibious bus through Old San Juan and the San Juan bay.

Encantos Ecotours
Tel: 272 0005; 808 0005
Outdoor activities, historical, cultural and nature tours throughout Puerto Rico. Activities include kayaking, snorkeling, biking, hiking and sailing lessons with gear rental. Serves San Juan metro area and southwest of island.

Rico Suntours
Tel: 722 2080
www.ricosuntours.com
Established company provides tours, and transfers, specializing in team building groups. Serves San Juan metro area, northwest, northeast and southwest of island. Accommodates travelers with wheelchairs.

United Tour Guides
Tel: 723 5578; 725 7605
www.unitedtourguides.com
Experienced tour operators for main cruise lines and groups. Tours in San Juan, Coamo, the northwest and the northeast of the island.

Wheelchair Getaway
Tel: 800-868 8028; 883 0131
Transportation and customized tours for disabled traveler, mostly in the San Juan metro area, but also more locations around the island.

Other Cruise Companies

The following cruise lines include San Juan as one of their regular ports of call.

Carnival Cruises
tel: 1-888-226 4825 (US); 020-7940-4466 (UK)
www.carnival.com

Celebrity Cruises
tel: 1-800-647 2251 (US); 0800-018 2525 (UK)
www.celebrity.com

Costa Cruises
tel: 1-800-477-6877 (US); 020-7940-5398 (UK)
www.costacruises.co.uk

Cunard Line
tel: 1-800-728-6273 (US); 0845-071-0300 (UK)
www.cunardline.com

Holland America Line
tel: 1-800-426-0327 (US); 020-7940-4466 (UK)
www.hollandamerica.com

Norwegian Cruise Line
tel: 866-234-0292 (US); 0845-658-8010 (UK)
www.ncl.com; www.uk.ncl.com

Princess Cruises
1-800-774-6237 (US); 0845-355-5800 (UK)
www.princesscruises.com

Radisson Seven Seas
tel: 1-877-505-5370 (US)
www.rssc.com

Royal Caribbean International
tel: 1-800-327-6700 (US); 0800-018-2020 (UK)
www.royalcaribbean.com

Seabourn Cruise Line
tel: 1-800-929-9391 (US)
www.seabourn.com

Silver Sea Cruise Line
tel: 1-800-722-9955 (US)
www.silversea.com

Windstar Cruises
tel: 1-800-258-7245 (US); 020-7292-2387 (UK)
www.windstarcruises.com

GETTING AROUND

On Arrival

Be sure to keep the ticket for your checked in luggage because airport officials in the baggage-claim area at the Luis Muñoz Marín International Airport will require this to verify ownership of your bags before allowing you to exit. Checked-in luggage is slow to start rolling out on to the baggage claim belts.

Porters or *maleteros* from the Operativa de Servicio de Equipaje are available in all baggage-claim areas, they will help carry bags for a fee of US$1 per bag, regardless of size. The *maleteros* can be identified by their light-blue shirts and dark-blue pants and an ID tag with "Operativa de Servicio de Equipaje".

If you arrive between 9am and 7pm, stop by the Tourism Company Information Center (tel: 791 1014) in concourse C at street level. Pick up a copy of *¡Qué Pasa!, Bienvenidos* or *Places to Go* magazines.

Airport/City Transportation

Taxis
The best way to get from the airport to your destination, if it's in the San

BELOW: Old San Juan harbor is the place to take a boat to modern San Juan.

Travel Times

Estimated travel times by car from Luis Muñoz Marín International Airport when traffic is not heavy:

Airport to Dorado	30 mins
Airport to Río Grande	45 mins
Airport to Fajardo	1hr
Airport to Humacao	1hr 20 mins
Airport to Isabela	2hrs 30 mins
Airport to Aguadilla	3hrs
Airport to Mayagüez	3hrs
Airport to Ponce	1hr 15 mins
Airport to Rincón	2hrs 30 mins

Juan tourist areas, such as Condado, Isla Verde and Ocean Park, is by taxi.

Taxis are regulated by Transportación Turística. To take a cab, you must stand in line and obtain a transportation voucher from the Ground Transportation stand (orange with the Tourism Company's logo), located at street level and on the second (first) floor of all terminal exits. The voucher indicates the price and address of your destination.

Taxis are plentiful, especially in tourist areas. Some metro-area taxi companies include:
Capetillo Taxi, tel: 758 7000
Major Taxi Cabs, tel: 723 2460
Metro Taxi, tel: 725 2870
Rochdale Radio Taxi, tel: 721 1900
Santana Taxi Service, tel: 547 1926

Fixed taxi rates apply under the Taxis Turísticos program, sponsored by the Puerto Rico Tourism Company. Participating taxis are white with the Taxis Turísticos logo on the door. Keep in mind that rush hour brings traffic jams and heavy rain also slows things down.

Note that all tolls must be paid by the passenger. The Teodoro Moscoso Bridge Toll is US$2. A surcharge of US$2 each applies to the sixth and seventh passenger in a vehicle, while US$0.50 is charged for each of the first three pieces of luggage and US$1 each for the fourth piece of luggage and thereafter. Tips are not included in the set fare.

Metered taxi rates apply outside of the set San Juan tourism zones. The initial charge is $1.75, with $0.10 charged for every ⅑ of a mile or every 25 seconds of waiting time. The same luggage charges as in the transportation zones are applicable, as are the fees for the sixth and seventh passenger. There is a $1 call charge, and the minimum charge for a trip is $3. Hourly rent charge is $36, and the night rate (from 10pm to 6am) is $1 over the meter charge.

If visitors wish to visit parts of the island outside the metropolitan area ask for a metered journey or negotiate a flat price with driver before setting off. However, such trips are expensive, so it is best to take a tour or rent a car for sightseeing trips around the island.

By Air

Most international and many domestic flights (including those from the United States) to San Juan land at Luís Muñoz Marín International Airport in Isla Verde, others use San Juan's second airport, Isla Grande, just across an estuary south of Puerta de Tierra. Ponce and Mayagüez have modern, small airports which provides access to the capital in 20 minutes.

Ponce's airport accommodates flights from Atlanta, Newark and New York in the US. Aguadilla airport, which was created from part of Ramey Air Force Base, also accepts flights from the US and Canada.

Vieques has a good airport and the **Vieques Air Link** (tel: 741 8331), which leaves Isla Grande daily is a pleasant way of getting to and from that lovely island.

Small planes can be chartered at Isla Grande Airport.

Airports

Arecibo
Antonio (Nery) Juarbe Municipal Airport
Tel: 881 2072. For private planes
Aguadilla
Rafael Hernández Airport
Tel: 890 6075
Culebra
Benjamín Rivera Noriega
Tel: 742 0022
Isla Grande
Isla Grande Airport
Tel: 729 8790
Isla Verde
Luis Muñoz Marín International Airport
Tel: 791 3840; 253 5695
Mayagüez
Eugenio María de Hostos Airport
Tel: 833 0148
Ponce
Mercedita Airport
Tel: 842 6292
Vieques
Antonio Rivera Rodríguez Airport
Tel: 741 8358; 741 0515

By Bus

There is a wide-ranging public transport system. Most towns have private bus services. The only public bus service is in the San Juan metro area. The Metropolitan Bus Authority has routes through Bayamón, Guaynabo, Río Piedras, San Juan, Carolina and part of Trujillo Alto. Adults pay US$0.75 per trip. Buses run daily from 4.30am–10pm, they are air-conditioned but can get crowded and don't operate on a set schedule. Buses can be hailed where you see signs: *Parada de Guaguas*. For information about bus routes and terminals:
Tel: 250-6064; 294 0500, ext. 524 or 514; 800-981 3021
www.ati.gobierno.pr

By Public Car

Puerto Rico's major cities are linked by *públicos*, independently owned small vans which can be found at stands all over San Juan and in the smaller cities. *Públicos* are good value and comfortable, and probably the best alternative to having one's own car. To arrange a pick up call one of the following companies:
Blue Line
Tel: 765 7733
Río Piedras, Aguadilla, Aguada, Moca, Isabela and others
Chofered Unidos de Ponce
Tel: 764 0540
Ponce and others
Línea Caborrojeña
Tel: 723 9155
Cabo Rojo, San Germán and others
Línea Sultana
Tel: 765 9377
Mayagüez and others
Terminal de Transportación Pública
Tel: 250 0717
Fajardo and others

By Urban Train

Puerto Rico's commuter rail system has 16 modern stations, it connects downtown Bayamón with eastern Santurce near Sagrado Corazón University, passing through the Torrimar neighborhood, the Centro Médico (the island's main medical center), the University of Puerto Rico at Río Piedras, and the financial district of Hato Rey. Route expansions are planned to Old San Juan, Carolina and Caguas. The fare is US$1.50 per ride on air-conditioned cars, which includes a bus connection. For information, contact: Tren Urbano, tel: 866-900 1284 or visit www.ati.gobierno.prs

By Water

Ferries

The country lacks the extensive water transportation networks of other islands in the Caribbean. But the ferry that operates from the tourist piers of San Juan to Cataño, a mile across San Juan Bay, is a time-saver (less than 10 mins) and a real bargain at US$0.50 per ride. The ferry runs from 6am–10pm. Call tel: 788 0940 for schedules.

Ferries also run from Fajardo to Vieques and Culebra and vice versa. They leave the docks at Fajardo for Vieques at 9.30am, 1pm, 4.30pm and 8pm weekdays; 9am, 3pm and 6pm weekends and holidays. Ferries leave Vieques for Fajardo at 6.30am, 11am, 3pm and 6pm on weekdays; 6.30am, 1pm and 5pm on weekends and holidays. Ferries from Fajardo to Culebra leave at 9am, 3pm and 7pm daily. Ferries from Culebra to Fajardo depart at 6.30, 1pm and 5pm daily. A one way journey takes approximately 1hour 15 minutes and costs US$2.25 per adult from Fajardo to Culebra or US$2 per person to Vieques. Children pay US$1 to either island. Seats can be reserved, but it's best to arrive an hour early. Ferries don't always stick to the schedule so leave extra time if making connections.

For information and reservations: **Fajardo port,** tel: 800-981 2005; 863 0852
Vieques, tel: 741 4761; 41-0233
Culebra, tel: 742 3161

A high-speed ferry also links Old San Juan with Culebra and Vieques, though it's pricey – $68 for a round trip to Culebra, $78 for a round trip to Vieques, $33 between Culebra and Vieques (excluding port fees). One-way fares are available. Service is seasonal, so check availability by visiting. For reservations call 877-899 3993 or visit www.islandhispeed ferry.com/puertorico

Boat Trips

Charter a boat in Mayagüez for the arduous but fascinating 45-mile (72-km) trip to the Isle of Mona. Companies that operate tours include:
Copladet, tel: 765 8595
www.copladet.com
Adventours or Excursiones Guariquén, tel: 530 8311
www.adventourspr.com

By Car

Car Rental

Puerto Rico has one of the highest per-capita rates of car ownership in the Americas, and an automobile is a necessity for anyone who wants to see the island. The drive from east to west across the island is little more than a 3-hour trip. Puerto Rico therefore has many car rental companies. Avis, Budget, Hertz and National have offices in the baggage claim area of terminal E at the Luis Muñoz Marín International Airport,

ABOVE: tropical car design in San Juan.

others are a short shuttle-bus trip away. Most have unlimited mileage. Smaller companies often have excellent automobiles and are less expensive. Even though insurance usually costs extra you would be advised to purchase it. And always carefully check the terms and conditions of the rental agreement detailing insurance coverage.

To rent a car visitors must be a fully qualified driver of at least 25 years old and agencies will usually require a deposit using a major credit card to secure the vehicle. However, some will accept a large cash deposit in lieu of the credit card. Foreign drivers must also produce either an international driver's license or a license from their home country. US licenses and international licenses are valid for use in Puerto Rico for up to 3 months.

Rules of the Road

Driving is on the right-hand side of the road. Speed limits are not often posted in Puerto Rico; they are listed in miles, paradoxically – distance signs are in kilometers. The speed limit on the San Juan–Ponce *autopista* is 55 mph (90 kph) although in some places the limit is 65 mph (100 kph). Limits elsewhere are lower, especially in residential areas, where speed-bumps *(lomos)* provide a natural barrier to excess.

Puerto Rico's older coastal highways are efficient routes but can be slow going, due to never-ending traffic lights. Roads in the interior are narrow, tortuous, poorly-paved, and dangerous. Often, they run along dizzying cliffsides. Frequent landslides mean that roads are often washed out during the rainy season. Hurricanes, too, take their toll on

the roads and traffic signals are regularly out of order so drivers go at their own pace, which usually means too fast, weaving in and out of traffic. Also be aware that road signage is poor and many of the smaller roads do not appear on any map. Be careful too with the many potholes you may encounter along the road.

By law, you must wear seat belts in Puerto Rico. As in some parts of the US, turning right on a red light when traffic allows is permitted – except at a few intersections, where a sign advising you not to do so is indicated. Be advised that hitchhiking and picking up hitchhikers can be extremely dangerous.

In general, most Puerto Rican drivers tend to follow the rules of the road, but a formidable group do not, which can make driving hazardous. The best advice is to be aware of where you are at all times, drive defensively and don't take anything for granted. Traffic signs and lights may not be heeded by other road users.

Be sure to carry change for the numerous tolls throughout the road network. If you breakdown and do not have roadside assistance try the following 24-hour towing companies:
Central Towing & Transport, tel: 800-981 0087; 744 5444
Grúas Pachi, tel: 728 8140
Metropolitan Tow Service, tel: 727 0573

Road Safety

Slow down if you see a sign indicating any of the following:

Desprendimiento	**Landslide**
Desvío	**Detour**
Carretera Cerrada	**Road closed**

A CCOMMODATIONS

HOTELS, YOUTH HOSTELS, BED & BREAKFAST

Choosing a Hotel

Puerto Rico has a wide range of accommodations, but big resorts set the tone. Still, guest houses, beach houses, grand hotels, and camping grounds, as well as a host of less conventional settings, round out a growing and expensive, lodging situation.

The island's large splashy **beach resorts** are mainly two types. The first comprises well-equipped, landscaped, pricey beachfront resorts with casinos, several bars, fine restaurants and most have beautiful golf courses. Each is characterized by excellent sports facilities such as large swimming pools, tennis courts, a gym, and long stretches of beach.

The second type of resort hotel is less lavish, may not have a casino and tend to be only half as expensive as the larger places. These include the big, white high-rises of San Juan's Condado and Isla Verde areas, which cater to a mixture of holiday-makers and business people.

Guest houses tend to be less costly, smaller and more intimate than the big resorts, with around a dozen rooms. Many have beach front locations that offer guests the opportunity to walk across the patio, rather than the lobby, for a morning swim. About half have bars; almost all have swimming pools.

If you prefer to be independent renting an **apartment** or **condominium** is a good self-catering option.

San Juan Vacations (tel: 727 1591; www.sanjuanvacations.com) has a comprehensive listing of condominiums available in Isla Verde and Condado.

Avoid the sleazy hotels, most are in major cities that tend to be full of bugs and dirt. However, they are extremely cheap and therefore attractive to budget travelers willing to brave the bugs.

The *parador* presents a unique lodging option in Puerto Rico. These family-run country inns, often old coffee or sugar *haciendas*, offer the authentic ambiance of Puerto Rican rural life. Beautiful old furniture and elegant dining facilities make them worth trying. Many of the *paradores* are located in particularly scenic areas. Rates are mostly very reasonable, often around US$70–90 per night for a double room, and the food is usually much better than what you may find at nearby restaurants.

Be warned however, some *paradores* have a distinctly utilitarian flavour with dormitory style rooms. It pays to do a little research, try to obtain photos of the establishment before making a reservation.

From the US mainland, *parador* reservations can be made through a central toll-free number: 800-866 7827. In Puerto Rico, call 800-981 7575 (toll-free). For more information visit www.gotoparadores.com.

The Puerto Rico Tourism Company currently certifies 23 paradores, which are listed in the box.

Paradores

Bahía Salinas, Cabo Rojo, tel: 877-205 7507, 254 1212; bahiasal@centennialpr.net **$$**
Baños de Coamo, Coamo, tel: 825 2186; hbcoamo@coqui.net **$**
Boquemar, Boquerón, tel: 851 2158; boquemar@prtc.net **$**
Caribbean Paradise, Patillas, tel: 839 5885; caribbean@isla.net **$**
El Buen Café, Hatillo, tel: 898 1000; www.elbuencafe.com **$**
El Faro, Aguadilla, tel: 866-321 9191; www.FaroHotels.net **$**
El Guajataca, Quebradillas, tel: 800-965 3065, 895 3070; rooms@elguajataca.com **$**
Hacienda Gripiñas, Jayuya, tel: 828 1717; www.haciendagripinas.com **$**
Hacienda Juanita, Maricao, tel: 838 2550; www.haciendajuanita.com **$**
Highway Inn, Cabo Rojo, tel: 851 1839; wbh@westernbayhotels.com **$**
J. B. Hidden Village, Aguada, tel: 868 8686; info@miparador.com **$**
Joyuda Beach, Boquerón, tel: 851 5650; www.joyudabeach.com **$**

La Cima Hotel, Aguadilla, tel: 890 2016; www.lacimahotel.com **$**
Palmas de Lucía, Yabucoa, tel: 893 4423; www.palmasdelucia.com **$**
Perichi's, Joyuda, tel: 851 3131; www.hotelperichi.com **$**
Pichis's, Guayanilla, tel: 835 3335; www.pichis.com **$**
Posada Porlamar, La Parguera, tel: 899 4015; www.parguerapuertorico.com **$**
Villa Antonio, Rincón, tel: 823 2645; www.villa-antonio.com **$**
Villa del Mar, La Parguera, tel: 899 4265; villamar@prtc.net **$**
Villa Parguera, La Parguera, tel: 899 3975; www.villaparguera.net **$**
Villas del Mar Hau, Isabela, tel: 872 2045; www.paradorvillasdelmarhau.com **$**
Villas Sotomayor, Adjuntas, tel: 829 1717; www.paradorvillassotomayor.com **$**
Vistamar, Quebradillas, tel: 895-2065; www.paradorvistamar.com **$**

ACCOMMODATION LISTINGS

OLD SAN JUAN

Chateau Cervantes
329 Recinto Sur Street
Tel: 724 7722 $$$
www.cervantespr.com
Boutique hotel in the heart of San Juan with six deluxe rooms and six suites, all simply yet elegantly decorated. There is also a good restaurant on the property.

Hotel El Convento
100 Cristo Street
Tel: 800-468 2779; 723-9020 $$$
www.elconvento.com
Convent dating to the 16th century, now a 71-room, gay-friendly hotel.

Sheraton Old San Juan Hotel
100 Brumbaugh Street
Tel: 866-653 7577; 721 5100 $$$
www.sheratonoldsanjuan.com

Hotel with 240 rooms, built as part of the waterfront expansion. With restaurant, lounge, roof-top pool and large casino.

The Gallery Inn
204 Norzagaray Street
Tel: 722 1808 $$
www.thegalleryinn.com
Art gallery and 22-room guest house in a 16th-century mansion. Eclectic funky elegance.

Howard Johnson Plaza de Armas
22 San José Street
Tel: 722 9191 $
www.hojopr.com
Convenient location near restaurants, bars, stores. With 51 rooms, rate includes continental breakfast.

METROPOLITAN SAN JUAN

PUERTA DE TIERRA

Caribe Hilton
Los Rosales Street
San Gerónimo Grounds
Tel: 800-468 8585; 721 0303 $$$
www.hiltoncaribbean.com/sanjuan
The 646-room Caribe Hilton is the only hotel in Puerto Rico with a private beach. Several restaurants and fitness center.

Normandie Hotel
499 West Muñoz Rivera Avenue
Tel: 877-987 2929; 729 2929 $$
www.normandiepr.com
Art Deco hotel, most of its 173 rooms include a parlor with a working and sitting area and sun room. Gay-friendly.

Atlantic Beach Hotel
1 Vendig Street
Tel: 721 6900 $$
www.atlanticbeachhotel.com
Beach hotel with 36 rooms. Rate includes continental breakfast, beach chairs and towels. Gay-friendly.

Best Western Pierre Hotel
105 De Diego Avenue
Tel: 800-528 1234; 721 1200 $$
www.hotelpierresanjuan.com
Traditional hostelry that caters to families and business clientele. Its 184 units are well-proportioned and equipped with air conditioning and cable TV.

Holiday Inn Express
1 Mariano Ramírez Street
Tel: 888-826 2621; 724 4160 $$

www.hiexpress.com
Simple chain hotel within walking distance of Condado Lagoon and beaches. The hotel has 115 rooms, a pool, and the price includes continental breakfast.

Radisson Ambassador Plaza
1369 Ashford Avenue
Tel: 800-468 8512; 721 7509 $$
www.radisson.com/SanJuanpr_ambassador
This 233-unit hotel has a pleasant piano bar adjacent to the casino, a restaurant and sports bar, and two lounges with live music. Features lavish concierge floor with two-room suites.

PRICE CATEGORIES

Price categories are for a double room in high season:
$ = under 150
$$ = 150–250
$$$ = 250+

San Juan Beach Hotel
1045 Ashford Avenue
Tel: 800-468 2040; 723 8000 $$
www.sanjuanbeachhotel.com
Located on the beach, with a swimming pool, this colorful 95-room hotel caters to tourists and business people.

At Wind Chimes Inn
1750 Ashford Avenue
Tel: 800-946 3244; 727 4153 $
www.atwindchimesinn.com

CONDADO

Condado Plaza Hotel & Casino
999 Ashford Avenue
Tel: 866-317 8934; 721 1000 $$$
www.condadoplaza.com
With 570 units, top-notch restaurants, large casino, pool and business center.

San Juan Marriott Resort & Casino
1309 Ashford Avenue
Tel: 800-464 5005; 722 7000 $$$
www.marriott.com/sjupr
Grand 525-room hotel that is popular with Puerto Ricans. Large casino and several fine restaurants on site.

BELOW: walking through Old San Juan.

TRANSPORTATION

ACCOMMODATIONS

EATING OUT

ACTIVITIES

A – Z

LANGUAGE

ABOVE: The Ritz-Carlton resort.

Lovely 22-room guest house on the Tourist Zone's main avenue.

Casa del Caribe
57 Caribe Street
Tel: 877-722 7139; 722 7139 $
www.casadelcaribe.com
The hotel has 13 intimate rooms decorated with Puerto Rican original art. Complimentary breakfast can be taken on the wrap-around veranda.

Comfort Inn San Juan
6 Clemenceau Street
Tel: 800-858 7407; 721 0170 $
www.choicecaribbean.com
Next to the Condado Lagoon, this watersports center has 56 rooms.

Diamond Palace Hotel & Casino
55 Condado Avenue
Tel: 800-468 2014; 721 0810 $
www.diamondpalacehotel.net
A good choice for budget travelers who want to be close to where it's happening. With 133 rooms and a small casino. Near popular restaurants.

El Canario by the Lagoon
4 Clemenceau Street
Tel: 800-533 2649; 722 5058 $
www.canariohotels.com
With 44 rooms, this comfortable bed and breakfast hotel is located on the Condado Lagoon.

El Canario by the Sea
4 Condado Avenue
Tel: 800-533 2649; 722 8640 $
www.canariohotels.com
Small 25-room guest house

near the beach. All rooms are air conditioned with private bath. Complimentary breakfast.

El Canario Inn
1317 Ashford Avenue
Tel: 800-533 2649; 722 3861 $
www.canariohotels.com
Lovely 25-room small hotel/bed and breakfast inn with lots of character.

Faro Hotels El Consulado
1110 Ashford Avenue
Tel: 289 9191 $
info@ihphoteles.com
Elegant European-style bed and breakfast with 28 rooms.

Hotel El Portal
76 Condado Avenue
Tel: 721 9010 $
www.hotelelportal.com
Traditional small hotel with 47 well-equipped rooms.

Iberia Hotel
1464 Wilson Avenue
Tel: 724 1040 $
hoteliberapr@hotmail.com
This 30-room hotel in a residential neighborhood includes air conditioning, phone and bath; decorated in cozy Spanish style.

Numero Uno Guesthouse
1 Santa Ana Street
Tel: 866-726 5010; 726 5010 $$
www.numero1guesthouse.com
Intimate beachfront inn with 14 comfortable and

tastefully decorated rooms, and restaurant. Gay-friendly.

Hostería del Mar
1 Tapia Street
Tel: 877-727 3302; 727 3302 $
www.hosteriadelmarpr.com
Delightful 24-room hostelry on the beach; breakfast included. Thrilling view of the Atlantic. Restaurant. Gay-friendly.

Courtyard by Marriott Miramar
801 Ponce de León Avenue
Tel: 800-289 4274; 721 7400 $$
www.courtyardsj.com
Business hotel with 140 rooms with easy access to Old San Juan, Condado and Puerto Rico Convention Center. Popular restaurant.

Hotel Miramar
606 Ponce de León Avenue
Tel: 977 1000 $
www.miramarhotelpr.com
Comfortable hotel accommodation; with 50 rooms.

Hotel Olimpo Court
603 Miramar Avenue
Tel: 724 0600 $
hotelolimpocourt@hotmail.com
In a residential area the 45-room hotel has guest rooms and studio apartments with fully equipped kitchenettes.

El San Juan Hotel & Casino
6063 Isla Verde Avenue
Tel: 866-317 8935; 791 1000 $$$
www.elsanjuanhotel.com
Lavish resort with 382 rooms and a casino. The resort also has some of San Juan's best restaurants.

Embassy Suites Hotel & Casino
8000 Tartak Street
Tel: 800-362 2779; 791 0505 $$$
www.embassysuitessanjuan.com
Spacious 300-room luxury resort with one-bedroom suites that include a living/working area. Large casino and huge banquet hall.

ESJ Towers
6165 Isla Verde Avenue
Tel: 800-468 2026; 791 5151 $$$
www.esjtowers.com

On the beach, this 450-room complex features air-conditioned studios and apartments with fully equipped kitchens and private balconies.

InterContinental San Juan Resort & Casino
5961 Isla Verde Avenue
Tel: 800-327 0200; 791 6100 $$$
www.ichotelsgroup.com
Beautiful, modern hotel with 402 rooms. Las Vegas-style entertainment at night. Five restaurants.

San Juan Water & Beach Club Hotel
2 Tartak Street
Tel: 888-265 6699; 728 3666 $$$
www.waterbeachclubhotel.com
Boutique hotel with 76 smooth-operator rooms, vibrant lounge bars and restaurant. Located on Isla Verde beach. Gay-friendly and pet-friendly.

The Ritz-Carlton San Juan Hotel, Spa & Casino
6961 Los Gobernadores Ave.
Tel: 800-241 3333; 253 1700 $$$
www.ritzcarlton.com/hotels/san_juan
Luxurious 416-room resort with casino, spa and fitness center, private dining room, and chic boutiques.

Hampton Inn and Suites
6530 Isla Verde Avenue
Tel: 800-426 7866; 791-8777 $$
www.hamptoninn.com
This 200-room resort features two-room suites with lounge, bar, meeting rooms and fitness center.

Best Western San Juan Airport Hotel
Luís Muñoz Marín International Airport
Terminal D, Second Floor
Tel: 800-981 1701; 791 1700 $$
www.bestwestern.com/pr/sanjuanairporthotel
Lodging with 125 soundproofed rooms. Flat-screen TV; breakfast included.

Borinquen Beach Inn
5451 Isla Verde Avenue
Tel: 728 8400 $
www.borinquenbeachinn.com
On tourist strip near beach; 12 rooms and free parking.

Casa Mathiesen Inn-Hotel
14 Mar Mediterráneo Street Villamar
Tel: 800-677 8860; 726 8662 $
www.coqui-inn.com
Lovely 30-room hotel located just off the beach. Two restaurants.

Coral by the Sea
2 Rosa Street
Tel: 791 3748 $
www.coralbythesea.com
This low-priced 68-room motel is best known for its restaurant. Basic rooms have Satellite TV; cocktail lounge and live entertainment.

Green Isle Inn
36 Mar Mediterráneo Street
Villamar
Tel: 800-677 8860; 726 4330 $
www.coqui-inn.com
Comfy 26-room hotel. One of the best deals in town.
Hotel Villa del Sol
4 Rosa Street
Tel: 791 2600 $

www.villadelsolpr.com
Spanish villa-style hotel with 24 rooms, one block from the beach; free parking.
Howard Johnson Hotel
4820 Isla Verde Avenue
Tel: 800-446 4656; 728 1300 $
www.hojo.com
This 115-room hotel has deluxe rooms on executive

floor complete with jacuzzi; cable TV. Restaurant.

THE NORTHEAST

El Conquistador Golf Resort & Casino
1000 El Conquistador Avenue, Fajardo
Tel: 866-317 8932; 863 1000 $$$
www.elconresort.com
This 972-room resort has a private island; a funicular transports guests to the marina. international tournaments at the 18-hole championship golf course.
Paradisus Puerto Rico
Route 3, Intersection with PR-955
Coco Beach, Río Grande
Tel: 866-436 3542; 657 1040 $$$
www.puertoricoparadisus.com

All-suite, all-inclusive beach resort with 486 rooms. Facilities include a spa, golf course, live entertainment and casino, six restaurants, and bars and lounges.
The Westin Río Mar Beach Golf Resort and Spa
Route 968, Km 1.4, Río Grande
Tel: 800-474 6627; 888 6000 $$$
www.westinriomar.com
Lovely setting, on the beach and among the hills, this resort with 600 rooms is ideal for a secluded getaway. Views of El Yunque from the two

championship golf courses. Tennis courts, a fitness center and a casino, and a choice of eight restaurants.
The Fajardo Inn
52 Parcelas Beltrán
Puerto Real Area, Fajardo
Tel: 860 6000 $$
www.fajardoinn.com
This 97-room hotel offers a panoramic view of the Atlantic and is located on five lush acres (2 hectares).
Anchor's Inn
Route 987, Km 2.7, Fajardo
Tel: 863 7200 $
www.anchorsinn.net

Small hotel located on a bluff overlooking the sea. This 14-room inn has simple rooms and features an excellent seafood restaurant.
Scenic Inn
52 Parcelas Beltrán
Puerto Real Area, Fajardo
Tel: 860 6000 $
www.fajardoinn.com
Small guest house with 10 rooms, ideal for travelers looking for simple but inexpensive lodging. Restaurant and swimming pool on the property.

THE SOUTHEAST

Four Points by Sheraton at Palmas del Mar
170 Candelero Drive, Humacao
Tel: 866-615 2323; 850 6000 $$$
www.fourpoints.com

This 107-unit suite resort includes two 18-hole golf courses, 16 tennis courts, horseback riding, scuba diving and restaurants.

Caribe Playa Beach Resort
Route 3, Km 112.1, Patillas
Tel: 839 6339 $
www.caribeplaya.com
Simple beachfront studios

with kitchens in the 30-room resort. Seaview terrace restaurant, barbecue, hammocks, and children's pool.

BELOW: Palmas del Mar.

THE NORTH AND THE WEST

DORADO

Embassy Suites Dorado del Mar Beach & Golf Resort
201 Dorado del Mar Boulevard
Tel: 800-362 2779; 796 6125 $$$
www.embassysuitesdorado.com
A great place for a getaway just a few blocks from Isla Verde beach. With 210 rooms in a modern block, an 18-hole championship golf course designed by local golf legend, Juan "Chi Chi" Rodríguez, and a beautiful lagoon-style pool with a fine ocean view. There are also tennis courts and two restaurants on the complex.
Hyatt Hacienda del Mar
301 Highway 693
Tel: 800-926 4447; 796 3000 $$$
www.hyatthaciendadelmar.hyatt.com
Large, luxury beachfront resort, which has been converted into a pricey timeshare complex. Fully equipped condominiums in modern tower blocks right on Dorado beach. There is a large swimming pool, a spa and fitness center, residents can also enjoy a plethora of watersports such as sailing and snorkelling nearby.

ISABELA

Costa Dorada Beach Resort
Route 466, Km 0.1
Tel: 800-975 0101; 872 7255 $
www.costadoradabeach.com
All 52 rooms have a view of the northern coast and offer standard amenities.

AGUADILLA

Cielo Mar Hotel
84 Montemar Avenue
Tel: 882 5959 $
www.cielomar.com
The hotel has ocean views; 72 rooms with amenities.
Hotel El Pedgregal
Route 111, Km 0.1, Cuesta Nueva Street
Tel: 888-568 6068; 891 6068 $
www.hotelelpedregal.com
Landscaped property with ocean views. Pool area, restaurant and snack bar.

RINCÓN

Casa Isleña
Route 413 Interior, Km 4.8
Punta Higüero, Barrio Puntas

Tel: 888-289 7750; 823 1525 $
www.casa-islena.com
Guest house with nine rooms. Romantic atmosphere and a friendly restaurant.
Horned Dorset Primavera
Route 429, Km 3.0
Tel: 823 4030 $$$
horneddorset@hotmail.com
With a reputation for privacy, elegance and fine service and 22 secluded suites. Restaurant.
Lazy Parrot Inn
Route 413, Km 4.1, Barrio Puntas
Tel: 800-294 1752; 823 5654 $
www.lazyparrot.com
Funky 11-room guest house with pool and shop.
Rincón of the Seas Grand Caribbean Hotel
Route 115, Km 12.2
Tel: 866-274 6266; 823 7500 $$
www.rinconoftheseas.com
Comfortable hotel with stylish Art Deco interior and 112 rooms. Restaurant. Ideal for families.
Villa Cofresí Hotel
Road 115, Km 12.3
Tel: 823 2450 $
www.villacofresi.com
On the beachfront on the south side of the point. A laid-back, family-oriented place with 68 rooms; continental breakfast included.

MAYAGÜEZ

Holiday Inn Mayagüez & Tropical Casino
2701 Hostos Avenue
Tel: 800-465 4329; 833 1100 $
www.holiday-inn.com/mayaguezpr
Centrally located hotel; 141 rooms with air conditioning, cable TV, lounge; and non-smoking rooms.
Howard Johnson Downtown Mayagüez
70 East Méndez Vigo Street
Tel: 832 9191 $
www.howardjohnson.com
Comfortable hotel with 39 rooms. Centrally located.
Mayagüez Resort and Casino
Route 104, Km 0.3
Algarrobo Sector
Tel: 888-689 3030; 832 3030 $$
www.mayaguezresort.com
Family hotel with 140 rooms set in 20 acres (8 hectares) of landscaped gardens. Lots of kids at the weekend. Restaurant.

BELOW: the elegant Horned Dorset Primavera, Rincón.

THE SOUTH

Copamarina Beach Resort
Route 333, Km 6.5, Guánica
Tel: 800-468 4553; 821 0505 $$$
www.copamarina.com
Luxury resort with 106 rooms set in mangroves and forest. Ideal for families.

Hilton Ponce Golf & Casino Resort
1150 Caribe Avenue, Ponce
Tel: 800-981 3232; 259 7676 $$
www.hiltoncaribbean.com/ponce

Luxurious hotel with 253 rooms and suites. Casino and 27-hole championship golf course nearby.

Holiday Inn & Tropical Casino Ponce
3315 Ponce Bypass, Ponce
Tel: 800-465 4329; 844 1200 $$
www.holiday-inn.com/ponce
Part of the international hotel chain. Some rooms overlook the Caribbean Sea.

Hotel Bélgica
122 Villa Street, Ponce
Tel: 844 3255 $
www.hotelbelgica.com
A simple 60-room hotel in the heart of town.

Hotel Meliá
75 Cristina Street
Degetau Plaza, Ponce
Tel: 800-448 8355; 842 0260 $
www.hotelmeliapr.com
Lovely hotel with 73 rooms.

Friendly staff and complimentary breakfast.

Howard Johnson Ponce
103 Turpo Industrial Park
Mercedita Area, Ponce
Tel: 866-668 4577; 841 1000 $
www.hojo.com
Family accommodations with 120 rooms near the airport, with restaurant and swimming pool. Includes continental breakfast.

CORDILLERA CENTRAL AND THE OUTER ISLANDS

CENTRAL

Monte Río Hotel
18 César González Street, Adjuntas
Tel: 829 3705 $
Hotel with 24 rooms, pool, and meeting facilities. Great views of the countryside.

Casa Grande Mountain Retreat
Route 612, Km 0.3, Utuado
Tel: 894 3939 $
This small mountain inn is located on a former coffee plantation. With 20 simple rooms surrounded by lush forest and landscaped gardens. Swimming pool and yoga center on the property. No air conditioning or telephone in rooms. Restaurant

THE OUTER ISLANDS

Culebra

Bahía Marina
Punta Soldado Road, Km 2.4
Tel: 742 0535 $$
www.bahiamarina.net
Laid-back apartment-hotel complex comprising 16 simple condos with kitchenette and sea views. Near to the beach and a nature reserve. Facilities include pool and watersports. Restaurant

Club Seabourne
Fulladoza Bay
Tel: 800-981 4435; 742 3169 $$
www.clubseabourne.com
An intimate boutique hotel

with 14 stylish and comfortable villas and rooms set in tropical garden. Facilities include swimming pool; watersports, hiking and cycling can be arranged. Restaurant; eat inside or out on the deck. Great views of the bay.

Hotel Costa Bonita
Carenero Point
Tel: 800-578 4487; 742 3000 $$
www.costabonitaresort.com
Laid-back resort with 164 studios and one-bedroom suites.

Vieques

Inn on the Blue Horizon
La Casa del Francés
Road 996, Km 4.3
Tel: 877 2583; 741 3318 $$$
www.innonthebluehorizon.com
Tastefully decorated 10-room guest house with a breathtaking view. Ideal for a getaway. Swimming pool and other facilities available.

Martineau Bay Resort & Spa
Route 200, Km 3.2
Tel: 866-837 4216; 741 4100 $$$
www.martineaubayresort.com
Part of a hotel group this health spa has 144 rooms and villa suites. Pretty beachfront and comfortable air-conditioned rooms. Fitness center and a spa offering a wide variety of treatments, some services available in-room. Watersports, tennis. Restaurant

Hacienda Tamarindo
Route 996, Km 4.5
Puerto Real sector

Tel: 741 8525 $$
www.haciendatamarindo.com
Lovely boutique hotel with 16 stylish, but simple rooms. The inn is on a hilltop so guests can enjoy great views.

Amapola Inn and Bilí Restaurant
144 Flamboyán Street
Esperanza sector
Tel: 741 1382 $
www.amapolainn.com
Simple beachfront guesthouse with eight small, yet efficient rooms and studios.

Hix Island House
Route 995, Km 1.5
Esperanza sector
Tel: 741 2302 $$
www.amapolainn.com
Simple, but stylishly

designed boutique hotel. Concrete buildings surrounded by lovely gardens contain 13 airy rooms with partially open showers for the nature lovers. The hotel has an eco-friendly philosophy and is a good choice for those wanting to get away from it all and holiday simply.

The Crow's Nest
Route 201, Km 1.5
Tel: 741 0033 $$
www.crowsnestvieques.com
The small inn provides basic accommodation with views of the countryside near Isabel Segunda and a short drive to a good beach. Rooms have a kitchenette, there is also a pool on the premises.

BELOW: and so to bed at Hix Island House, Vieques.

E ATING OUT

RECOMMENDED RESTAURANTS, CAFES & BARS

What to Eat

Aside from having a delectable and historic native cuisine, Puerto Rico benefits from its American and Caribbean connections in having just as many of the world cuisines as you'd find in the largest cities of the United States. Spanish, US, Mexican, Chinese, French, Italian, Swiss, Brazilian, Japanese and other food is plentiful, especially in San Juan.

Puerto Rican cuisine differs from that of its Spanish neighbors in the Caribbean almost as much as it differs from that of the mainland US. Relying heavily on rice, beans and whatever Puerto Ricans haul out of the sea, it is a mild, filling, well-balanced style of cookery. *See the feature on Puerto Rican Cuisine, page 75, for more details.*

Where to Eat

You find get Puerto Rican food in all manner of spots: in the modest urban *fondas*, where a rich *asopao de camarones* will cost you under five dollars; in the rural *colmados* where roast chicken is the order of the day; and in the posh restaurants of Old San Juan and the Condado, such as La Mallorquina *(see page 269)*, the Caribbean's oldest continuously operating restaurant. The restaurants of San Juan tend to be concentrated in certain areas.

While *fondas* are all over town, European cuisine tends to be concentrated in the trendier parts of Old San Juan and in the more expensive areas of the Condado and Santurce, such as Ashford Avenue. There must be a higher concentration of American fast-food joints than anywhere else on earth. These are in the Condado and the modern shopping malls in Carolina and Hato Rey. Bars are everywhere.

Healthy Options

There is a great movement toward health foods in Puerto Rico. Dozens of stores have cropped up dispensing vitamins, herbs and organically grown foods. These establishments also provide small restaurants where you may have lunch, which might consist of a soy burger and sprouts sandwich and natural orange juice. Recommended: **Mother Earth**, Plaza Las Americas, third level, tel: 754 1995; **Freshmart**, an organic food supermarket with stores located on Route 887, Carolina, tel: 762 7890 and also on Plaza Montemar, 201 Indo Costa Street, corner with Calaf Tres Monjitas, Hato Rey, tel: 282 9106.

RESTAURANT LISTINGS

OLD SAN JUAN

Aguaviva
364 Fortaleza Street
Tel: 722 0665
Open: L and D daily. $$$
Seaside Latino restaurant with chic and trendy decor. Mouth-watering seafood. Calling ahead to sign up on the waiting list is highly recommended.
Amadeus
106 San Sebastián Street
Tel: 722 8635
Open: L and D Tues–Sun. $$$
Puerto Rican restaurant with creative variations of traditional dinners, fresh seafood and delicious ceviche. The bar is always well stocked. Reservations recommended.
Barú
150 San Sebastián Street
Tel: 977 7107
Open: D daily. Last order at 12:45am Thurs–Sat. $$$
Caribbean- and Mediterranean-influenced tapas and a sexy lounge atmosphere. Reservations recommended.

Café Berlin
407 San Francisco Street
Tel: 722 5205
Open: B from 11am–12:30pm, L and D daily. $$
"Gourmet vegetarian" eatery offering fresh pastas, organic foods and a delicious salad bar.
Café Manolín
201 San Justo Street
Tel: 723 9743
Open: B and L from 6am–4:30pm daily. $
Puerto Rican restaurant with excellent authentic cuisine at reasonable prices, served in a relaxed atmosphere.
311 Trois Cent Onze
311 Fortaleza Street
Tel: 725 7959
Open: During summer, D Wed–Sat, Br and D Sun. $$$
Provence was the inspiration for this formal French restaurant set in a landmark building and decorated with tradition and style. Meals are sophisticated yet simple. Two outdoor patios add to

its charm. Reservations recommended.

Dragonfly
364 Fortaleza Street
Tel: 977 3886
Open: D only Mon–Sat. $$$
Sexy Asian-Latino fare in an intimate space. There are small dishes to share. Calling ahead to join the waiting list is highly recommended.

El Patio de Sam
102 San Sebastián Street
Tel: 723 1149
Open: L and D daily. $$$
Caribbean cuisine in a casual setting. Sam's hamburgers are legendary. Reservations recommended.

Il Perugino
105 Cristo Street
Tel: 722 5481
Open: L Thurs–Sat, D daily. $$$
Italian restaurant where chef-owner, Franco Seccarelli, prepares specialties such as *pasta a la vongole*, *carpaccio* of Angus beef and marinated salmon. Fine wine. Reservations required.

La Bombonera
259 San Francisco Street
Tel: 722 0658
Open: B, L and D daily. $$
Puerto Rican food is served in this traditional cafeteria-style bakery. The best place in Old San Juan for a inexpensive, satisfying *arroz con pollo*, and coffee with pastries, especially *mallorcas*.

La Mallorquina
207 San Justo Street
Tel: 722 3261
Open: L and D Mon–Sat. Closed Sept. $$$
Puerto Rican cuisine in the oldest restaurant on the island, dating from 1848. House specialties: *asopao de marisco* and *arroz con pollo*. Worth a visit if only for the interior courtyard. Reservations required.

Panza
329 Recinto Sur Street
Chateau Cervantes
Tel: 289 8900
Open: L and D Mon–Sat. $$
Fine dining, with creative international cuisine. Reservations are required.

Sofia
355 San Francisco Street
Tel: 721 0396

Open: L and D daily. $$$
Italian restaurant with pizzas, *linguini alla vongole* with *pancetta*, *churrasco*, veal chops, poached halibut and braised lamb shank. The setting is casual, in a restored colonial house. Call ahead to join the waiting list.

Tantra
356 Fortaleza Street
Tel: 977 8141
Open: L and D daily. $$$
Hindu-influenced food with modern flashes.

The Parrot Club
363 Fortaleza Street
Tel: 725 7370
Open: L and D daily, Br Sun. $$$
A contemporary Latin bistro and bar featuring live music. Call in advance to put your party on the waiting list.

PUERTA DE TIERRA

El Hamburger
402 Muñoz Rivera Avenue
Tel: 721 4269
Open: L and D daily. Open until 12:15am Sun–Thurs and 4am Fri/Sat. $
Before fast-food restaurants started to take over the island, El Hamburger was the place to go, and it still draws the crowds. Build your own burger and pick your favorite jukebox song.

Marisquería Atlántica
7 Lugo Viñas Street
Tel: 722 0890
Open: L and D Tues–Sun. $$$
This Spanish seafood eatery prides itself on being the "friendliest fresh food and fish restaurant in town." Try daily specials.

CONDADO/OCEAN PARK

Ajili Mójili
1006 Ashford Avenue, Condado
Tel: 725 9195
Open: L and D daily. $$$
Authentic local cuisine with a gourmet twist. Dishes include: *mofongo relleño*, *arroz con pollo*, *fricasé de cabrito*, *piononos*, *piñón* and *serenata de bacalao*. These local dishes cost far less in other places. Reservations recommended.

Antonio's Restaurant
1406 Magdalena Avenue, Condado
Tel: 721 2139
Open: L and D Mon–Fri, D only Sat. $$
Spanish gourmet cuisine in an elegant atmosphere. Table settings are majestic; service impeccable. Steaks, chicken and seafood complemented by Spanish wine. Reservations.

Bebo's Café
1600 Loíza Street
Tel: 726 1008
Open: B, L and D daily. Kitchen closes 12:30am. $$
Cheap and tasty local dishes offered like *pastelones*, *salmorejo de jueyes* and roasted *pernil*. Casual ambiance.

Cherry Blossom
1309 Ashford Avenue
San Juan Marriott Resort & Casino
Tel: 723 7300
Open: L and D Mon–Fri, D only Sat, L only Sun. $$$
Japanese steakhouse and sushi bar featuring *teppanyaki* preparation. Guests can order dinner from the bar on the second level. The service is fast and careful. Reservations.

Cielito Lindo
1108 Magdalena Avenue, Condado
Tel: 723 5597
Open: L and D Mon–Fri, D only Sat/Sun. $$
Authentic Mexican *cantina* with casual decor and dining. The festive atmosphere appeals to both tourists and locals. Less formal than most Condado restaurants.

Compostela
106 Condado Avenue
Tel: 724 6088
Open: L and D Mon–Fri, D only Sat. $$
Spanish restaurant highly rated by *San Juan City Magazine*. The Galician chef-owner, José Rey, prepares the freshest seafood with a deft hand and a creative contemporary spirit. Reservations required.

Dunbar's
1954 McLeary Street, Ocean Park
Tel: 728 2920
Open: L and D Wed–Sat, Br, L and D Sun. Open until midnight Wed, Thurs, Sun and until 1am Fri/Sat. $$
Daily specials include gnocchi, mahi-mahi, *filet mignon*, *bistec encebollado* and *fajitas*.

Green House
Ashford Avenue
Diamond Palace Hotel, Condado
Tel: 725 4036
Open: B, L and D daily. Open till 2am Sun–Thurs and till 5am Fri/Sat. $$
Short orders and full dinners

BELOW: al fresco dining in San Juan.

PRICE CATEGORIES

Prices for a three-course dinner per person with a half bottle of wine:
$ = under $20
$$ = $30–40
$$$ = $40+

at this popular place. Stop in after a hard night clubbing.
Ikakos
1108 Ashford Avenue, Condado
Tel: 723 5151
Open: L and D Sun–Fri, D only Sat.
$$$
Fresh Puerto Rican seafood served in an elegant setting. Reservations.
José José
1110 Magdalena Avenue, Condado
Tel: 725 8496
Open: L and D Tues–Fri, D only Sat, L only Sun. $$$
Named after its two owners, this restaurant serves international cuisine with a Creole touch, such as ostrich with chocolate foam and Port reduction. Reservations.
Mandalay
999 Ashford Avenue
Condado Plaza Hotel
Tel: 721 9140
Open: L and D daily. $$$
Oriental cuisine. The *New York Times* hails this as one of the best restaurants

in Puerto Rico. The menu features Szechuan, Hunan, Mandarin and Cantonese cuisine, as well as dim sum. Reservations.
Miró
76 Condado Avenue
Tel: 723 9593
Open: L and D Mon–Fri/Sun, D only Sat. $$$
Catalan/Spanish fresh fish and shellfish cooked Mediterranean style. Plates of squid, octopus, oysters, clams and langoustines abound. Reservations.
Portobello
55 Condado Avenue
Diamond Palace Hotel
Tel: 722 5256
Open: D daily. $$
Fine northern Italian and international dishes. Ravioli, gnocchi, seafood, and the best pasta sauce on the island. Also paella and *asopao*. Reservations.
Ramiro's
1106 Magdalena Avenue
Tel: 721 9049
Open: L and D Mon–Fri/Sun. $$$
Among Puerto Rico's finest restaurants featuring imaginative international specialties with a Spanish flair. Chefs/owners Oscar and Jesús Ramiro prepare memorable dishes.

Excellent desserts and wine list. Try the white sangria. Reservations.
Ristorante Tuscany
1309 Ashford Avenue
San Juan Marriott Resort
Tel: 722 7000 ext. 6219
Open: B, L and D daily. Open 6am–10pm. $$ (early-bird dinner) $$$ (à la carte).
Italian cuisine, fine dining with an excellent wine list. Reservations recommended.
Tony Roma's
999 Ashford Avenue
Condado Plaza Hotel
Tel: 722 0322
Open: L and D daily. $$$
Baby back ribs with barbecued beans and coleslaw are a pleasing lunch or dinner. The Cajun spiced ribs are great.
Via Appia
1350 Ashford Avenue, Condado
Tel: 725 8711
Open: L and D daily. $$
Always busy Italian sidewalk café with pizza and pasta dishes.
Zabó Creative
14 Candina Street
Tel: 725 9494
Open: D Tues–Sat. $$$
Restaurant in an old beach house in the heart of Condado. Choose from a variety of appetizers or a

selection of entrées. Reservations recommended.

MIRAMAR

Augusto's Restaurant
801 Ponce de León Avenue
Courtyard by Marriott
Tel: 725 7700
Open: L and D Tues–Fri, D only Sat.
$$$
Continental restaurant considered to be one of the best on the island. Winner of the prestigious Golden Fork Award. Reservations.
Bistro de Paris
801 Ponce de León Avenue
Courtyard by Marriott
Tel: 721 8925
Open: B, L and D daily, Br Sun. $$
Menu favorites such as French onion soup, crushed pepper tenderloin, flambé with cognac, cream and potatoes au gratin; apple tart. Reservations.
Chayote
603 Miramar Avenue
Olimpo Court Hotel
Tel: 722 9385
Open: L and D Tues–Fri, D only Sat.
$$$
Contemporary Caribbean cuisine in elegant but casual surroundings.

HATO REY, RÍO PIEDRAS AND PUERTO NUEVO

Nuevo
Café Valencia
1000 Muñoz Rivera Avenue
Hato Rey
Tel: 764 3790
Open: L and D Sun–Fri, D only Sat.
$$$
Traditional Spanish cuisine. Famous for its *paella*. Reservations recommended.
El Zipperle
352 F.D. Roosevelt Avenue
Hato Rey
Tel: 763 1636
Open: L and D daily. $$$
German/Spanish cuisine in an old-time eating and meeting place. Reservations.
Frida's Mexican Restaurant
128 Domenech Avenue, Hato Rey
Tel: 763 4827
Open: L and D Mon–Sat. $$$
Mexican cuisine, casual ambiance and fine dining. A local favorite. Reservations.

Jinya's Restaurant
1009 Piñeiro Avenue, Puerto Nuevo
Tel: 783 2330
Open: L and D Tues–Sat, 3pm–9pm Sun. $$$
Delicious traditional sushi rolls and *sashimi*, as well as "Japanrican" rolls with *chicharrón* and *bacalao*. This casual-elegant restaurant also has steak and chicken *teriyaki*, *tempura* and soft-shell crab. Daily specials. Reservations recommended on weekends.
Los Chavales Restaurant
253 F.D. Roosevelt Avenue
Hato Rey
Tel: 767 5017
Open: L and D Mon–Sat. $$$
Old-time popular gathering place with international Spanish cuisine and fresh seafood in an elegant setting. Reservations recommended.

Mangère
311 De Diego Avenue, Puerto Nuevo
Tel: 793 3697
Open: L and D daily. $$$
Italian cuisine with daily specials. Reservations.
Margarita's
1013 F.D. Roosevelt Avenue
Puerto Nuevo
Tel: 781 8452
Open: L and D daily. $$
Mexican, well known for its margaritas, *enchiladas* and *fajitas*. *Mariachi* band on the weekend.
Metropol 3
124 F.D. Roosevelt Avenue, Hato Rey
Tel: 751 4022
Open: L and D daily. $$
Cuban cuisine that's a long-time local favorite. Daily specials include meat, chicken and fish dishes with rice and beans and fried plantain. Try natilla

and Cuban coffee for dessert. One of three Metropols in Puerto Rico.
Tierra Santa
284 F.D. Roosevelt Avenue
Hato Rey
Tel: 763 5775
Open: L and D daily. $$$
Hummus, *tabuleh* and shish kebab are favorites here. Entrées include *kustaleta* (lamb chops) and *gambary* (shrimps Arab style). Belly-dancing on Fri/Sat. Reservations recommended.
Yuan Restaurant
255 Ponce de León Avenue
MCS Plaza, Hato Rey
Tel: 766 0666
Open: L and D daily. $$$
Set in attractive, dimly lit decor with roses on each table. Delicately prepared Chinese cuisine. Reservations recommended.

SANTURCE

La Casona
609 San Jorge Street
corner Fernández Juncos Avenue
Tel: 727 2717
Open: L and D Mon–Fri, D only Sat.
$$$
Spanish restaurant in an old Spanish-style home. Lobster salad, stuffed rabbit loin and the best paella in Puerto Rico make this a popular spot. Immaculate service. Reservations recommended.

Pikayo
299 De Diego Avenue
Museo de Arte de Puerto Rico
Tel: 721 6194
Open: L and D Tues–Fri, D only Mon/Sat. $$$
Creative cuisine combines gourmet recipes with local produce and fresh seafood. Considered to be one of the best restaurants in San Juan. Reservations recommended.

Isla Verde
Casa Dante
39 Isla Verde Avenue
Atlantic View sector
Tel: 726 7310
Open: L and D daily. $$$
Caribbean and international cuisine. Excellent *mofongo* dishes. Reservations.

Che's
35 Caoba Street
Punta Las Marías
Tel: 726 7202
Open: L and D daily. $$$$
Argentinean restaurant specialising in *parrilladas*, *churrasco* and *chimichurri* as well as grilled steaks and pasta. Reservations.

La Piccola Fontana
6063 Isla Verde Avenue
El San Juan Hotel & Casino
Tel: 791 0966
Open: D only daily. $$$
Elegant northern Italian fare in classic surroundings. Try

Fettuccini alfredo, veal *scaloppine* and tip-top caesar salad. Reservations.

Lupi's Mexican Grill and Sports Cantina
Road 187, Km 1.3
Tel: 253 2198
Open: L and D daily. Kitchen and bar open until 4am. $$
Mexican bar/sports *cantina* with a US flavor. Delicious *fajitas* and flying fish.

Ruth's Chris Steak House
5961 Isla Verde Avenue
InterContinental San Juan Resort
Tel: 253 1717
Open: D daily. $$$
American-style seafood. Reservations.

The Palm Restaurant
El San Juan Hotel & Casino
6063 Isla Verde Avenue
Tel: 791 3300
Open: D only daily. $$$
A classic American steakhouse known for its

ABOVE: drinking in a city bar.

gigantic steaks and lobsters. Reservations.

Yamato
El San Juan Hotel & Casino
6063 Isla Verde Avenue
Tel: 791 8152 Open: D only daily. $$$
Outstanding service in this *teppanyaki* and *sushi* restaurant. Try the *sake* and Sapporo beer. Reservations.

CATAÑO AND FAJARDO

La Casita
27 Manuel Enrique Street
Palo Seco, Catano
Tel: 788 5080
Open: L and D daily. $$$
Fancy restaurant in a poor

neighborhood serving delicious fresh fish; specialties include a delicious octopus cocktail and *mofongo relleno* with lobster. Reservations.

El Conquistador Golf Resort & Casino
1000 El Conquistador Avenue, Fajardo
Tel: 863 1000
Open: D only daily. $$$

Upscale resort with a choice of world-class restaurants as well as a variety of more casual places open for lunch and dinner.

JOYUDA AND PONCE

Pino's Restaurant
Route 102, Km 14.6, Joyuda
Tel: 255 3440
Open: L and D Wed–Sun. $$
Typical Puerto Rican seafood restaurant near Mayagüez, specializing in fish fillets and *mofongo relleno* with *mariscos* (mashed, spiced crab meat

and fried plantain stuffed with seafood).

Mark's at the Meliá
Hotel Meliá, 2 Cristina Street, Ponce
Tel: 284 6275
Open: L and D Tues–Sat. $$$
Elegant place with classic continental dishes made from local ingredients. Reservations.

Pito's Seafood
Route 2, Km 2.18, Las Cucharas, Ponce
Tel: 841 4977
Open: L and D daily. $$
This eatery's specialty is a favorite island dish: *Mofongo relleno* made with stuffed fried plantain, and seafood, meat or chicken.

Restaurant El Ancla
End of Hostos Avenue on Ponce Playa, Ponce
Tel: 840 2450
Open: L and D daily. $$$
Menu specialties include fish and seafood such as Caribbean lobster, red snapper and shrimps cooked Creole style.

VIEQUES

Café Media Luna
351 Antonio G. Mellado Street
Isabel II
Tel: 741 2594
Open: D only Thurs–Sun. $$
Eclectic menu with Asian dishes, fresh seafood and steak. Good reviews from *Gourmet*, *Food and Wine*, and *The New York Times*.

Carambola
Road 996, Km 4.3
Inn on the Blue Horizon
Tel: 741 3318
Open: L and D Thurs–Sun. $$$
Casual elegance and exquisite cuisine such as coconut curry chicken, seafood *mofongo* and grilled *churrasco*.

Chez Shack
Route 995, Km 1.8
Tel: 741 2175
Open: D only Thurs–Mon. Closed Sept and Oct. $$
Caribbean seafood and steak.

The Blue Moon Bar & Grill
Road 996, Km 4.3
Inn on the Blue Horizon

Tel: 741 3318
Open: L only Tues–Sun, D Tues/Weds. $$
American food with a Puerto Rican twist. This busy island rendezvous features a 60-ft (18-meter), custom-made, mural bar top. Tapas served Tuesday and Wednesday nights.

ACTIVITIES

THE ARTS, NIGHTLIFE, FESTIVALS, SHOPPING AND SPECTATOR SPORTS

THE ARTS

General Information

Visitors may pick up free publications which provide useful information on places to go, sights to see, history, and general information about the island. Most readily available are *¡Qué Pasa!*, *Bienvenidos* and *Places to Go*. These are usually found at the larger hotels and tourist offices. La Princesa in Old San Juan is the main tourist office, while a small kiosk near the Condado Plaza Hotel also stocks a variety of tourist literature. The Luis Muñoz Marín International Airport also has a tourism office, which is located at street level in Terminal C.

BELOW: a ceremonial mask costume.

Museums

Puerto Rico's museums place great emphasis on the colorful history of the island and its people. The island's most famous museum, the **Ponce Art Museum**, is primarily devoted to classic paintings which represent schools from around the world. The **Museo de Arte de Puerto Rico** *(see page 143)* in Santurce opened in the summer of 2000 and houses masterpieces by Puerto Rican artists. San Juan's **Museo de Arte e Historia** *(see page 134)* depicts the story of the city dating back to the 16th century, while the **Museo de las Américas** *(see page 131)* houses a collection of items from New England to Mexico, with a strong emphasis on Puerto Rican life. Most of the island's museums do not charge admission and are open daily. Try to plan a museum trip on a weekday when there are usually fewer visitors.

Art Galleries

Almost all of Puerto Rico's cities sell local crafts and art, from Aguadillan lace to Loízan *vejigante* masks, but an art "scene" exists only in the city of San Juan. Here, the combination of a radiant light and an active network of patronage has drawn most of the finest painters of Puerto Rico and many from North America and Europe. Sculpture thrives, as do the crafts of Puerto Rico and other Latin American nations. Most galleries are huddled together on a few of Old San Juan's streets, but you'll also find galleries in San Juan's other neighborhoods and even out on the island. Following is a list of some of the better galleries in the metropolitan area:

Art Students League
Beneficiencia Street
Old San Juan
Tel: 722 4468
A small, changing display of some of San Juan's up-and-coming artists, with a tendency towards the vanguard and the experimental. Open: 9am–5pm Monday to Saturday.
Galería Botello
208 Cristo Street
Old San Juan
Tel: 723 9987
www.botello.com
Fine international paintings, sculpture, *santos* and graphic art. Open: 10am–6pm Monday to Saturday.
Galería W. Labiosa
200 Tetuán Street
Old San Juan
Tel: 721 2848
Prints, silk screens and original paintings. Open: 9am–6pm Monday to Saturday.
Galería Palomas/San Juan Frames
259 Tetuán Street
Old San Juan
Tel: 724 8904
A fine collection of Puerto Rican paintings, graphics, prints, drawings and *santos*. Open: 9:30am–6pm Monday to Saturday.
Galería San Juan
204 Norzagaray Street
Old San Juan
Tel: 722 1808
www.thegalleryinn.com
A sizable changing collection of fine paintings in an elegant, old building that doubles as a hotel and is always open.
Viota Art Gallery
793 San Patricio Avenue
Las Lomas, San Juan
Tel: 782 1752
www.viotagallery.com

The gallery features the work of contemporary Puerto Rican artists and foreign artists residing on the island. Open: 9am–6pm Monday to Saturday.

Concerts

Since its inception the Puerto Rico Symphony Orchestra has progressed to a position of great respectability. Frequent concerts are held in the **Fine Arts Center** Festival Hall, known locally as the "Bellas Artes," in Santurce. Chamber music ensembles are numerous at the university and among private concert-givers. The highlight of the classical music year comes during the **Casals Festival** in February/March, when the Puerto Rico Symphony's performances at Bellas Artes are complemented by guest appearances from musicians from around the world, including renowned Itzhak Perlman and Maxim Shostakovich.

For information on concerts taking place at Bellas Artes, call 620 4444.

Ballet

There are plenty of opportunities to see ballet in San Juan. The San Juan Ballet periodically hosts performances at **Bellas Artes**. Ballet Concierto has a classic repertory. The San Juan City Ballet is performs regularly at the restored **Tapia y Rivera Theater** in Old San Juan. Rounding out dance offerings are the modern dance shows given at the **Julia de Burgos Amphitheater** in Río Piedras as part of the University of Puerto Rico (UPR) Cultural Activities.

Bowling

Galaxy Lanes, on the third level of Plaza Las Américas, is a multi-purpose bowling alley with a capacity for 1,000 people. It opened in the summer of 2006 and has 32 bowling lanes, two entertainment levels, two restaurants and two bars and billiards. Giant projection screens add to the fun, along with a dance floor and DJ.

Movies

Independent movie theaters have gone the way of the movie multiplex. Santurce, once crowded with such theaters, now has only one, as does Miramar. Cinemas within **shopping centers** are much more common today, most notably in **Plaza Las Americas** and **San Patricio**.

A Fine Arts Cinema Café with leather seats and a deli/café serving drinks opened in the **Popular Center**'s North Tower in Hato Rey. Check local newspapers for a complete list of theaters, current movie listings and show times.

NIGHTLIFE

The nightlife of Puerto Rico ranges from the tranquility of coffee and conversation to the steamy, fast-lane excesses of San Juan's clubs. On cool nights in the Cordillera, nightlife resembles what Puerto Ricans have probably enjoyed for decades, if not centuries. Townspeople gather round local plazas and sing with guitars, finding time between tunes for a couple of sips of Don Q or Medalla.

San Juan duplicates much of this rural nightlife – on weekends in the old city, youths of high school and college age mill about the Plaza San José by the hundreds in bars, restaurants and coffee houses.

But in San Juan and other big cities, partying is generally taken with more reckless abandon. The whole city is crowded with bars and dancing establishments of all description.

In Old San Juan, **Nuyorican Café**, **Los Hijos de Borínquen** and **El Patio de Sam** provide good spots for drinking and chatting.

What's On

Free publications such as *¡Qué Pasa!* and *Bienvenidos*, usually found at hotels and tourist offices, provide up-to-date information on local nightlife. Gay and lesbian travelers can pick up a copy of *Puerto Rico Breeze*, which can be found at the gay-friendly Atlantic Beach Hotel in Condado.

Nightclubs and Discos

Old San Juan

Café Bohemio
100 Cristo Street
El Convento Hotel
Open: daily
Tel: 723 9300
Professional and gay-friendly crowd, popular on Tuesday.

Carli Café Concierto
Corner of Recinto Sur and San Justo streets
Plazoleta Rafael Carrión
Tel: 725 4927
Open: Mon–Sat
Dining club with live jazz by former Beach Boys pianist Carli Muñoz.

Club Lazer
251 Calle Cruz
Tel: 721 4479
www.clublazer.com
Open: Friday–Sunday

ABOVE: a night out at Club Lazer.

Loud youthful disco with hip-hop, R&B and reggaeton. Open late.
El Batey
Cristo Street
Open 24 hours.
Small, loud dive. Great classic rock juke box.
Hard Rock Café
253 Recinto Sur
Tel: 724 7625
www.hardrock.com
Open: daily
Delicious food accompanied by loud music, with rock 'n' roll memorabilia.
Kudetá
314 Fortaleza Street
Tel: 721 3548
Open: Thursday–Saturday, till late on Friday/Saturday.
Two-floor club with dance floor on the second level and a VIP lounge on the third. Music includes hip-hop, house, techno and progressive. Dress fashionably; attracts a youngish crowd, age range 18–30.
Nuyorican Café
312 San Francisco Street, entrance through the alleyway
Tel: 977 1276; 366 5074
www.nuyoricancafepr.com
Open: daily till late
House band plays classic salsa on Wednesday/Friday. Other nights feature Latin jazz, rock or Latin fusion. Poetry and theater as well. A casual, popular bar and restaurant popular with a diverse crowd.
Pool Palace
Lobby of Paseo Portuario Building, 330 Recinto Sur Street
Tel: 725 8487
www.poolpalacepr.com
Open: Thursday–Saturday, till late on weekends

ABOVE: out for drinks in Plaza del Mercado.

Something for every taste – a sports bar with 12 billiard tables and gaming systems (open daily), dance floor, lounge and restaurant. Thursdays feature live salsa music and lessons, on Friday and Saturday there is a variety of live bands or DJs. The age range is 21 up. Dress up.
Rumba
152 San Sebastián Street
Tel: 725 4407
Open: Thursday–Saturday
Dance to live salsa on Friday and Saturday with an over 25 crowd. Music varies on Thursdays and the crowd is younger. Popular with locals and tourists alike. Casual attire.

Puerta de Tierra
N-Lounge
Normandie Hotel
499 West Muñoz Rivera Avenue
Tel: 729 2929
www.normandiepr.com
Open: Tuesday–Sunday
Electronic lounge music, casual ambiance; lounge and terrace. The age of the crowd is 23 and over.
Condado and Ocean Park
Dunbar's
1954 McLeary Street
Tel: 728 2920
Open: Wednesday–Sunday
This hangout for visitors is a well-known pick-up joint. The menu has buffalo chicken wings and a game of darts is usually on the go. Informal with live music every night. Attracts a diverse crowd from 25–45 years old.
Kali
1407 Ashford Avenue
Tel: 721 5104
Open: Tuesday–Sunday
Dress to impress for this cool restaurant and bar where folks chill to lounge, hip-hop and electronic music.

The place attracts a diverse crowd from 25–50 years old. Open late.
Moorings
1214 Ashford Avenue
Tel: 725 2192
Open: Wednesday–Sunday, till late on weekends
Bar and grill with 1980s rock, salsa, merengue and reggaeton, plus karaoke on Wednesday. The crowd ranges from 22–28 years old.
The Lobby Bar at San Juan Marriott
1309 Ashford Avenue
Tel: 800-464 5005; 722 7000
www.marriott.com/sjupr
Open: Wednesday–Sunday
Dance the night away to live salsa and merengue Attracts a diverse crowd from 25–60. Dress up.

Hato Rey
Club Boccacio
1–2 El Centro Building
Tel: 299–1745
Open: Friday–Saturday till late
A casual club that plays merengue, salsa and dance music. The place to be on Friday for gays and lesbians; the crowd is 21-45 years old.
Coaches Sports Restaurant
137 F.D. Roosevelt Avenue
Tel: 758 3598
www.coachespr.com
Open: Wednesday–Sunday
Sports bar and restaurant. Rock music in Spanish and English, with a crowd aged 25–30.
Medusa
Roosevelt Avenue and 7 América Street
Tel: 764 9230
www.medusatheclub.com
Open: Thursday–Saturday
Happening gay club with hip-hop, house, reggaeton and tribal music. Dress up.

Santurce
Krash Klub
1257 Ponce de León Avenue
Tel: 722 1131
www.krashpr.com
Open: Wednesday–Saturday
Formerly known as Eros, this club plays hip-hop, house, reggaeton and is popular with gay men aged 18–60.
La Placita
Open: Thursday–Saturday
Historic open-air plaza, during the day a farmers' market; at night the square is filled with young professionals, fondas, restaurants and live music.
Tía María's Liquor Store
326 José de Diego, Stop 22
Tel: 724 4011
Open: daily, till late on weekends
Casual pub with billiards. During business hours there is a mixed heterosexual crowd, after 7pm it attracts a gay crowd.

Isla Verde
Brava
El San Juan Hotel & Casino
Tel: 791 1000
www.bravapr.com
Open: Thursday–Saturday
Elegant yet fun, an old-style disco for night owls aged 23 and over.
Lupi's
Route 187, Km 1.3
Tel: 253 2198
Mexican bar and sports cantina. Delicious margaritas, fabulous fajitas and live music.
San Juan Water and Beach Club Hotel
2 Tartak Street
Tel: 728 3666
www.waterbeachclubhotel.com
Open: Tuesday–Saturday
House, R&B and techno music is played in the lobby bar and lounge called **Liquid**, which is open till very late. The rooftop bar and lounge, called **Wet**, features a sushi bar, a spectacular view and is open daily.
Shots
677 Isla Verde Avenue, Isla Verde Mall
Tel: 253 1443
Open: Wednesday–Sunday till late
Sports bar and restaurant featuring salsa on Thursday, Friday and Saturday with a variety of live bands. The crowd is aged 18–35 years old. Dress is casual attire.
The Lobby at El San Juan Hotel & Casino
6360 Isla Verde Avenue
Tel: 791 1000
It feels as if all of San Juan heads for the lobby on Saturday night for salsa and merengue at **El Chico Bar** and drinks and music at the **Oval Bar**. Dress to impress.

Casinos

Gambling is legal in Puerto Rico. Casinos have blackjack, roulette, poker, slots and games of chance.

Casinos are permitted only in hotels and usually tend to be open from noon until the early hours.

FESTIVALS

Annual Events

Almost every holiday is the occasion for a festival in Puerto Rico, many of them legislated, others informal. Every town has its patron saint, and every saint a festival. These, known as *patronales*, are the biggest events of the year in their respective towns. The most famous is probably Loíza's **Fiesta de Santiago Apostól** in July. The largest is certainly San Juan's **Noche de San Juan Bautista** in late June, and a very popular one with islanders is the **San Sebastián Festival** in Old San Juan in mid-January.

The **Le Lo Lai Festival** is a year-round festival program established by the Puerto Rican Tourism Company. It involves evening shows of Puerto Rican music and dance staged in hotels and in Old San Juan. For details contact: Puerto Rico Tourism Company (tel: 721 2400, ext. 2715 or 800-866 7827).

SPORTS

Outdoor Activities

Freshwater Fishing

There are 12 private clubs devoted to freshwater fishing, in the island's man-made lakes and reservoirs.

Bass, both large-mouth and peacock, are local favorites, though at least four other recreational species like sunfish, tilapia and catfish are fished as well. Plastic worms are the most popular choice of bait among bass fishermen. The reservoirs are stocked with more than 2,000 fish from the Maricao Fish Hatchery (Los Viveros).

Only four reservoirs are open to the public and are managed by the Department of Natural and Environmental Resources (DNER). Facilities include boat ramps, information centers and restrooms. For reservoir fishing regulations or for directions to the facilities, call the DNER's Reserves and Refuges Division, tel: 999 2200, ext. 2713; www.drna.gobierno.pr

The four reservoirs open to the public are:

Cerrillos Lake
Ponce
Tel: 259 9979
Fairly deep and large. Facilities include a barbecue. Accessible by Route 139.

Guajataca Lake
Quebradillas
Tel: 896 7640
One of the largest reservoirs in Puerto Rico, receives 27,000 visitors per year. Off Route 119 in San Sebastián.

La Plata Lake
Toa Alta
Tel. 983 7215
Measuring 26 sq. miles (67 sq. km), this is Puerto Rico's second-largest lake. It is located between Toa Alta, Bayamón and Naranjito, and accessible by Route 167.

Lucchetti Lake
Yauco
Tel. 856 4887
Fed by the Yauco River and located 4 miles (6 km) outside the town of Yauco. It has a camping area, barbecue and bathrooms with showers. Accessible through Route 128, Km 12.3.

Salt-water Fishing

Salt-water fishing, particular deep-sea fishing, is also popular, with several bill fish tournaments held off the coast. Shallow-water fishing is also practiced on the island, and there's excellent tarpon fishing. For shallow-water fishing, take a skiff to the coastal mangroves.

For deep-sea fishing, boats can be chartered in San Juan, Fajardo and Arecibo, which are close to the Atlantic's Puerto Rico Trench, dubbed Blue Marlin Alley. Today, most caught marlin are tagged and released. To fish wahoo, head to deep waters off Humacao. For tuna, head to the Mona Passage on boats departing from Rincón, Mayagüez, Cabjo Rojo and La Parguera. The best months to catch blue marlin are August and September, while yellow and blackfin tuna, mahi mahi, wahoo and bonito have their own seasons.

Deep-sea and shallow-water fishing charters are available from:

Adventures Tourmarine
Cabo Rojo
Tel: 375 2625

Caribbean Outfitters
Carolina
Tel: 396 8346

Castillo Tours & Watersports
San Juan
Tel: 791 6195

Light Tackle Adventure Fishing
Cabo Rojo
Tel: 849 1430

Parguera Fishing Charters
La Parguera
Tel: 382 4698

Tropical Fishing Charters
Fajardo
Tel: 379 4461

Hiking

There are several hiking trails in Puerto Rico and many afford spectacular vistas. There are particularly good hikes in the Caribbean National Forest at El Yunque, as well as in the Guánica State Forest and on Mona Island. Río Camuy Cave Park and Las Cabezas de San Juan Nature Reserve have have what are considered walks rather than hikes, but are still enjoyable. The Puerto Rico Department of Natural Resources in San Juan (tel: 999 2200, ext. 5156, www.drna.gobierno.pr) can provide more information on many of the country's trails.

Horseback Riding

Hacienda Carabalí
Luquillo
Tel: 889 5820.
With Paso fino horses and an excellent reputation.

Rancho Buena Vista
Palmas del Mar Resort
Humacao
Tel: 479 7479.
Upscale.

Tropical Trail Rides
Isabela
Tel: 872 9256.
Horseback riding through forest and on beaches.

Golf and Tennis

Golf courses and tennis courts are scattered throughout the island, though most of the better ones are in the large, expensive resorts. These hotels sometimes allow access to non-guests for a fee.

Resorts with 18-hole championship golf courses include:

Embassy Suites Dorado del Mar
Dorado
Tel: 796 3070

Westin Río Mar
Río Grande
Tel: 888 6000

Palmas del Mar
Humacao
Tel: 285 2256

Kayaking

Kayaks are an ecologically friendly way of exploring the island's mangroves and its coast. They're also an excellent way to check out the bioluminescent bays in Vieques and Fajardo. Companies that rent kayaks or offer tours include the following:

San Juan Waterfun
San Juan
Tel: 643 4510
Travesías Isleñas Yaureibo
Vieques
Tel: 939-630 1267
Yokahú Kayak Trips
Fajardo
Tel: 604 7375

Sailing

Most of Puerto Rico's sailors head to Fajardo or Ponce for weekends on the water. Try one of the charter companies below:
Ventajero Sailing Charters
Fajardo
Tel: 645 9129
Boats of all sizes and descriptions available for rental. Tours.
Puerto del Rey Marina
Fajardo
Tel: 860 1000
Ponce Yacht & Fishing Club
Tel: 842 9003

Scuba Diving

Puerto Rico is prime scuba territory. Some operators offer sailing, snorkeling and fishing in addition to scuba diving. Try: **Caribbean School of Aquatics**, tel: 728 6606; 383 5700; www.saildiveparty.com Located in San Juan, it also serves Fajardo, Culebra and Vieques. Dive lessons from the following:

San Juan

Caribe Aquatic Adventure
Park Plaza Normandie Hotel
Puerta de Tierra
Tel: 281 8858

Culebra and Rincón

Culebra Divers
Dewey
Tel: 742 0803
Taíno Divers
Rincón
Tel: 823 6429

Fajardo

Fajardo is probably the island's capital for watersports. Contact:
Catamaran Getaway
Villa Marina Yacht Harbor
Fajardo
Tel: 860 7327

Snorkeling

Equipment can be rented or bought at dive shops and department stores. Some companies that offer snorkeling tours are:
Adventures by the Sea
San Juan
Tel: 374 1410
Paradise Scuba & Snorkeling
La Parguera
Tel: 899 7611

Surfing

Puerto Rico has almost ideal conditions for surfing – warm water, brilliant sunshine and heavy but even tubular surf. Many of the most popular spots are convenient to San Juan: Aviones, off Route 187 in Piñones, is probably the most renowned, and so named because of the airplanes that fly over from nearby international airport. La Ocho, in Puerta de Tierra's Escambrón Beach is also popular and crowded on weekends. In the northwest, Punta Higüero, off Route 413 in Rincón, is famous, while Jobos Beach proves popular among Aguadilla and Isabela residents.

Swimming

Puerto Rico has sandy beaches, some crowded, others secluded and quiet. Many are *balnearios* with public bathing facilities that include lifeguards, refreshment stands and dressing rooms. Around San Juan most popular are Luquillo and Vega Baja. All beachfront, except the beach at the Caribe Hilton, is public.
    Swimmers are advised to be careful of strong surf and undertow at beaches, especially in the northwest. Swimmers should head to Escambrón beach, a short walk from the Normandie Hotel or the Caribe Hilton in Puerta de Tierra.

Windsurfing and Kiteboarding

Windsurfing and kiteboarding are popular island-wide. Ocean Park in San Juan and La Parguera are ideal places to practice both sports. For rentals and lessons try:
Kiteboarding PR
#2 Santa Ana Street
1A, Ocean Park
Tel: 374 5329
www.kiteboardingpr.com
KitesurfPR
2434 Loíza Street #2
San Juan
Tel: 221 0635
www.kitesurfpr.com
Vela Uno
2430 Calle Loíza
Punta las Marías
Tel: 728 8716
www.velauno.com

Health Clubs & Spas

Bodyderm Spa
Copamarina Beach Resort
Guánica
Tel: 821 0505
Golden Door Spa at Las Casitas Village
El Conquistador Golf Resort & Casino
Fajardo
Tel: 800-468 8365; 863 1000 ext. 7300

Mandara Spa
Westin Río Mar Beach, Golf and Resort Spa
Río Grande
Tel: 888 6000
N'Spa
Normandie Hotel
Puerta de Tierra
Tel: 729 2929
Secrets of Eden Spa
331 Recinto Sur Street
Old San Juan
Tel: 721 6400
The Ritz-Carlton Spa
Ritz-Carlton Hotel
Isla Verde
Tel: 253 1700 ext. 4131
Zen Spa & Health Studio
1054 Ashford Avenue
Condado
Tel: 722 8433

SPECTATOR SPORTS

Baseball and Basketball

Puerto Rico's national pastime is baseball. The island has produced some of the great stars of the game.
    The Puerto Rico Winter League season runs from November to February, with teams in Santurce, Caguas, Ponce, Manatí, Mayagüez and Arecibo. The league has no official website, although www.hitboricua.com is a good resource sanctioned by the league.
    Many aspiring big-leaguers (and not a few has-beens) play in Puerto Rico. Games are almost daily, and tickets generally inexpensive. Those who want to keep abreast of American and National Leagues will find complete box scores in the local papers. Also, cable TV brings a variety of big-league games.
    Basketball is another popular team sport. The Superior Basketball League (www.bsnpr.com) has teams in almost all the larger cities .

Horseracing

Horseracing in San Juan is at **El Comandante Racetrack** in Canóvanas, 10 miles (16 km) east of the city. Races are held on Monday, Wednesday, Friday and Saturday at 2.30pm, Sunday at 2.15pm; admission is free. For more information on races, tel: 876 2450 or www.comandantepr.com

Cockfighting

For a truly Puerto Rican sporting experience, cockfighting is hard to match. Although the sport is viewed inhumane to many, its popularity on the island cannot be denied. In this sport, dozens of the proudest local cocks are matched one-on-one in a tiny ring, or *gallera*. A predominantly male crowds are almost as interesting as the fights themselves. These knowledgeable enthusiasts are familiar with a cock's pedigree through several generations. The shouts are deafening, the drinking is reckless, and the betting is heavy. Betting is done on a gentlemanly system of verbal agreement, and hundreds of dollars can change hands on a single fight.

Galleras are scattered all over, and the fights in even the most rural areas can draw hundreds. Admission can be expensive but the beer is cheap. For information on cockfighting in the San Juan area:

Club Gallístico de Puerto Rico
Isla Verde Avenue, Isla Verde
Tel: 791 1557
Club Gallístico Río Piedras
Route 844, Km 4.2, Trujillo Alto
Tel: 760 6815

SHOPPING

Where to Shop

In San Juan, the more upmarket shopping areas tend to be concentrated in the Old City and the Condado. Old San Juan has the more boutiquey atmosphere of the two. There are plenty of shops selling tourist baubles, curios and T-shirts. Among the better stores in the Old City are its jewelry shops, especially numerous along Fortaleza Street, which have signs reading *Joyería*. Other specialties include leather and arts and crafts, ancient and modern. There are also outlet shops and designer-clothing stores such as Polo Ralph Lauren, Coach, Donney & Bourke and Versace. If you're looking for authentic Puerto Rican goods places to visit in Old San Juan are:
Bared (jewelry)
Fortaleza and San Justo streets
Tel: 724 3780
Club Jibarito & Hellenis
202 Cristo Street
Tel: 724 7797
Joyería Riviera
257 Fortaleza Street
Tel: 725 4000
Puerto Rican Arts & Crafts
204 Fortaleza Street
Tel: 725 5596
Rums of Puerto Rico
la Casita at Old San Juan
Spicy Caribbee
154 Cristo Street
Tel: 725 4690
The Condado lures customers with slightly more money to spend.

Clothing, porcelain, crystal, jewelry. There's less of a market ambiance in Condado, which has a touristy tone.

Hato Rey, Santurce and Isla Verde are workaday places for residents.

An exception is **Plaza Las Américas**, the Caribbean's largest shopping mall, in Hato Rey. This is the best place on the island for shopping. It is rivaled by the **Plaza Carolina** shopping center in Carolina. Other malls include the **Plaza del Caribe** in Ponce and the **Mayagüez Mall** in Mayagüez. Cities as small as Caguas and Cayey have malls.

Some of the larger malls are:
Belz Factory Outlet World Puerto Rico
Route 3, Km 18.4, Canóvanas
Tel: 256 7040
Designer-name factory outlet stores, food court, movie theaters, about 40 minutes outside of San Juan.
Plaza Carolina
Intersection of 65th Infantry Avenue and Roberto Clemente Street, Carolina
Tel: 768 0514
Second-largest shopping mall in Puerto Rico with two department stores, over 200 specialty shops, movie complex and food court.
Plaza Las Américas
Intersection of Roosevelt Avenue and Las Américas Expressway, Hato Rey
Tel: 767 1525
Largest shopping mall in the Caribbean.

For traditional (barter) shopping in San Juan, the best marketplace is the **Plaza del Mercado**, a bustling outdoor affair in Río Piedras. Primarily a fruit market, the Plaza has in merchandise of all kinds. Prices

are often unlisted and haggling can be intense. Santurce also has a smaller market.

What to Buy

Cigars are a good purchase, and in spite of laws prohibiting smoking in public tobacco and cigar shops have sprung up. There are many shops in Old San Juan, such as **The Tobacco Shop** on the first level of Plaza Las Américas. It is well-stocked, but prices are a bit high. **Habana Cuba**, is on San Patricio Avenue in San Patricio, the **International House of Cigars** is on Avenida Miranda in Río Piedras. **El San Juan Hotel & Casino** has a "cigar boutique," which sells fine cigars from the Dominican Republic, Honduras and Jamaica.

Locally made arts and crafts are another good choice sold. Contact the Puerto Rico Tourism Company's Cultural Affairs Division (tel: 723 0682) for advice.

Books

The following have a good selection of books in both English and Spanish:
Bookworm, 1129 Ashford Avenue, Condado, tel: 722 3344.
Borders, Plaza Las Américas, Hato Rey, tel: 777 0916; Plaza Escorial, Carolina, tel: 701 6200.
By the Book, 304 Ponce de León Avenue, Hato Rey, tel: 777 0485.
Castle Books, San Patricio Shopping Center, tel: 774 1790.
La Tertulia, 204 O'Donnell Street, Old San Juan, tel: 724 8200.

BELOW: kiteboarding off the coast.

A – Z

A HANDY SUMMARY OF PRACTICAL INFORMATION, ARRANGED ALPHABETICALLY

A dmission

Some nightclubs and pubs have admission fees, usually between $8 and $10. Public beaches administered by the National Parks Company also charge a small fee for parking ($2 for motorcycles, $3 for cars, $4 for vans). Pedestrians can enter free of charge into these public beaches.

B usiness Hours

Business hours follow the US rather than the Latin tradition, and the afternoon siesta is generally not practiced. Most stores are open Monday–Saturday 9am–6pm, banks open Monday to Friday 8:30am–2:30pm; certain branches of each bank may open on Saturday and evenings. Some selected stores of major supermarket chains are open 24 hours a day, 7 days a week.

C limate

Puerto Rico has one of the most pleasant and unvarying climates in the world, with daily highs almost invariably at 70–85°F (9-21°C). The island is at its wettest and hottest in August, with 7 inches (18 cm) the average monthly rainfall and 82°F (28°C) the average daily high. During the rainy season, sudden late-afternoon squalls are common.

Regional variations are noticeable: Ponce and the southern coast are warmer and drier than San Juan and the north. It is coldest in the higher altitudes of the Cordillera, where the lowest temperature in the island's history was recorded near Barranquitas: 39°F (4°C).

Average daily high temperatures for San Juan range from 75°F (24°C) in January and February to 82°F (28°C) from June through to September.

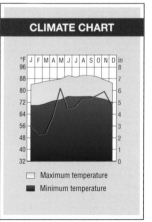

CLIMATE CHART

☐ Maximum temperature
■ Minimum temperature

Crime and Safety

In recent years, the serious crime rate in Puerto Rico has skyrocketed, but following a crackdown by police the annual murder rate has dropped. It is a place with high unemployment and a tourist population that is often gullible and vulnerable. Travelers would be wise to take precautions, such as staying in well-lit and populated areas when walking at night.

Petty theft and confidence scams are more prevalent than violent crimes. Always lock your room, especially in smaller lodgings. Never leave luggage unattended or out of your sight. Most hotels will store bags at the front desk, as will many restaurants and shops. Never leave any valuables in your room. It is advisable to leave your room key at the front desk when you go out.

Always lock automobiles, regardless of whether you have left any valuables inside, as the car radios that come with most rented vehicles are extremely valuable, easily sellable and much coveted by thieves. If you do leave valuables in a car, place them out of sight.

Travelers checks are accepted in Rico, so there is no reason to carry more cash than you need.

Puerto Rico has an island-wide emergency number: 911. Most dispatchers understand some English.

Customs

Customs regulations resemble those of the United States, and are carried out with similar thoroughness. It is illegal to transport perishable foods, plants, drugs or animals into or out of Puerto Rico except with prior permission. This stipulation applies to those traveling to and from the United States as well. For more information, call the **Transportation Security Administration** (TSA), tel. 253 4591, or the **US Department of Agriculture**, tel: 253 4651.

Canadians are allowed to bring back duty-free one carton of cigarettes, one can of tobacco, 40 imperial ounces of liquor, and 50 cigars. All valuables should be declared on the Y-38 form before departure from Canada, including serial numbers of valuables already owned, such as expensive foreign cameras. For more information, contact the **Canada Customs and Revenue Agency**, tel: 800-461 9999 in Canada, or 204-983 3500, or visit www.ccra-adrc.gc.ca.

UK citizens have a customs allowance of 200 cigarettes, 50 cigars or 250 grams of smoking tobacco; 2 liters of still table wine; 1 liter of spirits or strong liqueurs (over 22 percent volume); 2 liters of fortified wine, sparkling wine, or other liqueurs; 60 ml perfume; 250 ml of toilet water; and £145 worth of all other goods. For more information, contact **HM Customs & Excise**, National Advice Service, Dorset House, Stamford Street, London SE1 9PY, tel: 020 8929 0152 or visit www.hmce.gov.uk.

Australian citizens can bring in 250 cigarettes or 250 grams of loose tobacco, and 1,125 milliliters of alcohol. If you're returning with valuable goods you already owned, such as foreign-made cameras, you should file form B263. For more information, contact the **Australian Customs Service**, GPO Box 8, Sydney NSW 2000, tel: 02-6275 6666, or see www.customs.gov.au.

The duty-free allowance for New Zealand is 200 cigarettes or 50 cigars or 250 grams of tobacco (or a mixture of all three if their combined weight doesn't exceed 250g); plus 4.5 liters of wine and beer or 1.125 liters of liquor. Fill out a certificate of export, listing the valuables you are taking out of the country; that way, you can bring them back without paying duty. For more information, contact the **New Zealand Customs Service**, The Custom House, 17–21 Whitmore Street, Box 2218, Wellington, tel: 04-473 6099, or see www.customs.govt.nz.

Duty-free shops are open for all international flights, and for flights to the United States and US possessions in the Caribbean.

D isabled Travelers

The Americans with Disabilities Act (ADA) applies to all public facilities in Puerto Rico. Most businesses can accommodate travelers with disabilities.

For general information or to file complaints, call the local Handicapped Advocate, tel. 800-981 4125; 725 2333. The hearing impaired can call 725 4012 or 725-0613. You may also find information at www.oppi.gobierno.pr. The Handicapped Advocate's central office is located on 670 Ponce de León Avenue, Caribbean Office Plaza, 2nd floor, Miramar. Regional offices are also in Aguada, Arecibo, Humacao and Ponce.

The Handicapped Advocate has a guide of locations and services that can accommodate handicapped travelers, including hotels, paradores, vacation centers, restaurants, sights, transportation and medical services. The guide is available at the central office in Miramar, or it can be mailed if requested.

It is recommended that you call your accommodations ahead of time to verify that they accommodate handicapped travelers.

Parking for disabled travelers is available in most places, and many towns have ramps that accommodate wheelchairs. However, Old San Juan is known as a difficult place to navigate for travelers in wheelchairs. As of this writing, ferry services were also not accessible to those in wheelchairs.

The beaches of Luquillo and Boquerón have facilities that allow people in wheelchairs to bathe in the ocean.

For transportation and tours, call Wheelchair Getaway, tel: 800-868 8028/883 0131.

Care Vacations of the Caribbean rents out medical equipment for disabled travelers on cruises or staying at hotels, tel. 877-661-6496; 761-8870, www.carevacation.com.

E conomy

Manufacturing is the largest sector of the local economy. Puerto Rico is the world's largest producer of pharmaceuticals; tourism is a growing industry and the island is a banking center for most of the Caribbean.

Puerto Rico's per-capita income is $18,500 a year, according to fiscal year 2005 statistics – lower than the United States. Thirty percent of the workforce is employed by the government. The island's gross domestic product in fiscal year 2005 was about $72.37 billion, by far the largest in the Caribbean and one of the largest in Latin America.

Electricity

The voltage in Puerto Rico is the same as in the mainland United States (110 volts, 60 cycles a.c.).

Embassies and Consulates

Because Puerto Rico isn't an independent nation, it cannot have diplomatic relations with anyone. Hence, there are no embassies in San Juan – but plenty of consulates and honorary consulates. These are listed in the yellow pages of the phone book under Consulados and in the directory's "Newcomers' Guide," found between the yellow and white pages. You may also call the State Department's Service for the Foreign Citizen, tel. 723 2727, www.estado.gobierno.pr.

Some of the consulates follow: **Canada**, 268 Ponce de León Avenue, Suite 802, San Juan, tel: 753 8060. **UK**, Chardón Tower, Suite 1236, 350 Chardón Street, tel: 758 9828.

Emergency Numbers

San Juan

Emergency, tel: 911.
Police, tel: 343 2020.
Fire Department, tel: 343 2330.
Medical Center of Puerto Rico, tel: 777 3535.
Assist (for medical emergencies), tel: 754 2550.
US Coast Guard, tel: 729 6770.
Rape Hotline, tel: 765 2285/800-981 5721.
Poison Control Center, tel: 726 5660/800-222 1222.
American Red Cross, tel: 759 7979.
Operator/Information, tel: 411.

E tiquette

Puerto Ricans are lively, friendly and hospitable. Don't be surprised if a group of locals becomes noisy and boisterous while talking, particularly when discussing island politics; it is rarely as argumentative as foreigners assume. Puerto Ricans are also known for gesturing animatedly with their hands while they talk.

Upon meeting one another, Puerto Ricans like to shake hands, then give one kiss on the cheek, and they always greet each other with "Buenos días" ("Good morning"), "Buenas tardes" ("Good afternoon") or "Buenas noches" (Good evening), also said upon parting company.

G overnment

Puerto Rico is a territory of the United States. Since 1952 it has its own constitution and its official status is "Free Associated State." It is commonly referred to as the "Commonwealth of Puerto Rico." Puerto Ricans were granted US citizenship in 1917 and have almost all the economic and personal rights and responsibilities pertaining thereto.

Heading the island's government is an elected governor; Puerto Rico has an elected Senate and House of Representatives, which work much like the US system.

Puerto Ricans are not permitted to vote in national elections. However, they are represented in the US Congress by a Resident Commissioner who can sit on committees but cannot vote. Puerto Rican residents do not pay federal income tax.

Gay and Lesbian Travelers

Attitudes towards gays and lesbians in Puerto Rico are similar to those in the states, though less accepting than in places like New York City, Miami and San Francisco.

San Juan is the more gay-friendly area of the island, with many bars, restaurants and hotels in Condado, Ocean Park and Old San Juan owned by gays and lesbians. Many have "gay-nights." The beach at Ocean Park especially attracts gay travelers.

The first Sunday in June features a gay pride parade in Condado, as well as many activities in the week leading up to it.

Other areas that welcome gays and lesbians are Boquerón (southwest), Fajardo (northeast) and the small island of Culebra.

For listings of gay-friendly bars,

accommodations and places to go, visit www.orgulloboricua.net. When you get to the island, pick up a copy of the free and bilingual newspaper "Puerto Rico Breeze," found at the Atlantic Beach Hotel in Condado and at Condom World stores. It has current listings of events, restaurants, and stores.

H ealth & Medical Care

Puerto Rico's health care resembles that of the United States in that it has no national health service, and the sick are cared for on a pay-as-you-go basis.

In practice, however, Puerto Rico's health care is administered on a far more lenient basis than in the United States. In general, fees are much lower and, since many Puerto Ricans have medical insurance, being hospitalized is far less of a financial nightmare than it is in the continental United States. Most hospitals have 24-hour emergency rooms but, if possible, check the yellow pages of the telephone book under Hospitales, or search for "sala emergencia" in www.superpagespr.com.

Puerto Rico is full of competent medical professionals. If you could choose where to fall ill, you'd doubtless elect San Juan, as the number of universities and clinics there make it full of doctors and medical personnel. Still, facilities in other areas, though often old and disheartening, are generally run by capable physicians and nurses.

On the next page are listed some of the larger hospitals with emergency rooms and some of the more popular (not necessarily 24-hour) pharmacies in San Juan. For listings in provincial cities, check the yellow pages in the phone book.

Hospitals

Ashford Presbyterian Community Hospital, Condado, tel: 721 2160. Hospital Auxilio Mutuo, Hato Rey, tel: 758 2000.
Hospital San Pablo, Bayamón, tel: 740 4747.
Hospital Pavía, Santurce, tel: 727 6060.
Río Piedras Medical Center Central Emergency Room, Américo Miranda Avenue, Río Piedras, tel: 777 3535.
San Jorge Children's Hospital, Santurce, tel: 727 1000.

Special Considerations

Puerto Rico has few dangerous bacteria and diseases, but one deserves a special mention. Almost all of the island's rivers are infected with schistosomes, parasitic

flatworms that cause schistosomiasis (bilharzia), which can lead to severe damage to internal organs. Some say that river water is safe to drink and swim in on the upper altitudes of mountains, provided it is running swiftly, but this guide does not recommend it. Tap water is safe.

I nternet & Websites

Most of the larger hotels provide guests with internet access either in their rooms or at least in a communal area. A random selection follows:
At Wind Chimes Inn
1750 Ashford Avenue, Condado
Tel: 727 4153.
Caribe Hilton
Los Rosales Street, Puerta Tierra
San Gerónimo Grounds
Tel: 721 0303.
Embassy Suites Hotel & Casino
8000 Tartak Street, Isla Verde
Tel: 791-0505.
Hilton Ponce Golf & Casino Resort
1150 Caribe Avenue, Ponce
Tel: 259 7676.
Horned Dorset Primavera
Route 429, Km 3.0, Rincón
Tel: 823 4030.
Hostería del Mar
1 Tapia Street, Ocean Park
Tel: 727 3302.
Sheraton Old San Juan Hotel
100 Brumbaugh Street, Old San Juan
Tel: 721 5100.
Internet cafés are not very common

Useful Websites

Arecibo Observatory:
www.naic.edu
Casa Bacardi Visitor Center:
www.bacardi.com
Culebra Island: www.culebra-island.com, www.culebra.org
Puerto Rico Coliseum:
www.coliseodepuertorico.com
Puerto Rico Convention Bureau:
www.meetpuertorico.com
Puerto Rico Convention Center:
www.prconvention.com
Puerto Rico Golf Association:
www.prga.org
Puerto Rico Hotel & Tourism Association: www.prhta.org
Puerto Rico Information:
www.enjoypuertorico.com
www.puertorico.com
www.puertoricowow.com
Puerto Rico Tourism Company:
www.gotopuertorico.com
San Juan Tourism:
www.sanjuan.org
Vieques Island:
www.enchanted-isle.com

on the island. But there is a short listing below:

CyberNet Café
1128 Ashford Avenue,
Condado
Tel: 724 4033, and
5575 Isla Verde Avenue
Isla Verde
Tel: 728 4195

Crew Station Internet Café
111 Paseo Concepción de Gracia, in front of the Old San Juan piers
Tel: 289 0345.

L ost Property

To contact the Luis Muñoz Marín International Airport police call 791 0098.

For property left in taxis, call the Tourism Transportation booths in the Luis Muñoz Marín International Airport, tel: 253 0418, or email lostandfound@prtourism.com or transportationclaims@prtourism.com

To report lost or stolen credit cards and travelers checks, call:
American Express, tel: 800-327 1267
MasterCard, tel: 800-307 7309
Visa, tel: 800-847 2911

If you lose your US passport, call the State Department, tel: 722-2121; other nationalities should contact the relevant consulate.

For property left on airplanes or airline area, call the airline directly.

M edia

Print

Puerto Ricans are avid readers of periodical literature, and the national dailies, published in San Juan, cover the spectrum of political opinion.

Of the Spanish papers, *El Nuevo Día* is probably the most popular, a meaty tabloid with special features and book excerpts. *El Vocero* is a slim paper with more local, sensational news; while the recently established *Primera Hora* is beginning to make waves. The *San Juan Star* publishes editions in English and Spanish.

Puerto Rico produces few magazines, but gets most of the weeklies from the United States and Spain. American newspapers are available here on the day of publication: in Spanish, *Diario Las Américas*, published in Miami; in English, *The New York Times*, *The New York Post*, *The Miami Herald* and *The Wall Street Journal*.

Television and Radio

Puerto Rico has more than 100 radio stations, including the English-language WOSO (1030 on the AM dial),

which is quite versatile, combining fine local coverage with network news. English-language WBMJ is a religious station, and the St. Thomas station may be picked up by some radios, particularly in the eastern part of Puerto Rico. Recommended Spanish music stations are Radio Uno and, on FM, Radio Fidelity.

The island has at least half a dozen Spanish-language TV stations of its own, but there are no English-language stations, save for the offerings on cable and satellite TV, which come from the United States and include all the American television networks. The government station, WIPR, broadcasts local programs in Spanish and some Public Broadcasting Service (PBS) programs in English.

Money Matters

All business in Puerto Rico is transacted in US dollars, and visitors are advised to buy travelers checks in that currency if you prefer not to carry cash or withdraw money from cash machines. Travelers checks are accepted all over the island.

Most restaurants, hotels and stores in well-traveled areas accept American Express, MasterCard, Visa, Carte Blanche, Discovery and Diner's Club.

Some American Express Travel Services are offered through the Bithorn Travel agency in Isla Verde Mall, Suite 201, tel: 791 2951.

The Banco Popular at the Luis Muñoz Marín International Airport provides currency exchange, tel: 791 0326.

Banking

Puerto Rico is the banking center of the Caribbean Basin and as such has branches of almost all of the leading North American banks, as well as many European and Puerto Rican institutions. ATMs (called ATH – *aa-teh-acheh* – in Puerto Rico) are installed in most towns around the island.

Banking hours are Monday to Friday 8.30am–2.30pm. Certain branches of each bank may open for part of the day on Saturday and, some evenings.

P harmacies

San Juan

Puerto Rico Drug
157 San Francisco Street, corner with Cruz Street
Old San Juan
Tel: 725 2202.
Walgreens
1000 Ave Ponce de Leon
Tel: 721 5302

also at 1130 Ashford Avenue
Condado (open 24 hours)
Tel: 725 1510.
Farmacías El Amal
617 Pavía Street
Santurce
Tel: 728 1760.

Mayagüez

Walgreens
Mayagüez Mall (open 24 hours)
Tel: 831 9251.

Ponce

Farmacias El Amal
Valle Real Shopping Center (open 24 hours)
Tel: 844 5555.
Walgreens
Fagot Avenue (open 24 hours)
Tel: 841 2135.

Postal Services

Puerto Rican postal services are administered by the US Postal Service. Regulations and tariffs are the same as those on the mainland. Stamps may be purchased at any post office; most are open from Monday to Friday 8am–5pm and on Saturday from 8am–noon. Stamps may also be purchased from vending machines located in hotels, stores and airports.

The US Postal Service Authorized Abbreviation for Puerto Rico is PR.

United Parcel Service (UPS) and Federal Express (FedEx) also provide service in Puerto Rico, as do some private mail service centers.

Phone numbers for the main mail carriers are:
Federal Express: 800-463 3339
General US Postal Office (information): 622 1756
UPS: 800-742 5877

BELOW: religious icons.

Public Restrooms

Restrooms are identified as such in English or in Spanish as "baños." If identified in Spanish, the ladies' room is marked with "Damas" and the men's room with "Caballeros."

Some public restrooms are better maintained than others, but a general rule of thumb is to not sit on the toilet seat. Many times you won't find toilet paper in public restrooms, except in good restaurants and larger hotels, so it's always a good idea to carry some tissue paper or napkins with you just in case.

All of the public beaches administered by the country's National Parks Company have public restrooms.

Public Holidays

The annual public holidays are:

1 January	New Year's Day
6 January	Three Kings Day
January	Eugenio María de Hostos Birthday
January	Martin Luther King, Jr. Day
February	Presidents' Day
March	Celebration of the abolition of slavery
March/April	Good Friday
April	José de Diego Day
May	Memorial Day
4 July	US Independence Day
July	Luís Muñoz Rivera Day, José Celso Barbosa Day
25 July	Puerto Rico's Constitution Day
September	Labor Day
October	Columbus Day
November	Veterans' Day
19 November	Celebration of the "discovery" of Puerto Rico
3rd Thursday in November	Thanksgiving Day
25 December	Christmas Day

R eligion

Puerto Rican history is steeped in religion, particularly the Roman Catholic tradition, as the Spanish monarchs at the time of colonization sent "conquistadores" along with priests to convert their new territories.

Roman Catholics still make up the majority of the population, approximately 85 percent, while Protestant churches and other groups such as Muslims and Jews represent about 15 percent of the population.

Most religious denominations on the island offer services in English. For more information, check the

listings on the yellow pages under Iglesias or in the English-language blue pages under Churches. Some services in English that are close to the San Juan tourist areas follow. Call to verify service times, as they may be subject to change.

Baptist

The Isla Verde Baptist Church (Sun 11am), tel: 726 3055.

Episcopal

St John's Cathedral, Santurce (Sun 8am, 11am), tel: 722 3254.

Inter-denominational

The Union Church of San Juan, Punta Las Marías (Sun 10.30am), tel: 726 0280.

Jewish

The Jewish Reform Congregation of Temple Beth Shalom, Santurce (Fri 8.30pm, Sat 10am), tel: 721 6333.
The Jewish Community Center at Shaare Zedeck Synagoge (English/Spanish/Hebrew on Fri 6.30pm, Sat/Sun 9am), tel: 724 4157.

Lutheran

Grace Lutheran Church, Santurce (Sun 10.30am), tel: 722 5372.

Methodist

The Holy Trinity Methodist Church, Old San Juan (Spanish with English translation on Sun 11am), tel: 722 5372.

Presbyterian

O'Neill Memorial Presbyterian Church, Old San Juan (Sun 9am), tel: 977 2405.

Roman Catholic

Nuestra Señora del Perpetuo Socorro, Miramar (Sun 10.30am), tel: 721 1015.
Stella Maris, Condado (Sun 9.30am, 12.30pm), tel: 723 2240.

S moking

As of this writing, Puerto Rico was slated to implement a law that prohibits smoking in virtually all public areas on March 3, 2007. The law doesn't allow businesses to designate areas for smokers, as was previously the case on the island. According to the regulation, smoking is prohibited in restaurants, bars, casinos, clubs, pubs and liquor stores. It is also not permitted in businesses dedicated to the sale of food, public buildings and transportation vehicles, convention centers, shopping malls and outdoor cafés if an employee takes an order

there, among other places. People may smoke in areas that are in the open air, out of work areas, in private homes, in vehicles when a child under the age of 13 is not present and in freestanding tobacco shops. Fines for violating the law start at $25 for individuals. Tourism had yet to develop a regulation for hotel rooms as of this writing, although smoking is prohibited in hotel common areas.

T ax

For the first time in its history, Puerto Rico implemented a 5.5 percent commonwealth sales tax starting on November 15 2006. At the time of writing, some municipalities had planned to also charge an additional sales tax of up to 1.5 percent. The sales tax is applicable to jewelry, electronics, rental vehicles and most goods and services. Medical services, prescription medicine, products derived from petroleum and non-processed foods are exempt from the tax. Other groceries are subject to the sales tax. There are additional taxes on alcohol and cigarettes, though these are included in marked prices and do not appear as surcharges. An excise tax applies to incoming automobiles.

There is also a room tax in Puerto Rico, which varies according to the kind of accommodation and its facilities. As of this writing, San Juan was slated to impose an additional occupancy tax of between $2 and $5 per night to hotels in the municipality.

Telecommunications

The international area codes for Puerto Rico are **787** and **939**. All numbers listed in this guide require a 787 area code unless otherwise indicated.

Coin-operated telephones are common and cost 50¢ for local calls, depending on the particular pay phone. When you hear the dial tone, you may dial the area code followed by the seven-digit number. If the call is outside the area you are calling from, you will need to dial 1-787 followed by the seven-digit number. If the call is long-distance within Puerto Rico, extra charges will apply. For calls to the US Virgin Islands, dial 1-340 and the number; to the Dominican Republic, dial 1-809 and the number. Every Caribbean island now has its own area code; check your directory for the complete list. For calls to the US and Canada, dial 1, then the area code, then the

number. An operator will tell you how much money to deposit.
If you wish to place a call through an operator, dial "0." Directions are usually printed on the phone, and are always printed in the first pages of the phone directory.

The phone directories in Puerto Rico are in Spanish, with a special wine and blue-colored section in English providing commercial and government telephone numbers and giving translations of the Spanish headings under which information can be found.

Telegraph facilities are available through Western Union or Telex. Western Union telegraphs (tel: 800-325 4045) and cash transfers arrive at food stores of the Pueblo chain. International Access Codes for phone cards are:

MCI 1-888-757 6655
Sprint 1-800-877 8000
AT&T 1-800-CALL-ATT

ABOVE: Our Lady Guadalupe Cathedral, Ponce.

Tipping

Puerto Rico has a service economy resembling that of the United States, and this means tipping for most services received. Some hotels and hotel restaurants include a 15 percent to 17 percent service charge to the bill, so always check your bill. Otherwise, follow the American rules of thumb: 15 percent in restaurants, including fondas and colmados but not fast-food joints; 10 percent in bars; 10–15 percent for cab drivers, hairdressers and other services. Fifty cents per bag is a good rule for hotel porters, and a few bucks should keep the person who cleans your room happy.

Time Zone

Atlantic Time Zone, four hours behind GMT and one hour ahead of Eastern Standard Time.

Tourist Offices Abroad

On the US mainland, call the Puerto Rico Tourism Company toll-free at 800-223 6530 (toll-free). Offices are located in Miami, tel: 800-815 7391 and Los Angeles, tel: 800-874 1230.
Outside the United States:
Canada
(postal address)
6-295 Queen Street East, Suite 465
Brampton, Ontario
L6W4S6
Tel: 416-580 6287.
UK
c/o Activate Sales & Marketing
2nd Floor, 67a High Street
Walton-on-Thames
KT12 1DJ

Tel: 01932 253302
Email: puertoricouk@aol.com

Local Tourist Offices
The Puerto Rico Tourism Company has its main office at:
La Puntilla building
2 Paseo de La Princesa,
Old San Juan
Tel: 721 2400.
Tourists may also get information at
La Casita,
Dársenas Plaza, next to Pier 1
Old San Juan
Tel: 722 1709.
There is a Tourism Company Information Center at the airport, on the first level of concourse C (tel: 791 1014).

Visas & Passports

No visa or passport is required for US citizens entering Puerto Rico from the United States. Visitors and cruise passengers planning to go to other Caribbean islands, excluding the US Virgin Islands, must have a valid passport to return to US territory. Those with permanent residence, however, are advised to bring their green cards.

Foreign nationals are required to present the same documentation and papers required for entry into the continental US.

Countries whose citizens are exempted from tourist visa requirements, for stays of up to 90 days, include Australia, Ireland, New Zealand, and the UK.

To qualify for visa-free travel, you need an unexpired passport, must hold a return or onward ticket, a completed form I-94W and enter aboard an air or sea carrier participating in the Visa Waiver Pilot Program if entering by air or sea (lists of participating air or sea carriers are available from most travel agents).

Weights & Measures

The British Imperial system is used in Puerto Rico for most things. Distances are measured in kilometers, but speed limits are in miles. Weight is measured in pounds and gas is sold in liters; most other things use the British Imperial system.

What to Wear/Bring

Puerto Rican dressing is casual yet mostly conservative: jeans, shorts and long trousers are common. Only in a very small number of clubs are jackets and ties really required, and businessmen often remove their jackets in the course of the workday. However, shed the shorts and tennis shoes when you go out at night, as Puerto Ricans like to dress up. Colorful, medium-length dresses are versatile evening wear for women. Anything more than a light sweater is seldom necessary, even on winter nights in the Cordillera. An umbrella will come in handy, especially in rainy late summer on the island's northern coast.

However, a high factor sunscreen and a hat are essential for those who plan to spend even a minimal amount of time outdoors.

L ANGUAGE

UNDERSTANDING THE LANGUAGE

General

The language of Puerto Rico is Spanish. While it is by no means true that "everyone there speaks English," a majority of Puerto Ricans certainly do, especially in San Juan. Almost everyone in a public-service occupation will be able to help in either language.

The Puerto Rican dialect of Spanish resembles that of other Antillean islands, and differs from the Iberian dialect in its rapidity, phoneme quality and elisions. For a more detailed look at this rich tongue, *see The Language of Puerto Rico on page 69*.

There are many excellent Spanish-English dictionaries, but Barron's, edited at the University of Chicago, is particularly recommended for its sensitivity to the vocabulary and syntax of the Latin-American idiom. Cristine Gallo's The Language of the Puerto Rican Street is an exhaustive lexicon of the kind of Puerto Rican slang most dictionaries would blanch at printing.

Basic Rules

English is widely spoken in most tourist areas, but even if you speak no Spanish at all, it is worth trying to master a few simple words and phrases.

Generally, the accent falls on the second-to-last syllable, unless it is otherwise marked with an accent (´) or the word ends in D, L, R or Z.

Vowels

a as in father
e as in bed
i as in police
o as in hole
u as in rude

Consonants

Consonants are approximately like those in English, the main exceptions being:
c is hard before a, o or u (as in English), and is soft before e or i, when it sounds like s. Thus, censo (census) sounds like senso.
g is hard before a, o, or u (as in English), but where English g sounds like j – before e or i – Spanish g sounds like a guttural h. g before ua is often soft or silent, so that agua sounds more like awa, and Guadalajara like Wadalajara.
h is silent.
j sounds like the English h.
ll sounds like y.
ñ sounds like ny, as in the familiar Spanish word señor.
q is followed by u as in English, but the combination sounds like k instead of like kw.
r is often rolled.
x between vowels sounds like a guttural h, as in México or Oaxaca.
y alone, as the word meaning "and", is pronounced ee.

Note that **ch** and **ll** are separate letters of the Spanish alphabet; if looking in a phone book or dictionary for a word beginning with ch, you will find it after the final c entry. A name or word beginning with ll will be listed after the l entry.

When addressing someone you are not familiar with, use the more formal "usted". The informal "tú" is reserved for relatives and friends.

Words and Phrases

Hello Hola
How are you? ¿Cómo está usted?
How much is it? ¿Cuánto es?
What is your name? ¿Cómo se llama usted?
My name is... Yo me llamo...
Do you speak English? ¿Habla inglés?
I am British/American Yo soy británico/norteamericano
I don't understand No entiendo
Please speak more slowly Hable más despacio, por favor
Can you help me? ¿Me puede ayudar?
I am looking for... Estoy buscando...
Where is...? ¿Dónde está...?
I'm sorry Lo siento/Perdón
I don't know No sé
No problem No hay problema
Have a good day Que tenga un buen día, or Vaya con Diós
That's it Ese es
Here it is Aquí está
There it is Allí está
Let's go Vámonos
See you tomorrow Hasta mañana
See you soon Hasta pronto
See you later Hasta luego
Show me the word in the book Muéstreme la palabra en el libro
At what time? ¿A qué hora?
When? ¿Cuándo?
yes sí
no no
please por favor
thank you (very much) (muchas) gracias
you're welcome de nada
excuse me con su permiso
OK bien
goodbye adiós
good evening/night buenas tardes/noches
here aquí
there allí
today hoy
yesterday ayer
tomorrow mañana (note: mañana also means "morning")
now ahora
later después
right away ahora mismo
this morning esta mañana

TRANSPORT

ACCOMMODATION

EATING OUT

ACTIVITIES

A – Z

LANGUAGE

this afternoon esta tarde
this evening esta tarde
tonight esta noche

On Arrival

I want to get off at... Quiero bajarme en...
Is there a bus to the museum? ¿Hay un autobús al museo?
What street is this? ¿Qué calle es ésta?
How far is...? ¿Cuán lejos queda?
airport aeropuerto
customs aduana
baggage claim reclamo de equipaje
suitcase maleta
train station estación de tren
bus station estación de autobuses/guaguas
metro station estación de tren urbano
bus autobús/guagua
bus stop parada de guaguas
ticket boleto/ticket
round trip ticket boleto de ida y vuelta
hitchhiking auto-stop/pon
toilets servicios/baños
This is the hotel address Ésta es la dirección del hotel
I'd like a (single/double) room Quiero una habitación (sencilla/doble)
... with shower con ducha
... with bath con baño
... with a view con vista
Does that include breakfast? ¿Incluye desayuno?
May I see the room? ¿Puedo ver la habitación?
washbasin lavabo
bed cama
key llave
elevator/lift ascensor/elevador
wheelchair silla de ruedas
stairs escaleras
wheelchair ramp rampa de impedidos
air conditioning aire acondicionado
internet connection conección a la red cibernética
trip viaje
business negocio
pleasure placer
vacation vacación

Emergencies

Help! ¡Socorro!/¡Auxilio!
Stop! ¡Alto!/¡Pare!
Call a doctor Llame a un médico
Call an ambulance Llame a una ambulancia
Call the police Llame a la policía
Call the fire brigade Llame a los bomberos
Where is the nearest telephone? ¿Dónde está el teléfono más cercano?

Where is the nearest hospital? ¿Dónde está el hospital más cercano?
I am sick Estoy enfermo/a (male/female)
I have lost my passport/purse (bag) He perdido mi pasaporte/cartera

On the Road

Where is the spare wheel? ¿Dónde está la rueda de repuesta?
Where is the nearest garage? ¿Dónde está el taller más cercano?
Our car has broken down Nuestro carro se ha dañado
I want to have my car repaired Quiero que reparen mi carro
It's not your right-of-way Usted no tiene prioridad/derecho de paso
I think I must have put diesel in my car by mistake Me parece haber echado combustible de motor diesel por error
the road to... la carretera a...
left izquierda
right derecha
straight on derecho
far lejos
near cerca
opposite frente a
beside al lado de
parking lot/car park estacionamiento
over there allí
at the end al final
town map mapa de la ciudad
road map mapa de carreteras
street calle
square plaza
give way ceda el paso
exit salida
dead end calle sin salida
wrong way va contra el tránsito
no parking prohibido estacionar/no estacione
motorway/expressway autopista
toll highway autopista/expreso
toll peaje
tyre/tire goma/llanta
speed limit límite de velocidad
petrol/gasoline station gasolinera
petrol/gasoline gasolina
unleaded sin plomo
diesel diesel
water/oil agua/aceite
air aire
puncture pinchazo
bulb bombilla
lights luces
breaks freno

On the Telephone

How do I make an outside call? ¿Cómo hago una llamada al exterior?
What is the area code? ¿Cuál es el código de área?
I want to make an international (local) call Quiero hacer una llamada internacional (local)

I'd like a wake-up call for 8 tomorrow morning Quiero que me despierten a las ocho de la mañana
Hello? ¿Díga?/¡Aló!
Who's calling? ¿Quién llama?
Hold on, please Un momento, por favor
I can't hear you No le oigo
Can you hear me? ¿Me oye?
He/she is not here Él/ella no está aquí
The line is busy La línea está ocupada
I must have dialed the wrong number Debo haber marcado un número equivocado

Shopping

Where is the nearest bank? ¿Dónde está el banco más cercano?
I'd like to buy Quiero comprar
How much is it? ¿Cuánto es?
Do you accept credit cards? ¿Aceptan tarjetas de crédito?
Can I pay with a check/cheque? ¿Puedo pagar con cheque?
I'm just looking Sólo estoy mirando
Have you got...? ¿Tiene...?
I'll take it Me lo llevo
I'll take this one/that one Me llevo éste/ese
What size is it? ¿Que talla es?
size (clothes) talla
small pequeño
large grande
cheap barato
expensive caro
enough suficiente
too much demasiado
a piece una pieza
each cada uno/la pieza/la unidad
bill la factura (shop), **la cuenta** (restaurant)
bank banco
bookshop librería
chemist/pharmacy farmacia
hairdressers peluquería
post office correo
department store tienda por departamentos
closed cerrado
open abierto
holiday feriado
business hours horas de oficina

Market Shopping

Supermarkets (*supermercados*) are self-service, but often the best and freshest produce is to be had at the town market (*mercado*) or the street market (*mercadillo*). Prices are usually by the pound (*por libra*) or by the unit (*por unidad*).

fresh fresco
frozen congelado
organic orgánico/biológico
basket cesta

bag bolsa
bakery panadería
butcher's carnicería
cake shop repostería/pastelería
fishmonger's pescadería
grocer's verdurería
tobacconist tabaquero/estanquero
junk shop/thriftshop tienda de segunda mano

Sightseeing

mountain montaña
hill colina
valley valle
river río
lake lago
lookout mirador
old town casco antiguo
monastery monasterio
convent convento
cathedral catedral
church iglesia
palace palacio
hospital hospital
town hall alcaldía
nave nave
statue estátua
fountain fuente
tower torre
castle castillo
Iberian ibérico
Phoenician fenicio
Roman romano
Moorish moro
Romanesque románico
Gothic gótico
museum museo
art gallery galería de arte
exhibition exposición
tourist information office oficina de turismo
free gratis
admission/admission fee entrada/precio de entrada
every day diario/todos los días
all day todo el día
swimming pool piscina
to book reservar

Dining Out

breakfast desayuno
lunch comida/almuerzo
dinner cena
meal comida
snack merienda
appetizer aperitivo
first course primer plato
main course plato principal
dessert postre
drink included bebida incluída
wine list carta de vinos
the bill la cuenta
fork tenedor
knife cuchillo
spoon cuchara
plate plato
glass vaso
wine glass copa

napkin servilleta
ashtray cenicero
straw sorbeto
waiter, please! camarero, por favor!
coffee café
...black negro
...with milk con leche
...decaffeinated descafeinado
sugar azúcar
tea té
herbal tea infusión
milk leche
mineral water agua mineral
...fizzy con gas
...non-fizzy sin gas
juice (fresh) jugo (natural)
beer cerveza
soft drink refresco
with ice con hielo
wine vino
red wine vino tinto
white blanco
rosé rosado
dry seco
sweet dulce
house wine vino de la casa
sparkling wine vino espumoso
Where is this wine from? ¿De dónde es este vino?
Cheers! ¡Salud!

Table Talk

I am a vegetarian Soy vegetariano
I am on a diet Estoy a dieta
What do you recommend? ¿Qué recomienda?
Do you have local specialties? ¿Hay especialidades locales?
I'd like to order Quiero pedir
That is not what I ordered Ésto no es lo que pedí
May I have more wine? ¿Me da más vino?
Enjoy your meal Buen provecho
That was delicious Eso estuvo delicioso/sabroso/rico

Menu Decoder

Breakfast and Snacks

azúcar **sugar**
bocadillo **sandwich in a bread roll**
bollo **bun/roll**
jalea/mermelada/confitura **jam**
huevos **eggs**
...cocidos **boiled, cooked**
...fritos **fried**
...revueltos **scrambled**
tocineta **bacon**
mantequilla **butter**
pan **bread**
integral **whole wheat/wholemeal**
avena **oatmeal**
pimienta **black pepper**
sal **salt**
sandwich **sandwich in square slices of bread**
tostada **toast**
yogúr **yoghurt**

Main Courses

Carne/Meat

cabrito **kid**
carne picada **ground meat**
cerdo **pork**
chorizo **paprika-seasoned sausage**
chuleta **chop**
conejo **rabbit**
cordero **lamb**
costilla **rib**
cuerito **roast suckling pig's skin**
entrecot **beef rib steak**
filete **steak**
jamón **ham**
jamón cocido **cooked ham**
jamón serrano **cured ham**
lechón asado **roast suckling pig**
lengua **tongue**
lomo **loin**
morcilla **black pudding**
rez **beef**
riñones **kidneys**
salchichón **sausage**
sesos **brains**
solomillo **fillet steak**
ternera **veal or young beef**
a la brasa/parilla **charcoal grilled**
a la plancha **grilled**
al horno/asado **roast**
bien cocido **well done**
en salsa **in sauce**
frito **fried**
guisado **stew**
parrillada **mixed grill**
pincho **skewer**
poco cocido **rare**
relleno **stuffed**
término medio **medium**

Pollo/Poultry

codorniz **quail**
faisán **pheasant**
pato **duck**
pavo **turkey**
perdiz **partridge**
pintada **guinea fowl**
pollo **chicken**

Pescado/Fish

almeja **clam**
anchoas **anchovies**
anguila **eel**
atún **tuna**
bacalao **cod**
besugo **sea bream**
boquerones **fresh anchovies**
caballa **mackerel**
calamar **squid**
camarones **shrimp**
cangrejo **crab**
caracol **sea snail**
carrucho **queen conch**
cazón **dogfish**
centollo **spider crab**
cigala **Dublin Bay prawn/scampi**
dorado **dolphin fish, mahi mahi**
fritura **mixed fry**
gamba **prawn**
jibia/chopito **cuttlefish**
jueyes **land crab**

langosta **spiny lobster**
langostino **large prawn**
lenguado **sole**
lubina **sea bass**
mariscada **mixed shellfish**
mariscos **shellfish**
mejillón **mussel**
merluza **hake**
mero **grouper**
ostión **large oyster**
ostra **oyster**
pescadilla/pijota **small hake**
pez espada **swordfish**
pulpo **octopus**
rape **monkfish**
rodaballo **turbot**
salmón **salmon**
salmonete **red mullet**
sardina **sardine**
trucha **trout**
tiburón **shark**
viera **scallop**

ABOVE: delicious tropical fruit on sale.

Vegetables/cereals

ajo **garlic**
alcachofa **artichoke**
apio **celery**
arroz **rice**
berenjena **eggplant/aubergine**
cebolla **onion**
cereal **cereal**
coliflor **cauliflower**
crudo **raw**
champiñón/seta **mushroom**
ensalada **salad**
espárrago **asparagus**
espinaca **spinach**
garbanzo **chick pea**
guisante **pea**
haba **broad bean**
habichuela **bean**
habichuela colorada/roja **red bean**
judía **green bean**
lechuga **lettuce**
lenteja **lentil**
maíz **corn/maize**
papa **potato**
pepino **cucumber**
pimiento **pepper/capsicum**
puerro **leek**
rábano **radish**
repollo **cabbage**
tomate **tomato**
verduras **vegetables**
zanahoria **carrot**

Fruit and Desserts

aguacate **avocado**
albaricoque **apricot**
cereza **cherry**
china **orange**
ciruela **plum**
frambuesa **raspberry**
fresa **strawberry**
fruta **fruit**
granada **pomegranate**
guineo **banana**
higo **fig**
limón **lemon**
limón verde **lime**

mandarina **tangerine**
manzana **apple**
melocotón **peach**
melón **melon**
pasa **raisin**
pera **pear**
piña **pineapple**
plátano **plantain**
sandía **watermelon**
toronja **grapefruit**
uva **grape**
flan **caramel custard**
helado/mantecado **ice cream**
natilla **custard**
pastel **pie**
postre **dessert**
queso **cheese**
tarta/torta/bizcocho **cake**

Numbers, Days and Dates

0	cero
1	uno
2	dos
3	tres
4	cuatro
5	cinco
6	seis
7	siete
8	ocho
9	nueve
10	diez
11	once
12	doce
13	trece
14	catorce
15	quince
16	dieciséis
17	diecisiete
18	dieciocho
19	diecinueve
20	veinte
21	veintiuno
30	treinta
40	cuarenta
50	cincuenta

60	sesenta
70	setenta
80	ochenta
90	noventa
100	cien
200	doscientos
500	quinientos
1,000	mil
10,000	diez mil
1,000,000	un millón

week semana
weekday día de semana
weekend fin de semana
Monday lunes
Tuesday martes
Wednesday miércoles
Thursday jueves
Friday viernes
Saturday sábado
Sunday domingo

January enero
February febrero
March marzo
April abril
May mayo
June junio
July julio
August agosto
September septiembre
October octubre
November noviembre
December diciembre

Weather

sunny soleado
cloudy nublado
rain/rainy lluvia/lluvioso
humid húmedo
umbrella paraguas/sombrilla
storm tormenta
hurricane huracán
wind viento
waves olas

FURTHER READING

FURTHER READING

General

Adventure Guide to Puerto Rico, by Harry S. Pariser, Adventure Guide Series (1997). Traveling around the island with the author takes the reader to out-of-the-way spots as well as to the best known. As the title implies, this guide focuses on the unusual. Pariser explores parks, reserves and the offshore islands, while including fine dining and exclusive accommodations. Easy to read. Well-written impressions of Puerto Rico should motivate the reader to explore the island.

The Disenchanted Island: Puerto Rico and the United States in the Twentieth Century, by Ronald Fernandez, Praeger Publishing (1996). A study of the Puerto Rico/United States relationship which goes back to the beginning of the 20th century. The author asserts that despite the island's economic progress it is heavily dependent on the US. Fernandez, who is a professor of sociology at Central Connecticut State University – as well as the author of Los Macheteros, the Violent Struggle for Puerto Rican Independence, places emphasis on the independence movement, claiming that the US has hampered the Puerto Rican economy and has contributed to its social problems. Fernandez illustrates his claims with supportive figures.

Island Paradox: Puerto Rico in the 1990s (1990 Census Research Series), by Francisco Rivera-Batiz/Carlos E. Santiago, Russell Sage Foundation (1997). Rapid improvement in social and economic conditions also gives rise to problems of unemployment and wide divergences in income levels. The authors claim that growth brought about by United States assistance also has led to difficulties in establishing international connections, and improving living conditions has its drawbacks as political ideals may take a back seat. A must-read to better understand Puerto Rico's economic and social dilemma.

Puerto Rico: A Political and Cultural History, by Arturo Morales Carrion, W.W. Norton and Co. (1984). Island history as interpreted by Puerto Rico's leading historian. Carrion traces Puerto Rico from the early days of Spanish rule in the 1600s to the 1980s when modern trends considerably changed the way of life. Carrion is assisted by four other contributing writers. The text tends to favor the Commonwealth political status while ignoring many achievements of the Statehood Movement.

Puerto Rico: A Profile by Kal Wagenheim, Hudson Publishing (1974). Highly regarded history of the island. Told in simple language by a journalist who spent more than a decade on the island. Wagenheim is assisted by his wife, Olga Jimenez, who describes lifestyles in Puerto Rico. The simple text has been used by high schools in their history classes. One of the few books that gives an accurate account of the jíbaro (Puerto Rico's country peasant.)

Puerto Rico Mio, Four Decades of Change, photographs by Jack Delano (1990). A collector's item for lovers of Puerto Rico. Black-and-white photographs tell the story of Puerto Rico from the 1940s to the 1980s by one who loved the island and its people dearly.

Teodoro Moscoso and Puerto Rico's Operation Bootstrap, by A.W. Maldonado, University Press of Florida (1997). Puerto Rico made giant strides to pick itself up economically and socially in the 1950s to reach its secure position today. Operation Bootstrap was the brainchild of Teodoro Moscoso, who steered the island out of the backwaters of poverty into the sea of prosperity. The program was successful in that it attracted large groups of capital investors, which brought industrialization to the island. Moscoso, who rose to head of the Alliance for Progress, has his professional life recounted here.

Kicking Off the Bootstraps: Environment, Development and

Community Power in Puerto Rico, by Deborah Berman Santana (1996). University of Arizona Press. In the modern era, Puerto Rico faces new challenges, such as control of the environment, which has undergone major changes during the island's industrial period. Community relations have taken on a completely different look as populations shift from country to city and a measure of prosperity brings drastic changes at various social levels.

Fiction

Family Instalments, by Edward Rivera. New York: Morrow (1982)
Macho Camacho's Beat, by Luis Rafael Sánchez. New York: Pantheon (1981)

Cuisine

Puerto Rican Dishes, by Berta Cabanillas and Carmen Ginorio. Río Piedras: Editorial de la Universidad de Puerto Rico (1993)
The Spirit of Puerto Rican Rum: Recipes and Recollections, by Blanche Gelabert. San Juan: Discovery Press (1992)
Puerto Rican Cuisine in America, by Oswald Rivera. New York: Four Walls Eight Windows (1993)
Rice and Beans and Tasty Things: A Puerto Rican Cookbook, by Dora Pomano. San Juan (1986)
Puerto Rican Cookery, by Carmen Aboy Valldejuli. Gretna: Pelican Publishing (1993)

Arts, Customs & Social

Puerto Rican Woman, by Edna Acosta-Belén and Eli H. Christensen. New York: Praeger (1979)
Divided Borders: Essays on Puerto Rican Identity, by Juan Flores. Houston: Arte Publico (1993)
Puerto Rican Culture: An Introduction, by Raoul Gordon. New York: Gordon Books (1982)
Antonin Nechodoma, Architect 1877–1928, by Thomas S. Marvel. Gainesville: University of Florida Press (1994)
Puerto Rico 1900: Turn-of-the-Century Architecture in the Hispanic

Caribbean, by Jorge Rigau. New York: Rizzoli (1992)
Trapped: Puerto Rico Families and Schizophrenia, by Lloyd H. Rogler and August B. Hollingshead. Maplewood: Waterfront Press (1985)
When I Was Puerto Rican, by Esmeralda Santiago. Reading: Addison-Wesley Publishing (1993)

Other Insight Guides

Apa Publications offer the discerning traveler more than 400 titles in its three series of travel guide books. **Insight Guides** provide a full cultural background and top-quality photography; **Insight Compact Guides** combine portability with encyclopedic attention to detail and are ideal for on-the-spot reference; and **Insight Pocket Guides** highlight recommendations by a local host and include a full-size pull-out map.

Insight Guide: Caribbean
The vivid text and spectacular photography in Insight Guide: Caribbean is just one of the well-informed, up-to-date titles covering the region. It brings to life the serenity, the allure, the diversity of this part of the world – from the beauty of a Caribbean sunset to the charm of the Caribees.

Insight Guide: Belize
Discover the beauty of Belize with the aid of breathtaking photography and articles written by local experts.

Insight Guide: Costa Rica
This is a fascinating book full of creative pictures and interesting information about this small island of Costa Rica, its people and customs.

Insight Pocket Guide: Puerto Rico
A perfect companion, this book offers a series of tailor-made itineraries designed to help readers get the most out of a short stay in Puerto Rico. It also includes a large-scale pull-out map, which can be used independently from the guide.

Insight Pocket Guide: Bahamas
Insight Pocket Guide: Bahamas comes complete with a pull-out map. The book, written by a local host, is based on a series of itineraries designed to help visitors get the most out of the Bahamas during a short stay. The tours divide between four main bases: New Providence & Paradise Island, Eleuthera and the Family Islands and Grand Bahama.

Other Caribbean titles in the Pocket series are Insight Pocket Guide: Barbados and Insight Pocket Guide: Jamaica, again written by local hosts and with pull-out maps.

Insight Compact Guide titles which highlight destinations in this region include Bahamas, Barbados, Costa Rica, Cuba, the Dominican Republic and Jamaica.

Feedback

We do our best to ensure the information in our books is as accurate and up-to-date as possible. The books are updated on a regular basis, using local contacts, who painstakingly add, amend and correct as required. However, some mistakes and omissions are inevitable and we are ultimately reliant on our readers to put us in the picture. We would welcome your feedback on any details related to your experiences using the book "on the road". Maybe we recommended a hotel that you liked (or another that you didn't), as well as interesting new attractions, or facts and figures you have found out about the country itself. The more details you can give us (particularly with regard to addresses, e-mails and telephone numbers), the better. We will acknowledge all contributions, and we'll offer an Insight Guide to the best letters received.

Please write to us at:
Insight Guides
PO Box 7910
London SE1 1WE
United Kingdom
Or send e-mail to:
insight@apaguide.co.uk

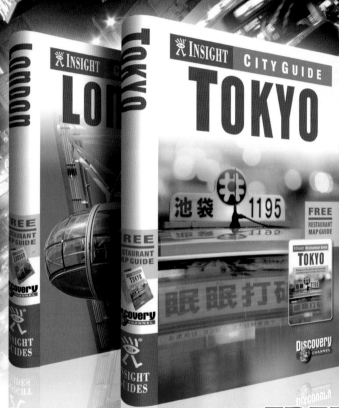

ART & PHOTO CREDITS

All photography by Bill Wassman
except for:
Stefano Amantini/4Corners Images
261, 271
APA Photo Agency 87
Archive Photos 46
Tony Arruza 1, 2B, 4B, 18/19, 28,
45, 49, 50, 58, 68, 70, 71, 74, 92,
93, 97, 100, 103, 104/105,
114/115, 121T, 130, 131,
152/153, 156T, 157, 159, 161,
162, 172/173, 174, 178, 180,
183, 185, 186, 188, 189T, 190,
191, 192/193, 197, 202, 202T,
214, 215T, 224, 224T, 225, 231,
239, 240L, 241, 241T, 253, 253T,
254, 255, 256, front flap top,
back cover center right
Mark Bacon/Alamy 167
Oliver Benn/Alamy 281
Pete Bennett/APA 259
**Brandon Cole Marine
Photography/Alamy** 200
Ian Cumming/Axiom 79
Danita Delimont/Alamy 6T, 8BL, 277
Steve Dunwell/Getty Images
136/137
Mary Evans Picture Library 20, 27
Everynight Images/Alamy 59, 273
**David R. Frazier Photolibrary, Inc./
Alamy** 287
Robert Fried 8TR, 51, 85, 90/91,
119, 132T, 143, 168T, 199T,
217, 218, 221, 248T, 250, 252,
264, 265

Stephen Frink 98/99
Stephen Frink Collection/Alamy 7TR
Glyn Genin 108/109
**Jorge R Collazo/
PhotosofPuertoRico.com** 269
Miquel Gonzalez/laif/Camerapress
181, 266, 274
Sylvain Grandadam/Hoa-Qui 263
**Jeff Greenberg/ The Image
Works/Topfoto** 78
Robert Harding Picture Library 14
Christian Heeb/laif/Camera Press
6BR
Robert Holmes/Corbis 9TR
Hulton Getty 34
Image Bank 21, 43, 95
**Courtesy of Jamaica National
Library** 36
Kim Karpeles/Alamy 272
Kobal Collection 47
Bob Krist 2/3, 5BL, 57, 69, 75,
77, 80/81, 82, 84, 94, 102,
122, 123, 125, 127, 141, 144,
145, 154, 158, 160T, 164/165,
171, 187, 223, 226, 227,
244/245
Larry Luxner 240R, 251
John Marshall 177
Michele Molinari/Alamy 283
**Reproduced from *Historia de
Puerto Rico*, by Salvador Bran**
34/35, 37, 38/39, 41
Greg Vaughn 96
Greg Vaughn/Alamy 267
isele Wulfsohn/South Light 111

PICTURE SPREADS

Pages 64/65: *Top Row, left to right*:
Tony Perrottet, Tony Arruza, Bob
Krist, Jose R. Channón
Bottom Row, left to right: Bob Krist,
Tony Perrottet, Tony Arruza
Pages 88/89: *Top Row, left to right*:
Bill Wassman, Tony Arruza, Tony
Arruza, Bill Wassman
Bottom Row, left to right: Bob Krist,
Bill Wassman, Tony Arruza, Tony
Arruza
Pages 150/151: *Top Row, left to
right*: Bill Wassman, Bill Wassman,
Private Archive
Centre Row, left to right: Bill
Wassman, Courtesy of Rum of
Puerto Rico
Bottom Row, left to right: Courtesy
of Rum of Puerto Rico, Bill
Wassman, Bill Wassman
Pages 208/209: *Top Row, left to
right*: Tony Perrottet, Bill Wassman,
Tony Arruza, Martin Rosefeldt/APA
Bottom Row, left to right: Tony
Arruza, Bill Wassman, Bill
Wassman, Tony Arruza

Map Production:
Berndtson & Berndtson Productions

INSIGHT GUIDE
PUERTO RICO

Cartographic Editor **Zoë Goodwin**
Production **Linton Donaldson**
Design Consultants
Klaus Geisler, Graham Mitchener
Picture Research **Hilary Genin**

INDEX

Numbers in italics refer to photographs

Punta del
Morro

Port of
San Juan
Lighthouse

El Morro

City Walls
(Murallas de San Juan)

Bastion de
San Antonio

✝ ✝ ✝ ✝
✝ SAN JUAN ✝
✝ CEMETERY ✝
✝ ✝ ✝ ✝

Bastion de
Santa Rosa

CEMENTERIO
DE SANTA MARIA
MAGDALENA DE PAZZIE

✝ ✝ ✝ ✝

Calle del Morro

Batería
San Fernando

La Perla

Bastion de
Santo Domingo

Calle Lucila Silva

Bastion de
Las Animas

Bastion de
Santa Elena

Calle Norzagaray

Plaza
del Quinto
Centenario

Dominican Convent,
Institute of Puerto
Rican Culture

Museo de Arte e
Historia de San Juan

Escuela de
Artes Plásticas

Cuartel de
Ballajá,
Museo de
las Américas

Totem
Telurico

San José

C. Virtud

Casa de las
Contrafuertes,
Pharmacy Museum

City Walls
(Murallas de
San Juan)

C. de Beneficiencia

Plaza San
José

Museo
Pablo Casals

Calle Cruz

Calle

Antiguo Asilo
de Beneficienca

Calle de las Monjas

C. San Sebastián

Iglesia
Metodista

Casa
Blanca

Dios de
Pentecostal

Calle Sol

Bastion de
San Augustin

Casa
Rosa

Calle Sol

Calle del Cristo

Calle San José

Hotel El Convento

La Rogativa

Caleta de las Monjas

Calle Hospital

City Hall
(Alcaldía)

Caleta de San Juan

San Juan Gate

Recinto Oeste

San Juan
Cathedral

Plaza de
Armas

El Museo Felisa
Rincón de Gautier

Calle R. Cordero

Calle Fortaleza

Centro Nacional de Artes
Populares y Artesanías

Calle Cruz

Palacio
Rojo

La Fortaleza

Casa
del Libro

Calle Tetuan

Calle

Cristo Chapel
(Capilla del Cristo)

City Wal
B
S

Siervas
de Marin

PARQUE DE
LAS PALOMAS

La
Princesa

Bastion de
Las Palmas

Paseo de la Princesa

Bahía de
San Juan

Calle Presidio

Trolley
Terminal

Arsenal de
la Marina

Calle Puntilla

N

US Co
Gu

Old San Juan

0   200 yds
0   200 m

La Pur